SAILING SHIPS

MetroBooks

1 The Sorlandet, flying the Norwegian flag, is a bark built in 1925. Once competing for the last loose cargoes, generally conquered directly at the quayside, she is seen here at sea, exploiting the gentle breeze at dusk.

2-3 The foresails of a large sailing ship: outer jib, flying jib, jib, jib foresail, and foresail. Five sails on the bowsprit of the Libertad, the Argentinean navy's sail training ship.

4-5 The Spanish sail training ship Juan Sebastian de Elcano is rigged with fore-and-aft sails on all four masts, a sail plan imposed in recent years by the need to reduce the size of crew needed to handle the canvas.

TEXT
FRANCO GIORGETTI
ERIK ABRANSON

EDITORIAL REALIZATION
VALERIA MANFERTO DE FABIANIS
LAURA ACCOMAZZO

GRAPHIC DESIGN
CLARA ZANOTTI

TRANSLATION
NEIL FRAZER DAVENPORT

© 2001 White Star S.r.l.
Via C. Sassone, 24 - 13100 Vercelli, Italy

This edition published by MetroBooks,
an imprint of Friedman/Fairfax
Publishers, by arrangement with White Star S.r.l.

Library of Congress
Cataloging-in-Publication
Data available
2001 MetroBooks

ISBN 1-58663-231-0
M 10 9 8 7 6 5 4 3 2 1

Printed in Italy

For bulk purchases and special sales, please contact:
Friedman/Fairfax Publishers
Attention: Sales Department
230 Fifth Avenue, Suite 700-701
New York, NY 10001
212/685-6610 Fax 212/685-3916

Visit our website:
www.metrobooks.com

Contents

Preface

The sailing ship, that vessel using the wind as a means of propulsion. The wind, a natural phenomenon, apparently extraneous to human life, rooted as it is to the earth, and yet so essential to the discovery of new lands and the transportation of the fruits of those lands. A phenomenon intimately bound up with the sea.

For centuries, man passively suffered the wind, patiently accepting contrary breezes, taking advantage of those in his favor. Small boats, already sporting sails, anxiously awaited these favorable winds, the only ones they would trust. Thus it was for centuries.

Then, apparently overnight, man learned to exploit the wind with ever larger and safer ships and, above all, with ever more efficient rigs: it was in the eighteenth century that man truly became a seaman and the ship became a sailing ship.

From then on, for a quarter of a millennium, clouds of canvas were put to sea throughout the globe, contributing stories of glory and great tragedy, romantic adventure and economic fortune, to the history of mankind. An era that will perhaps never be matched, with the enduring appeal of an activity fraught with physical hardship, death a frequent companion, but capable of holding sway over men who previously saw the wind and the sea as an impassable confine and cutting their atavistic ties to the land.

Today, the conditions which made that era possible no longer exist. Technological progress and a different conception of time are irreconcilable with adventure and challenge, factors inherent to the practice of sailing. Nonetheless, sailing still remains far more than a mere memory confined to museum halls or the pages of what, it has to be said, is a unique body of literature. Thus, despite the undeniable victory of mechanical propulsion over sail at the beginning of the twentieth century, still today those very same clouds of sail continue to propel vessels that embody the past and maintain an inextinguishable relevance to the present. Vessels on occasion recovered from ungenerous oblivion, other maintained in service out of affectionate respect, and still others built to replicate that which no longer exists.

These vessels are in the main sail training ships, training for life rather than the maritime profession, but there are also ships built for cruising at a more easy-going pace. And, lastly, there are ships whose reconstructed forms are intended as an active tribute to all that seamen and master carpenters, ship owners and shipbuilders, have contributed to humanity.

A tribute that this book is intended to echo, illustrating the sailing ships that sail today, that are still alive, as training ships, as cruise ships or replicas. Certainly, usages and customs have changed, navigation today no longer follows those paths that made going to sea both the most captivating and most hostile avenue open to man.

At fifteen years of age, Nelson was already a helmsman on an expedition to the freezing Arctic seas, paid and pittance and facing any number of potential dangers; his men were frequently pressed into service in an alcoholic daze, torn from some tavern and obliged to clamber along precarious footropes high above deck.

Navigating on the sailing ships of today, which explore the oceans for very different reasons, offers reasonable pay and considerable safety and is a choice made freely and after adequate schooling. Conditions on board ship are also very different and have nothing in common with the mere survival to which sailors often aspired up to the last days of sail, just a few decades ago.

However, these changing conditions have done nothing to erode the aesthetic appeal of the sailing ship and the intense communion with nature that is such a part of navigating under sail. It is in order to lend substance to these sentiments that this book, before illustrating what modern sail has to offer, re-examines the entire history of the sailing ship, taking an in-depth look at the historical and technical roots behind the various types and their development. While not presuming to cover every aspect of a world, that of the sailing ship, that in certain periods of history was its very motive power, ample space has been devoted to the fundamental stages of an evolutionary process that although slow, in as much as it has lasted almost 5,000

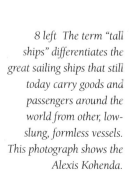

8 left The term "tall ships" differentiates the great sailing ships that still today carry goods and passengers around the world from other, low-slung, formless vessels. This photograph shows the Alexis Kohenda.

8-9 The wind is the engine, equally as efficient, at least in these conditions, as any mechanical unit, that drives the Pride of Baltimore II, a replica of an historic American ship, at her maximum rate of knots.

9 top right All sails are set, the crew is aligned on the yards and the bowsprit, all that is missing for the moment is a breath of wind to propel the Chilean navy's sail training ship Esmeralda across the seas once more.

years, has never stood still. In fact, the historical section is the true heart of the book, given that, while kept alive in the events illustrated in the second part, the sailing ship does indubitably now belong to history. It is to this fact that the book intends to bear testimony. Testimony in the form of a tribute to an appeal that the modernity of the other vessels that roam the seas today has failed to either extinguish or replace: the tall ship events are enjoying increasing popularity and there are ever greater numbers of young people attracted by a seafaring experience with an aura of authenticity. Sailing

ships are being built once again, for cruising as well as sail training, and the enthusiasm for replicas and the restoration of wrecks and abandoned hulks is ever greater. However, even if all this was not the case, and for some this interest in what, at the end of the day, was a simple means of transport (not that you should tell it to a sailor) is too much, universal admiration would remain to justify a tribute to pure beauty: among the inventions of human ingenuity, the sailing ship remains one of the most successful syntheses of technological, functional and aesthetic demands.

10-11 The Japanese ship Kaiwa Maru: amidst the masts of this large bark stands what is now an inevitable intruder, a funnel. The hull of this sailing ship in fact conceals an engine which is used as an auxiliary while maneuvering in overcrowded ports.

12-13 The West Indiamen which plied the routes to the New World were smaller than the East Indiamen with ratings of up to 500 tons. These small sailing vessels soon evolved into the famous packet ships.

Chapter 1

14-15 The great expanses of water created by the periodic and beneficial Nile floods were the setting for the first experiments with sail-powered transportation. While it is true that oars still are predominant in this illustration of one of the sacred Egyptian river's floods conserved in the museum at Palestrina, the presence of sailing vessels signifies that the Egyptians were already familiar with the technology.

15 This is the oldest known representation of a sailing ship. A small clay model dating from the fourth millennium BC, discovered in that cradle of human civilization, the basin of the two Mesopotamian rivers, the Tigris and the Euphrates. The model is today conserved in the Israel Museum of Jerusalem.

A man may carry a weight similar to his own, but only for brief periods. A wagon hauled by horses or bullocks may carry four or five quintals of goods. In contrast, a 32-foot canoe, powered by eight paddlers, carries four tons while a small sailing vessel with a crew of three, can handle over thirty. And both of the latter can keep it up indefinitely. This is the essential advantage of water transport, an advantage that has been recognized for millennia.

"Despatch forty ships laden with cedar trunks." This brief note by an Egyptian scribe who, in the year 2600 BC, wrote out an order given some time during the reign of Snefru, testifies to the capabilities of maritime transport and the ships of even that remote period of antiquity. The ships would have been sail-powered judging by the numerous wall paintings and written descriptions dating from the epoch of the great pharaonic dynasties.

The history of navigation has, therefore, paralleled that of man ever since the earliest days of the great civilizations. It is only logical that the development of water transport, whether by river or sea, would have always been the stimulus for the birth and evolution of those great civilizations rather than the contrary.

The first settlements, and those established up to the last of the great social upheavals, the industrial revolution of the eighteenth century, were all located close to water. This decision, which could hardly have been casual given its universal nature, could only have been taken as a consequence of the practical observation that water-borne travel or transportation was easier and more convenient than on dry land. Certainly, early man would have noticed how quickly a branch of wood dropped into a stream would have floated away from him. He would also have noted that if he grasped a floating tree trunk he would be

effortlessly transported downstream. Nor should it be forgotten that while the widespread diffusion of rivers, lakes and seas over the earth's surface constituted an obstacle to movement, then a prerequisite for survival, it was also an intellectual stimulus that natural perambulation over land did not provide.

It was thus that man began to travel on anything that floated such as a tree trunk, and subsequently a number of adjacent tree trunks forming rafts and canoes. The motive power for what was originally probably thought of as an extension of the body, were the hands and the feet, where the depth of the water permitted. Then came poles, oars and finally sails.

We have no information regarding the genesis or the precise era of the discovery of the sail as a means of propulsion. What we do know is that by time the pharaoh Snefru's scribe was copying out his orders, an efficient sailing rig had already been perfected if a fleet

The Origins - Antiquity

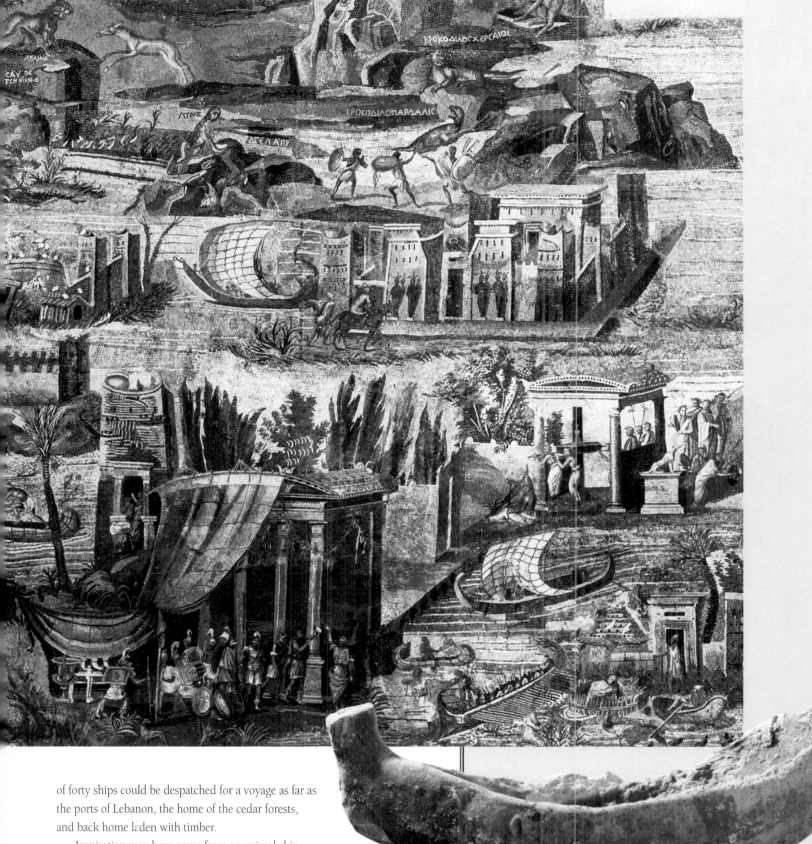

of forty ships could be despatched for a voyage as far as the ports of Lebanon, the home of the cedar forests, and back home laden with timber.

Inspiration may have come from an animal skin stretched out to dry and snatched away by a sudden gust of wind, or the great speed of a floating trunk that still had its full complement of foliage in windy conditions. What is indisputable is that by the fourth millennium before Christ, man already knew how to sail: this is confirmed by a clay model of a boat dating from circa 3500 BC found at the ancient Sumerian city of Eridu. The model features a precise location for stepping a mast, on the longitudinal axis slightly towards the prow, and holes in the planking that would appear to have held the ropes, or more correctly, the shrouds, destined to support it.

Water as a means of communications and transportation, indispensable in the search for

settlement sites, food and raw materials; floating as a means of carrying men and goods; the sail as an efficient and readily available means of propulsion. As long as six thousand years ago all the necessary elements were in place for the development of human society.

The sailing ship, as conceived in that remote epoch, was to assume diverse forms and rigs over the course of the centuries, following the progress achieved in science and engineering. However, the characteristic rectangular shape of the piece of canvas supported by a

horizontal pole is seen in the prehistoric rock engravings, in the drawings on the earthenware of the Mesopotamian and Egyptian civilizations, and still today in children's instinctive model boats. Passing from the Roman cargo vessels to the caravels of Colombus, from Nelson's great ships of the line to the last of the early twentieth century windjammers that carried phosphates from Chile and coal and iron from England, it is the square sail, the essence and symbol of the sailing ship, that catches the wind of our story.

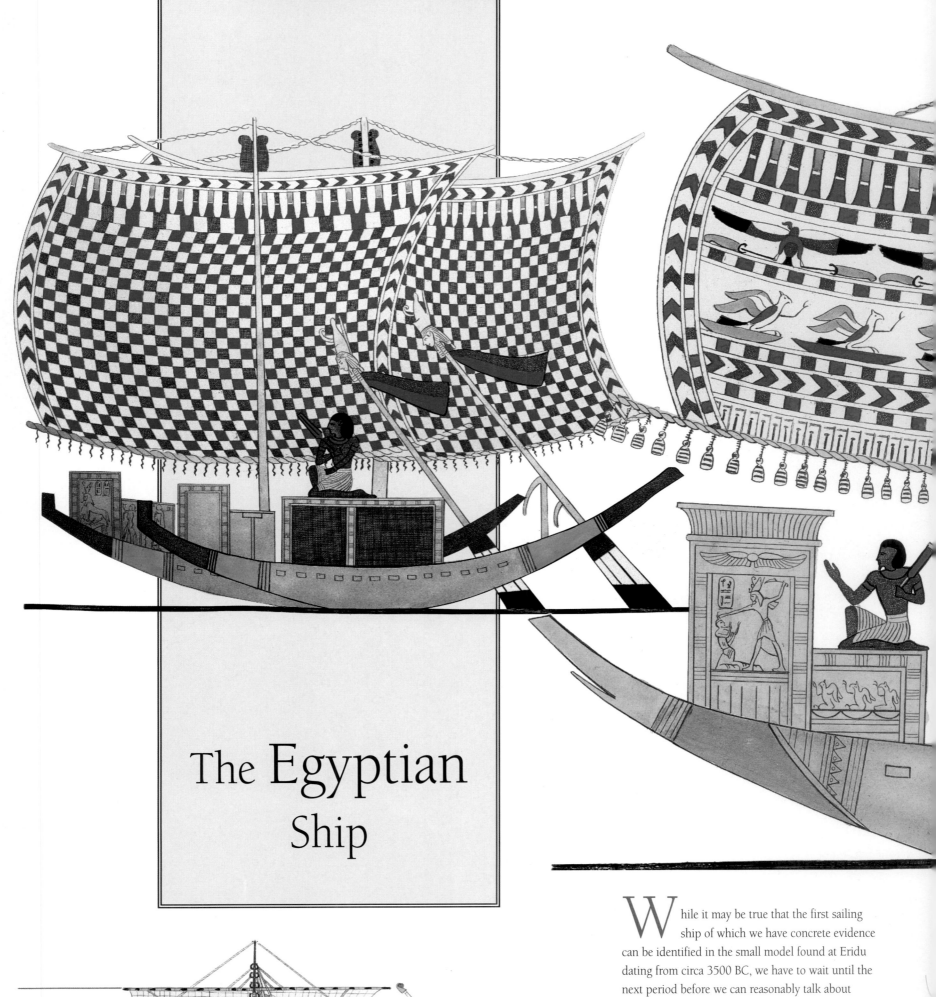

The Egyptian Ship

While it may be true that the first sailing ship of which we have concrete evidence can be identified in the small model found at Eridu dating from circa 3500 BC, we have to wait until the next period before we can reasonably talk about maritime navigation and true sailing ships. Above all, we have to look at the first great civilization to roam the waters of the Mediterranean sea, the Egyptian civilization.

The ship of Eridu was in reality a small cargo vessel designed to traverse the great rivers of the cradle of Mesopotamian development, the Tigris and the Euphrates, or at most to sail along them, linking the coastal settlements of the Persian Gulf.

The Egyptian sailing ship was a very different proposition as whilst it was initially conceived for sailing along the Nile, using the current to travel downstream and the prevailing winds to return

16 top and 17
These images, drawn from
Ippolito Rosellini's Historical
Monuments depict models—
found in the tomb of Ramses
III – of the earliest type of
Egyptian ship, built at a time
when there was no need for
hulls capable of resisting the
waves of the open sea. These
are royal barques, thus fitted
out for ceremonial duties, as
testified by the richness of the
decoration. The prow and
stern arch upwards, a form
probably dictated by the

material used for the
construction of the original
designs: bundles of papyrus
or river canes tied together.
Over time, wood began to be
used, but the form of the
vessels was not modified for
centuries.

16 bottom The image at the
bottom shows the maneuvre
required to set the sail: three
men, two sitting on the lower
yard of the square sail and
the other at the stern, are
adjusting the shrouds
supporting the mast; another
four are handling the
halyards of the upper yard,
while another is at the prow,
taking soundings.

against the flow, it soon found itself having to tackle different and more testing conditions in the Mediterranean and, above all, in the Red Sea and the Indian Ocean. The forms and techniques introduced by the Egyptian naval architects and boatbuilders to the sailing ship and sailing in general were, in fact, to remain essentially unchanged for millennia.

Despite what were still rough and ready construction methods, the Egyptian ship had an elegant, gondola-like form, with tapering extremities fore and aft. The sheerline was highly accentuated, lending the hull a characteristic arching profile that actually had a precise raison d'être: as the ship did not, in fact, have a load-bearing frame, a situation that was to persist for centuries, the planking performing this function.

This constructional technique involved the assembly of short planks of wood, set one against the other and joined with natural fiber cords for the longitudinal and vertical joints. The system derived from the technical impossibility at that time of cutting long planks and the difficulty faced by Egyptian boatbuilders in finding local trees with sufficiently tall trunks.

The planking assembled in this fashion was rendered watertight when the vessel was launched: the wood swelled and the cords shrank, thus sealing the joints between the various parts. At the same time, an arched, or banana-shaped form gave a degree of rigidity to a hull that was conceived as a unitary body with no separate chassis, to adopt automotive terminology. The load-bearing frame, and thus a body with no structural function was only to be introduced much later, in the medieval period.

In the ships of antiquity, the frame was inserted after the construction of the planking, and had, in effect, a function of localized stiffening and, above all,

of reinforcing the joins between the planks. There was thus no keelson but simply a frame of light ribs and beams, the latter supporting the deck where one was fitted and the loads carried by it.

When the Egyptian ship abandoned the calm waters of the Nile and ventured out into significantly more turbulent areas in order to guarantee the commerce, goods and wealth now indispensable to the progress of the kingdom, the structural robustness of their hulls, entrusted as we have mentioned, to the simple arched form, proved to be inadequate. The naval architects thus devised a solution of stunning simplicity, appropriate to the techniques and materials already in use: they linked the highest extremities of bow and stern with a heavy cable of twisted fibers.

The torsion on these cables, introduced by means of a wooden rod inserted through the fibers in the center, placed a load on the arch determined by the form of the hull, conferring a degree of rigidity sufficient to prevent it deforming as it passed over the waves.

The solution did, however, have one disadvantage in that it prevented a mast from being stepped on the longitudinal axis. This problem was overcome with the invention of the biped mast that also avoided the concentration of the dynamic load deriving from the system of sail-mast-stays on the keel of a hull that, as we have illustrated, had no longitudinal structure.

The biped mast and the heavy axial cable were to characterize Egyptian ships only, no other boatbuilders of antiquity adopting those features. The sails, on the other hand, had a typical square configuration, the most instinctive and easily produced solution.

With modest developments and sporadic attempts at fore-and-aft sail plans, the square rig was to remain unchanged up to the present day.

The sail of the Egyptian ship was set with two horizontal spars, one on the upper edge, one on the lower. Allowing for the limitations of the biped mast and, above all, the sailing techniques of the day which involved neither sailing against nor across the direction of the wind, this permitted the orientation of the surface to be adjusted.

Certain historical sources also provide us with information regarding the size of the sailing ships of ancient Egypt, the true forebears of the history of sailing. Generally speaking, they were small vessels, but the commercial expeditions would provision fleets of ships of up to 165 feet in length, a notable size and certainly close to the maximum achievable with wooden hulls.

The ship of Cheops, which was not actually designed to carry goods, was 141 feet meters long and 19 feet wide. A ship for the transportation of copper which was loaded on the coasts of the Sinai and sailed across the Red Sea, would reach up to 180 feet in length and have a beam of up to 59 feet. It would be crewed by around a hundred and twenty men.

These data come from the account of a shipwreck, certainly the first to be documented in the history of sailing, suffered by an Egyptian seaman. His ship was caught in a storm while crossing the Red Sea; the poor seaman managed to swim to the Sinai coast where he was picked up four months later by another Egyptian ship loading copper. This itself is evidence that such voyages took place with a certain regularity.

18-19 and 19 top Two models of Egyptian river boats: the left photograph shows the model of a royal sailing boat discovered in the tomb of Tutankhamun which provides confirmation of the images reproduced on the previous pages. Alongside is a model of what in all probability is a mercantile vessel, destined for the profitable traffic on the calm waters of the Nile, anticipating scenes that can still be witnessed on the same river today.

19 bottom Egyptian vessels soon began to venture out into the open sea: with the aid of the heavy rope stiffening the hull, large boats of up to 180 feet in length carried goods of all kinds along routes that regularly crossed the Red Sea and linked Egypt to the principal ports of the eastern Mediterranean. The image shows the work of loading and unloading an Egyptian ship moored. The stylized illustration, in accordance to the iconography of the time, reflects however the diffusion of naval transport which was still characterized by unevolved techniques of shipbuilding.

Meanwhile Calypso came back with some augers, so he bored holes with them and fitted the timbers together with wooden fastening pegs. He made the raft as broad as a skilled shipwright makes the beam of a large vessel, and he filed a deck on top of the ribs, and ran a gunwale all round it. He also made a mast with a yard arm, and a rudder to steer with. He fenced the raft all round with wicker hurdles as a protection against the waves, and then he threw on a quantity of wood. By and by Calypso brought him some linen to make the sails, and he made these too, excellently, making them fast with braces and sheets. Last of all, with the help of levers, he drew the raft down into the water.

While this may read like a manual of naval engineering, it is actually a passage from Homer's

20 top This painting clearly illustrates the important development introduced by the Greeks, the ram. An offensive weapon, without doubt, it was nonetheless a consequence of the elimination of the raised prow characteristic of Egyptian ships.

20 bottom The Greek myth of Ulysses is seen here in a mosaic from the Roman era. The ship too is Roman: while having a hull typical of those used in Aegean, is fitted with a foresail only introduced some centuries later.

The Greek Ship

20-21 In this Minoan fresco from the fourteenth century BC, depicting the entrance to the port of Santorini, we can see the two types of hulls then in use: in the center a ship with raised extremities, as used by the Egyptians and Middle Eastern fleets in general, on the left, the prow of a Greek ship with the threatening ram splitting the water.

Odyssey, a perfect description of how the sailing ships of ancient Greece were constructed.

The inhabitants of the mountainous peninsula jutting southwards into the eastern Mediterranean had learned the art of sailing and navigation from the Cretans, a people who during their ephemeral domination had come to the fore as the first maritime power in history.

Crete represented the hub of all water-based commerce in the eastern Mediterranean, an area that between 2000 and 1500 BC was the center of civilization, being the home of the Egyptians, Mesopotamians, Libyans and the Greeks.

The maritime power of the Cretans justified, moreover, their role as guardians of sea traffic which was already suffering from the pirate activities of a number of coastal peoples from what is now known as the Middle

East. This was the situation at least until the Greeks occupied Crete and took over the military and commercial positions previously occupied by the locals.

More or less in parallel with the establishment and subsequent consolidation of Greek naval power, another of the Mediterranean peoples, the Phoenicians, developed a formidable talent for sailing They, however, restricted their maritime activities to trading and the consequent foundation of colonies, spreading throughout the Mediterranean and beyond the Pillars of Hercules.

Herodotus described, in reliable detail, the circumnavigation of Africa completed by a Phoenician fleet around 600 BC: the Phoenicians descended the Red Sea as far as the Indian Ocean before wintering in an African bay to the south of the equator (throughout the period of antiquity, sea-going navigation was

restricted to the summer months, late spring and early autumn. In late autumn the ships were hauled out of the water and laid up until the following spring). In Africa, they sowed and harvested corn and then left the following spring. Two years after their departure, they reached the Pillars of Hercules. They were to return home, having traversed the Mediterranean, the following year.

Despite all the evidence that has been handed down to us, in the form of the numerous colonies founded as well as Herodotus' account, the history of Phoenician sailing is still shrouded in mystery. It may reasonably be supposed that their ships were not dissimilar to the contemporary Greek and Cretan vessels which had replaced the primitive Egyptian model that was in truth rather unsuitable for sea-going duties.

Thanks to the Greek constructors and naval

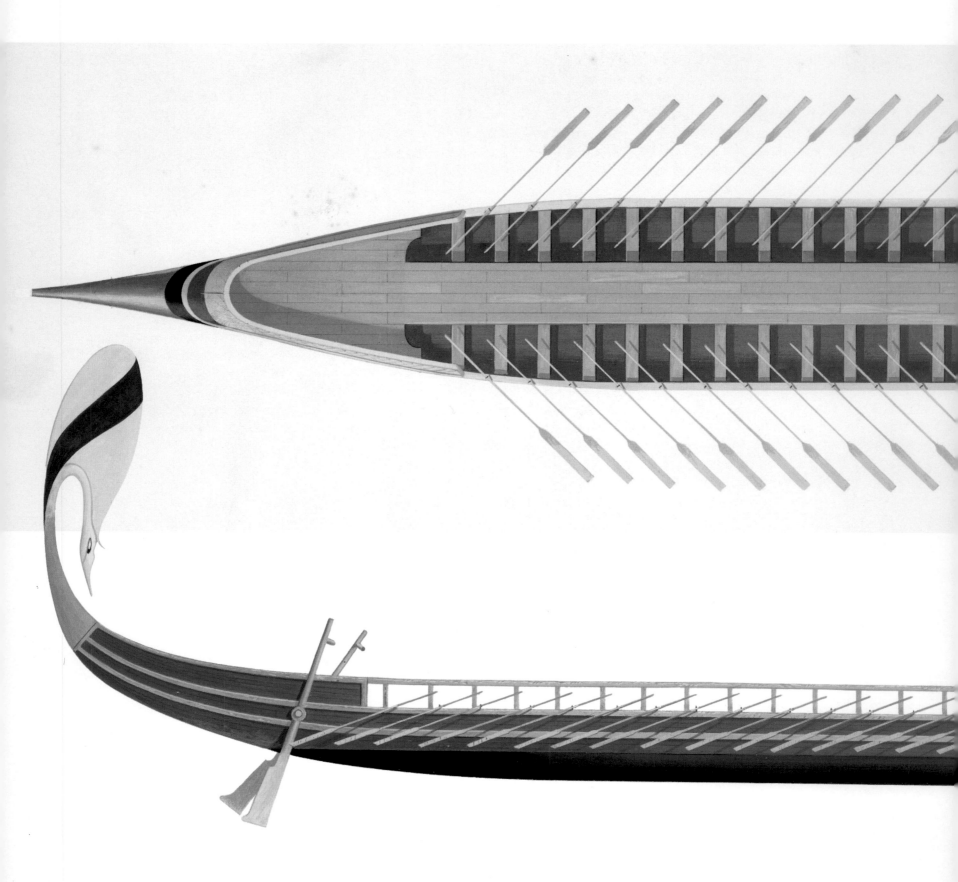

architects, shipbuilding in the second millennium AD was already a major factor in national economies. Corinth, which was long the leading shipbuilding center, had yards capable of producing a great number of vessels, while in a single year those at Athens managed to build 360 triremes, 50 quadriremes and 7 quinquiremes.

The constructional method described by Homer, while remaining based on structural planking as in the Egyptian ships, had introduced systems of connection between the planks that made the hull much stiffer: mortise and tenon joints locked together the various strakes which were fixed to the frame with wooden pins. Moreover, the planks themselves were no longer the short, Egyptian-style boards, but had acquired much more useful lengths thanks to the abundance of long timber.

Initial consequences of the greater longitudinal rigidity were the disappearance of the heavy tensioning cable running between stem and stern, the great invention of the Egyptian naval architects, and the changing shape of the hull, no longer arching or crescent shaped but long, tapering and low in the water.

Only the elongated stern overhang was retained in the Greek ships and terminated high above the water with decorative motifs. At the prow, in contrast, the most eye-catching and significant innovation in naval architecture was the introduction of the pointed ram.

The ram was essentially an instrument of warfare and, in fact, appeared only on those vessels built to this end: thus was born the galley, a type of ship that was only superseded with the introduction of the cannon after the sixteenth century of the modern era. The sailing warship was then, in reality, a ship that relied on oars for motive power, the sail being an auxiliary means of propulsion intended to allow the oarsmen some respite during long voyages, and only in favorable conditions. In battle, when maneuvring and when there was a need to move quickly, the oars were the ship's "engine."

Galleys with two, three or even five rows of oars were built in the search for ever greater speed and, above all, increased power and maneuverability in battle: it was the ram that had to inflict the decisive blow. In contrast, the sail was actually lowered, complete with the mast, when the enemy was spotted and retained the archaic square shape. The Greek ship

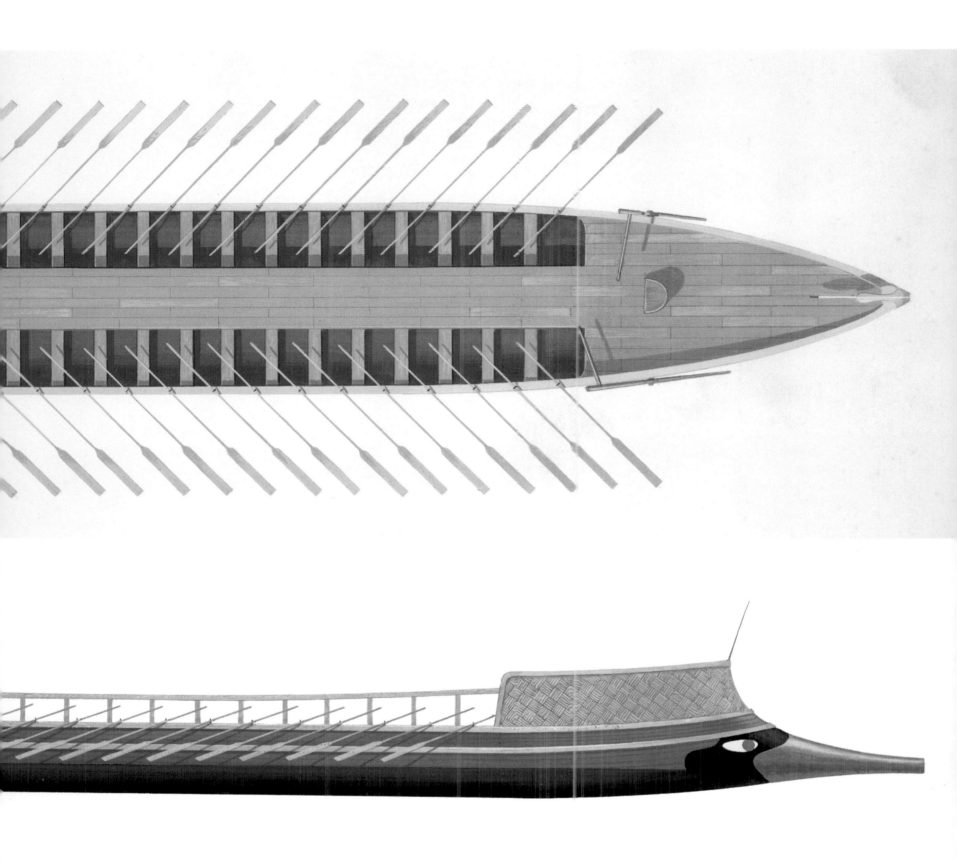

had a single yard, hoisted to the top of the mast, oriented with the same system of sheets used with the twin yards and sail of the Egyptian vessels. The windward sheet was fixed while the leeward one was adjusted by the helmsman.

In order to shorten sail when the wind was too strong for the ship, the crew drew up the lower corners with the lines attached to them that passed over the yard before descending to the deck. A similar system is used today to raise and lower Venetian blinds.

Sails were generally made of linen, composed of cloths with overlapping edges sewn together. Two types of fabric were used, a light and a heavy grade. We do not know whether the different fabrics were used in various areas of the same sail or rather for

different sails used according to the wind conditions, as we do today. It would be logical to lean towards the first theory given that sail propulsion was, in fact, auxiliary and that there would have been little space aboard, amidst all the oarsmen and the arms, to store spare sails.

The situation was, of course, different for merchant vessels which, having less streamlined forms and naturally lacking a ram, could devote their entire internal volume to cargo (replacing the rowers who would have taken up excessive space and been too heavy, not to mention expensive as they had to be fed). Cargo ships were therefore essentially sail-powered, patiently waiting for winds that were favorable in relation to the desired route.

Fortuitous archaeological discoveries have

THE GREEK GALLEY

22-23 The galley was a Greek invention: a type of ship characterized by great length with respects to its beam and draft, whose speed derived principally from rowing and thus the number of oarsmen it embarked. The galley was very agile and conceived to attack enemy ships efficiently by piercing their flanks with its ram. The eye painted on the prow (the hull was generally black due to the pitch with which it was treated) was intended to instill fear. The symbol is still used today on many small Mediterranean fishing boats, albeit with rather different symbolism.

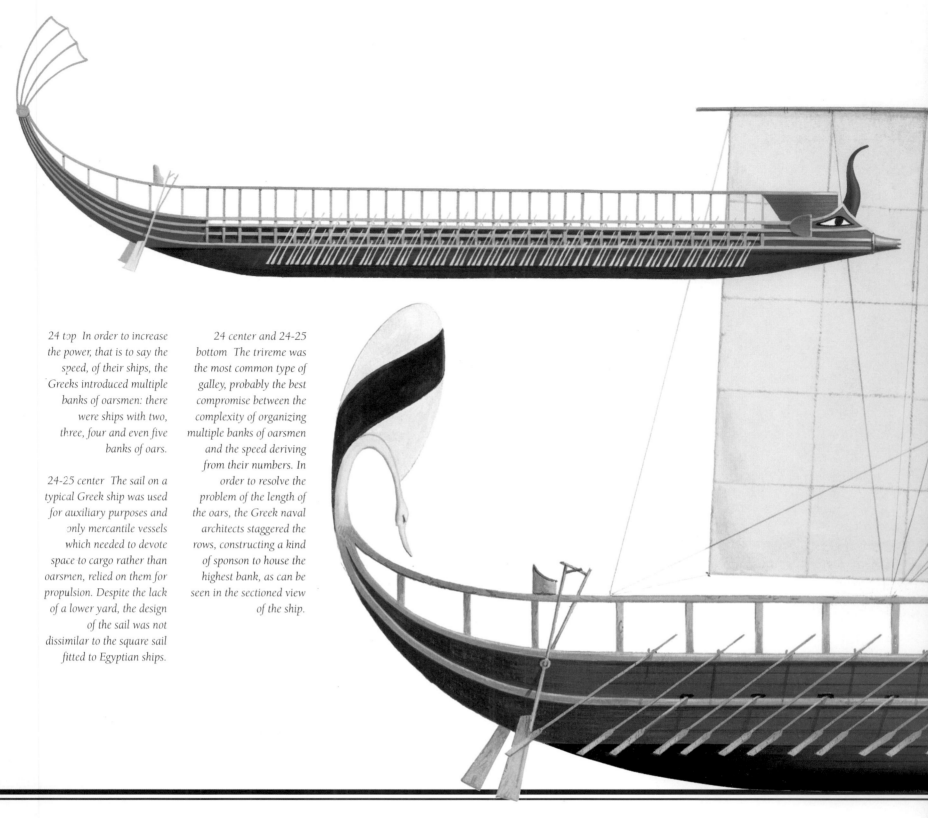

24 top In order to increase the power, that is to say the speed, of their ships, the Greeks introduced multiple banks of oarsmen: there were ships with two, three, four and even five banks of oars.

24-25 center The sail on a typical Greek ship was used for auxiliary purposes and only mercantile vessels which needed to devote space to cargo rather than oarsmen, relied on them for propulsion. Despite the lack of a lower yard, the design of the sail was not dissimilar to the square sail fitted to Egyptian ships.

24 center and 24-25 bottom The trireme was the most common type of galley, probably the best compromise between the complexity of organizing multiple banks of oarsmen and the speed deriving from their numbers. In order to resolve the problem of the length of the oars, the Greek naval architects staggered the rows, constructing a kind of sponson to house the highest bank, as can be seen in the sectioned view of the ship.

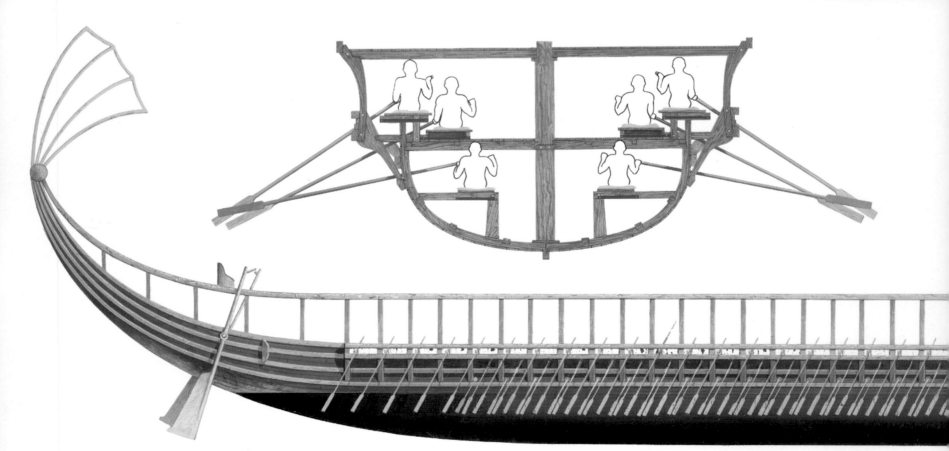

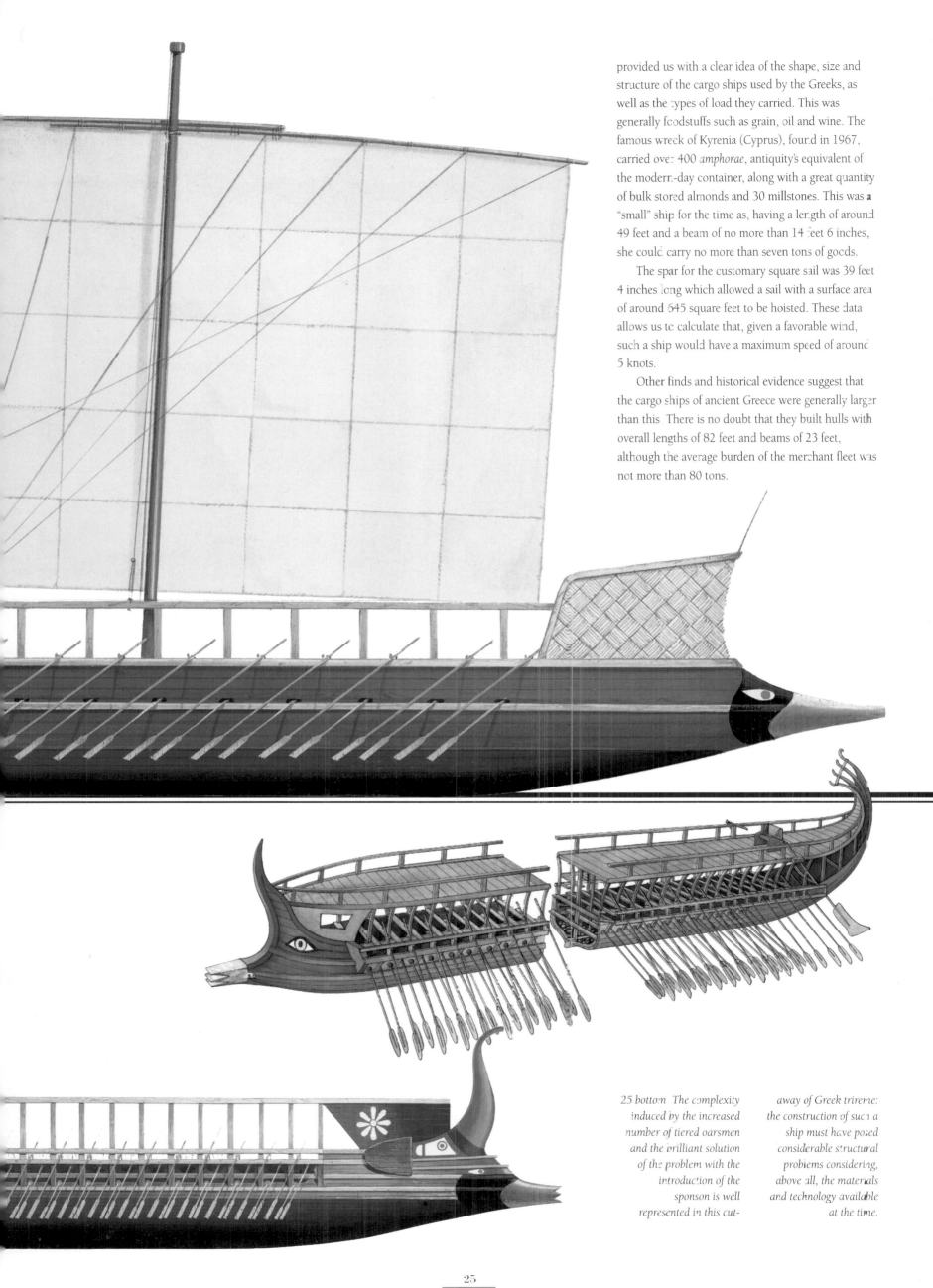

provided us with a clear idea of the shape, size and structure of the cargo ships used by the Greeks, as well as the types of load they carried. This was generally foodstuffs such as grain, oil and wine. The famous wreck of Kyrenia (Cyprus), found in 1967, carried over 400 *amphorae*, antiquity's equivalent of the modern-day container, along with a great quantity of bulk stored almonds and 30 millstones. This was a "small" ship for the time as, having a length of around 49 feet and a beam of no more than 14 feet 6 inches, she could carry no more than seven tons of goods.

The spar for the customary square sail was 39 feet 4 inches long which allowed a sail with a surface area of around 645 square feet to be hoisted. These data allows us to calculate that, given a favorable wind, such a ship would have a maximum speed of around 5 knots.

Other finds and historical evidence suggest that the cargo ships of ancient Greece were generally larger than this. There is no doubt that they built hulls with overall lengths of 82 feet and beams of 23 feet, although the average burden of the merchant fleet was not more than 80 tons.

25 bottom The complexity induced by the increased number of tiered oarsmen and the brilliant solution of the problem with the introduction of the sponson is well represented in this cut- away of Greek trireme: the construction of such a ship must have posed considerable structural problems considering, above all, the materials and technology available at the time.

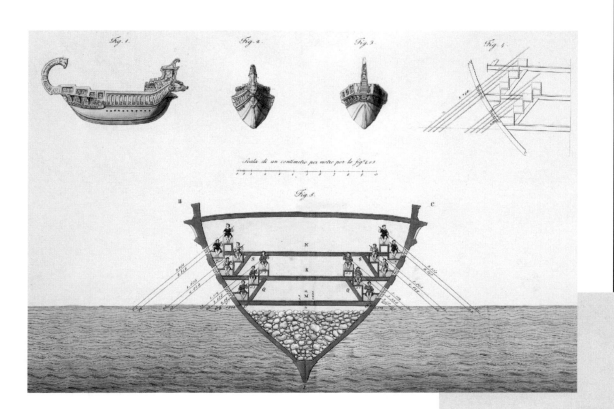

26-27 *These details of Roman ships are taken from Simonetti's* Storia delle nazioni. *The most interesting among them is the "arched" rig of the model to the bottom left, confirmed by contemporary sources, which could be considered as the first development of the ubiquitous square sail rig.*

The Roman Ship

26 top The Romans followed the Greek lead and developed large vessels with multiple banks of oars and auxiliary sails, at least for the warships. However, this sectional view is due more to the draftsman's imagination than historical fact: seven banks of oarsmen would seem to be excessive.

26 center In contrast, there is no doubting the impetus given by the Romans to the development of ports: this print, taken from Georg Braun's sixteenth century Civitates Orbis Terrarum, *while conceding much to the fertile imagination of the author, provides realistic testimony as to the size and facilities of the port of Ostia during the Roman epoch.*

From the third century BC onwards, and for the next five hundred years, the Mediterranean was to become to all intents and purposes a great lake traversed by military fleets and, above all, by regular commercial sailings, both belonging to the latest people to have taken control of the entire area, the Romans.

As was the case at the dawn of the preceding civilizations, in this initial period the Romans had concentrated on land rather than sea. However, as soon as demands and appetites deriving from political expansion and social progress began to make themselves felt, then the Romans too had to tackle maritime questions. They did so with such dogged determination that within the course of a single century they had become the first true naval power in history, finding themselves in a position comparable in terms of magnitude and effects to that enjoyed by the British navy around two thousand years later.

With the Romans, in fact, sailing adopted trends and techniques that were to remain unchanged up to the modern period. The ports, for example, which until then had been little more than beaches overlooked by towns, began to be embellished with those functions and features that were to become typical. The port of Ostia witnessed a building boom as soon as it became a terminus for the trade routes that converged there from throughout the Mediterranean in order to supply the goods required for the development of Rome.

Huge buildings, veritable human hives, were constructed to provide lodgings for the passing seamen and merchants. On the ground floors of these buildings flourished stores, shops and taverns of dubious morality. At the same time, at least seventy companies, comparable in terms of their activities to our import-export houses, were established in Ostia, along with those associations which eventually became the maritime mutual aid funds: there was one for each category of worker, from the caulkers to the seamen, from the fishermen to the stevedores, from the storemen to the customs officers.

This situation came about after the Romans had developed their capabilities in the fields of shipbuilding and navigation, drawing on the Greek and Phoenician traditions in the absence of native experience. The former they found virtually on their own doorstep following the conquest of the territories comprising the Greek colonies in southern Italy. The Phoenicians had instead been obliged to share their secrets following the Punic wars, fought by the Phoenician colony of Carthage which then dominated the waters of the central Mediterranean and thus obstructed the expansionist aims of Rome.

Taking the models and techniques of the Phoenicians and combing them with the experience of Greek workers, the Romans built their own fleets and, as already mentioned, established the first great navy.

The Roman ships were, in fact, based on those of the preceding civilizations. But, apart from certain instruments and techniques of warfare, it was the

Romans who developed the techniques of sail-power navigation, just as British were to do at a later date.

While the Roman sailing ship continued to rely on a large square sail as its means of propulsion, the seamen were not slow to recognize the limited maneuverability of the system: a second mast made its appearance at the bow of the ship to carry a second sail. This foresail was able to assist the steering of the vessel.

This short mast was the original foremast and as early as the first century BC was, on occasion, joined by a third at the stern, the mizzen. Naturally, only the largest cargo ships could afford to be rigged with two or three masts. Smaller vessels for fishing or coastal work, continued to be rigged with a single large mast in the center of the hull. However, on some of these ships, sails began to be used with a spar whose base pivoted on the mast: this was the fore-and-aft mainsail, or more precisely, a kind of spritsail, a format that was better suited to sailing into the wind or, at least more efficient when sailing with the wind abeam. Subsequently, this innovation was to spread throughout the Mediterranean basin as

the lateen sail.

A triangular topsail also made its appearance on the largest ships, rigged from the head of the mast and attached to the two extremities of the square sail's yard. This was an efficient system augmenting sail area as a means of increasing the speed of ships that were now carrying significant loads on long routes across the Mediterranean. With these new sails the Roman ship had a previously unheard of potential for development.

A good, albeit tragic, example of the efficacy of

this sail plan and one which at the same time illustrates the seamanship that accompanied its introduction, is provided by a third-century bas-relief. Similar in effect to the individual frames of a film, the sculpture describes the attempted rescue of a boy fallen overboard at the very entrance to the port of Rome. Two ships, a large cargo vessel with a square sail and foremast and a smaller vessel rigged with a spritsail, race from the port to the boy's aid just as a second large cargo ship is entering the port. The wind is blowing from the port out to sea and two ships, the in-bound cargo vessel and the smaller boat risk colliding. The fore-and-aft rigged boat luffs hard, a maneuvre favoured by this type of sail pattern, whilst the cargo ship sets her foremast and shortens square sail to turn rapidly.

We do not know how the situation unfolded, although it must have had a tragic finale, as the bas-relief decorates the boy's tomb. However, what we are left with is sufficient to allow us to evaluate the skill of the Roman fleet's crews who had clearly developed advanced sailing techniques rather than relying purely on the direction of the wind.

28 top A caulker at work: his gestures and tool, a characteristic axe, are the same as those employed for centuries up to the advent, two thousand years later, of iron and steel hulls.

28-29 The famous bas-relief depicting the dramatic attempted rescue of a boy fallen into the sea. The work is from a Roman funerary monument of the Imperial period. It is, to all intents and purposes, a compendium of the naval art of that civilization. The cargo ship is particularly large and is using its foresail to facilitate maneuvring. The smaller boats use different types of sails, a form of spritsail in fact, that is easier for small crews to handle.

29 top While the cargo, exotic animals in this case, destined for the circuses, is still being loaded, the sailors appear to be preparing to hoist the sails: they are anxious to depart, perhaps justified by a favorable wind, a factor too valuable in that era for the helmsman to waste.

30-31 The Roman bireme had a ram like the earlier Greek warships. The second ram fitted to the stern of this ship does not instead appear to be faithful to the original model; moreover, it would seem to be of limited utility with this kind of vessel. It does, however, add a degree of grace to the lines, an aesthetic question somewhat at odds with the usual pragmatism of Roman shipbuilders who were more preoccupied with increasing the offensive capabilities of their vessels, something they did most effectively. A case of artistic license, therefore, that can also be seen in the ship in the background which has been attributed with cargo carrying duties in spite of the presence of a ram and a bank of oarsmen.

In terms of hull shape, the cargo ship had large volumes and a significant freeboard while the naval vessels were "long ships" with two, three, four or even five layers of oars.

Although the techniques of sail propulsion had been perfected, offensive capabilities still relied on the ram invented by the Greeks and the maneuverability guaranteed by a large number of experts rowers. The Roman galley was similar in size to its Greek counterpart, but the situation with regards cargo ships was rather different. The large Roman merchant vessels destined to shuttle back and forth between Alexandria in Egypt and Rome had displacements of up to 1,600 tons.

The *Isis*, regarding which we have reliable information, was around 180 feet long, 46 feet beam and a burden of 1,200-1,300 tons. This large ship had a single stern cabin, destined for the commander and the helmsmen: the passengers, frequently carried in that period, merchants heading to the Middle East to trade in spices, fabrics, jewels and all those luxury goods which had become indispensable to the sophisticated Roman society, travelled on-deck, sheltered by precarious awnings when the warm Mediterranean climate turned nasty.

Drinking water was carried in capacious cisterns stowed at the bottom of the ship, while cooking was carried out on braziers in a sheltered area of the deck.

With only slight modifications, this type of ship was to continue to perform the same role throughout the Mediterranean for a further

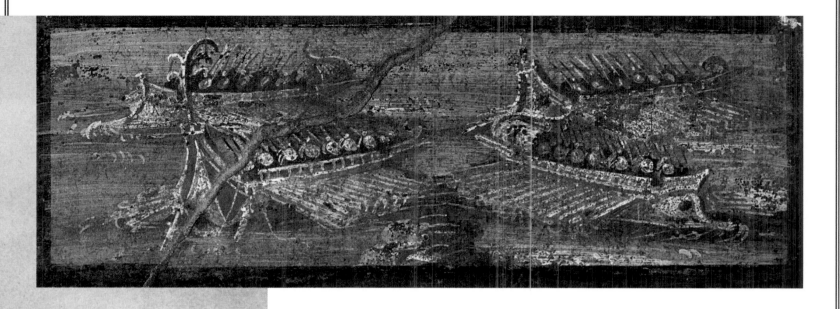

millennium. As mentioned earlier, shipbuilding technology continued to draw on the Greek and Phoenician traditions. The Roman ship still had structural planking: the wood used was fir, pine or cedar and the planks were not generally caulked but joined via the classical mortise and tenon system. The bottom was on occasion covered with lead installed over a layer of cloth soaked in pitch to protect the wood from the marine flora and fauna. The topsides were instead treated with melted wax mixed with pigments or again dressed with black pitch. Floors, ribs and keelson were made of oak and connected to the hull planking via copper nails and the topsides with hardwood pins. The sailmakers used linen fabrics, while the rigging was made of hemp, twisted papyrus fibers and even strips of leather.

The craft techniques and the materials employed had been refined, but the constructional technology was unchanged. Thanks to improvements in equipment, however, the Roman sailing ships enjoyed considerably better performance than their predecessors and were quite remarkably efficient when compared with those that followed in successive centuries: while the average speed was around 4 knots, some merchant vessels covered the distance between Tunisia and the coast of the Lazio region, or that between Sicily and Egypt, in times corresponding to average speeds of 6 knots!

A precious aid in obtaining this kind of performance was the Romans' portfolio of maps and charts. The commander of a large Roman cargo ship would have had little to envy with respects to his colleagues of the next millennium.

31 bottom left The Roman warship – as it appeared in a bas-relief – with a ram, a deck crowded with infantry and a castle from which arrows and darts could be launched at the enemy.

31 bottom right Another bas-relief depicts the characteristic cargo vessel which privileged sail propulsion and rounder forms and had no oarsmens

31 top In spite of its undoubted utility in naval battles, in reality the Roman ship was long conceived as a troop carrier, the soldiers embarked being used to attack and board enemy vessels. This is well illustrated by the forest of spears and shields that clutters the decks of these two biremes.

The Ship of the First Millennium

Before the first millennium AD, the Phoenicians had already circumnavigated Africa, as documented by Herodotus. The Greek explorer, Scylax of Caryanda had already compiled and published the *Periplus Maris Erythraei*, the first true portolan in history, with precise notes and information for sailors regarding the coasts, ports and prevailing winds, and Pytheas of Marseille (in his days a Greek colony named Massalia) had identified the Pole Star, had determined the geographical position of his city and had sailed beyond Gibraltar as far as the coasts of Norway, the first man to roam the seas for geographical purposes (his expedition had actually been organized and financed to search for tin mines!). In short, by the dawn of the first millenium AD seafaring had become a well established way of life; furthermore it was the fundamental instrument for expansion and the development of civilization itself.

The Romans were masters of both the Mediterranean and the northern seas where they met different cultures that had produced different types of ships suited to seas in which conditions were frequently hostile. It was not, however, until the Middle Ages that these new influences made themselves felt; the *Pax Romana*, had in effect petrified technological progress in the field of sailing. Up until the fifth or sixth centuries, military vessels had only had patrol duties to perform and the model developed by the Roman naval architects and admirals was even

excessive; at the same time, cargo ships efficiently performed transportation duties between the various provinces of the empire and the capital.

There was no evolution on the seas, the great historical and social changes were all taking place on dry land: what actually occurred was an involution, with the barbarian invasions and the consequent collapse of the Roman empire.

The epicenter of civilization shifted from the Italian peninsula, eastwards again to Byzantium and, for the first time, to the northern regions of Europe.

The Byzantine society actually used types of sailing ships that had already been seen. This could hardly be otherwise, given the centuries that had passed and the great civilizations that had alternated in the development of sail power. The symbol of the Byzantine fleet was the dromon, a large galley that considerably relied on oars for its motive power. Its sail plan was based on the convenient lateen sail that was easy to set and adjust in the case of favorable winds, and just as easy to strike in battle.

The dromon, or galley, was to be the sailing warship up to the sixteenth century, and was only to be made obsolete by the advent of the cannon and the type of ship better suited to the deadly new instrument of warfare, the galleon.

The dromon is certainly a kind of ship that represents more of a continuity that an evolution with respects to the preceding model. The Greek word *dromon*, derives from the term *dromos* meaning "running", just as galley in Greek means a fast animal.

Probably, and the doubt arises because we have no images or descriptions of the early dromons, they were none other than the ancient bireme, of Greek origin and refined by the Romans. What was new, and this was an important innovation, was the type of sail. With the end of the Roman empire, the square sail disappeared, except in the case of a few small merchant vessels. Through to the end of the Middle Ages, the Mediterranean was to see, above all, fast galleys, firstly Byzantine and then Venetian. Genoan, Spanish and Arab versions, all rigged with lateen sails. The precise origin of this type of sail is unknown, but although there is evidence that it was used during the Roman period, it certainly came out of the Arab world given that it is still widespread there today and, in the past, it was adopted by all those countries that were influenced by Arab expansion either through direct conquest or contiguity.

The lateen rig is characterized by a long yard,

supported at the center by the masthead, as with the square sail, but strongly sloping towards the bow where one end is fixed. The other end pointing skywards is oriented and moved from one side of the ship to the other. In this way the sail could be trimmed efficiently to allow the vessel to sail to windward, albeit not to the angles permitted by the rigs of modern sailing boats.

The mast itself was inclined slightly forward and supported by shrouds that could, in contrast with contemporary northern versions, be adjusted by means of tackles. The lateen sail is, in fact, hoisted forward, outside the shrouds, with those to leeward being slackened off to trim the sail towards the center of the ship when sailing into the wind. In contrast, the handling was complicated when one wanted or was obliged to tack: firstly the tacks (the lines adjusting forward end of the sail) and the sheets (those adjusting the stern end) were let out; after having let go a little the yard's halyard, a seaman than brought the yard vertical against the mast. At that point, the wind filled the sail towards the bow and, as the helmsman continued to tack, the seaman brought in the sheets on the other side. In short, the ship was tacked from the stern. This was, of course, also true of square-rigged vessels and the description is probably more complex than the actual operation. In one way or another, the lateen sail spread throughout the Mediterranean, and not only aboard the military galleys. Cargo ships, which with their rounder hulls and higher freeboard, still resembled their Roman equivalents, were also rigged with lateen sails.

During the period of the crusades, ships with two decks were developed that were suitable for carrying the then inseparable troops and horses. They were actually quite small compared with the ships that carried grain to Rome: the Venetian crusaders' ship, for example, was not more than 85 feet long and with a beam of about 20 feet. It had two masts, one taller and strongly inclined forward, both rigged with lateen sails. At the rear appeared a stern castle, which housed

32-33 The Republic of Venice's predominance came about thanks to its efficient fleet of naval and mercantile vessels such as the military galley, here reconstructed from contemporary models. Both types of ships were fitted with lateen sails which provided superior performance, especially when sailing into the wind, with respects to square sails.

33 top This painting by Raphael clearly illustrates the capabilities of the lateen sail: the ship is advancing, its oars clear of the water, the wind abeam, the sheet hauled in at the center, and the yard parallel to the longitudinal axis of the hull.

the captain's accommodation and the helmsman who still steered the ship with two lateral oars, as in the Egyptian era.

In the meantime, a strong maritime tradition had also developed in the seas of northern Europe. Committed to Roman expansion towards Germany and the British Isles, Julius Caesar had already encountered ships "that had a flatter hull to make them easier to haul onto the beach and easier to maneuver over tidal shoals (tides were virtually unknown to the Romans). With high bows and sterns identically shaped to better tackle the waves of those seas. With keels of oak to resist any impact. Built with ribs of wood a foot square in section, fixed to the planking with iron nails an inch thick; the sails made of hides or softened leather." This was the Scandinavian or Viking ship, propelled by a large square sail, well suited to coping with stormy seas in which oars would frequently be inefficient.

The Viking ship has two features which, to the expert as well as to the layman's eye, make it immediately recognizable: firstly the clinker planking, where the individual planks rather than being laid side-by-side instead overlap, the bottom edge of one plank over the upper edge of the one below it, nailed in place without caulking, and secondly the steering of the ship entrusted to a single steering-oar, always located on the starboard side (the name for the ship's rudder in Norwegian is *styri*, providing the origin of the English words "steer" and "steer-board" which of course evolved into starboard).

In the second half of the first millennium AD, with this type of long, low and clinker-built ship, the Scandinavian seamen completed voyages of exploration and conquest as far afield as England, Ireland, Iceland and the coasts of North America on the other side of the North Atlantic and well before Columbus.

From a constructional point of view, and apart from their clinker planking, other design details distinguished the Nordic vessels from their Mediterranean counterparts. While the planking still had a structural function, structural elements destined to form the load-bearing frame of the ship appeared: the heavy, robust keelson, as noted by Julius Caesar, that was not simply intended to

34 top With their longships the Vikings sailed the seas of northern Europe, reaching the coasts of Greenland and, as has now been proved, the American continent, well before Columbus. During those voyages across freezing seas, the only protection was a canvas awning hung above the thwarts.

34-35 bottom This drawing highlights a constructional feature typical of the Nordic boats: the keel, a longitudinal structure that emerged from the planking the full length of the ship, lending it strength and rigidity.

34-35 top The Nordic ship was long and light like the Mediterranean galley: it differed in that it was still fitted with a square sail due to the minor role played by oars for propulsion, a system less effective in the rougher northern waters, and its clinker construction.

"resist any impact," but also provided longitudinal stiffness and strength for the whole ship. Then there were the so-called "strong-planks," planks of greater thickness and with an inverted "L" shape that were located in correspondence with the waterline (providing supports for the principal transverse elements. the floor timbers) and the gunwales. The mast was stepped on, and transmitted the tensions of the propulsive system to, a true mast step which in turn rested on the keelson and involved four or five floor timbers.

The shape of the hull was very elongated at the waterline, hence the name "longship" generically attributed to the Viking vessels. In reality, they would not have been particularly long overall. They were, above all, low in the water, which may give an impression of length, and fairly beamy even though they failed to reach the typical proportions for the ships of the period when the ratio between length and breadth was in the order of 3 to 1, and with very fine and high extremities. The fore- and stern-castles typical of

medieval ships were to develop out of the high bows and sterns.

The longships were defined by the number of spaces or thwarts destined for the rowers: on average a ship had between thirty and forty thwarts which, as archaeological finds have demonstrated, were generally just over a yard long, meaning that the Viking sailing ship was probably no more than 115 feet long.

Around the thirteenth century, the northern seas became the dominion of the peoples who had settled in the areas of present-day England, northern France and the Hanseatic nations which had based their economies and security on sea power.

The ship that accompanied the development of those societies was based in terms of shape and construction, on the Viking model. Castles fore and aft soon appeared for military purposes, as had already occurred in the era of the Roman warship, but were also fitted to vessels destined for transportation and exploration. The ships were clinker-built, with tall, tapering bows and sterns. A single lateral rudder and a square sail were employed.

Out of these basic specifications was born the typical ship of the late Medieval period, common

36 bottom In the Mediterranean the fast military galley was flanked by the "round ship" with a greater carrying capacity, designed and developed to transport troops, horses, pilgrims and various followers of the crusades to the Holy Land. Like the galleys, the round ships were rigged with lateen sails.

37 The larger ships destined for more demanding voyages developed higher freeboards and imposing sail plans: the carrack of southern Europe like the one represented in this fifteenth century painting by Lorenzo Costa, and the northern cog, were both rigged with square sails and both featured high castles at stem and stern.

36 top The ships of the second millennium, at least in the types used in northern Europe, were revolutionized by the introduction of the sternpost rudder in place of the two steering oars (one in the Nordic tradition) mounted either side of the stern.

36 center The Mediterranean was also the cradle for innumerable types of smaller boats which, replicating the technology of the larger vessels, developed along the coasts and with only modest evolutionary changes have survived to the present day. The boat seen here, only the stern section having changed, can still be seen sailing along the coasts of the central and eastern Mediterranean.

throughout the northern seas, and soon influential on naval architecture further afield, thanks to commercial demands that led the northern shipowners to the Mediterranean and their colleagues from Genoa to the English ports. This was the cog.

A ship depicted on a number of seals from as early as the thirteenth century, while clearly displaying Viking influences, had more prominent castles than in the past, a bowsprit and fuller forms. Moreover, two images, one on a bas-relief from a late twelfth century baptismal font in Winchester cathedral, the other on a mural painting in the church of Fide on Gotland from the early thirteenth century, are the oldest despictions of the most important nautical invention since the era of the famous plaited cable that allowed Egyptian ships to leave the waters of the Nile and to sail the open sea: the sternpost rudder.

4,500 years had passed since the depiction of the first sailing

ship: during all that time, the ship, whether powered by sail or by oars, had always had two lateral steering oars in the Mediterranean and one in the northern seas.

When the civilizations of the north decided to expand their trading interests they could only do so by crossing the seas, and thus searched for technical improvements that could render their ships more efficient. Of these, the sternpost rudder was the most innovative and the most significant. The lateral steering oars, however effective they may have been on rowed galleys with even-keeled hulls, were not efficient when the ship was under sail and heeling. The windward steering oar would, in fact, find itself out of the water, while the leeward one would tend to flex or even break under strain given that it had only a single high pivot. The centerline rudder, fixed to the sternpost with metal hinges along its length, was always in the water and did not flex. The feature was to be adopted throughout the world and on all types of vessels, especially as the development of sailing in open and oceanic waters was to emphasize the limitations of oared propulsion.

The northern nations, faced with wave patterns that made rowing difficult, and committed to increasingly long voyages, developed their sailing techniques and gradually abandoned oars and oarsmen.

In terms of technology, the cog thus represents the prototype for the modern sailing ship: it had no

thwarts for rowers, but rather an efficient sail system, it boasted previously unheard of carrying capacity and, above all, was well equipped to tackle the high seas.

While the cog hulls were still clinker-built their framing was substantial and eventually became load bearing. The extremities were still tapered, but apparently not so markedly higher than the sides. In reality, the sides of the ships had actually been raised to increase the carrying capacity. The forecastle was now a small superstructure, while its equivalent at the stern increased in importance and gradually became an integral part of the hull.

The size of these vessels was generally modest: the cog of the fourteenth century had an overall length of just under 100 feet and a maximum beam of 23 feet. It was thus a slimmer ship than the Mediterranean cargo vessels, but had a draft of 10 feet and a similar freeboard. This meant that it had a large cargo capacity despite its modest dimensions. When these dimensions eventually increased, evidently to meet increased demands for trade and navigation, the cog evolved into the hulk, while retaining the same shape and rig.

The cog and the hulk, in fact, always had a single mast with a single large square sail that could be increased or shortened by adding or removing the "bonnets," bands of canvas that were laced along the foot of the sail.

Fixed reef points also soon appeared, but apart from this and the refinement of sail handling techniques, no modifications were made to the rig.

Only the encounter with the contemporary Mediterranean vessel, the carrack, which will be discussed separately, led to the birth of the three-masted sailing ship. Then again, it was also the reciprocal encounter with the cog that led to the reintroduction of the square sail to the Mediterranean's mercantile fleet after it had been forgotten following the disappearance of the typical Roman cargo ships.

The cog, and its larger sister the hulk, monopolized traffic in the northern seas. They were operated by the English merchants of the five Ports (Dover, Sandwich, Hythe, Romney and Hastings) who had come together to better manage and, above all, protect, their commercial interests. The cog was even more widespread among the German trading cities of the Hanseatic League: still today this kind of vessel is frequently referred to as the Hanseatic trader.

In the meantime, however, the Mediterranean was emerging from the obscurity of the Middle Ages and Venice and Genoa, and to an even greater extent, Spain and Portugal, were despatching their carracks on previously unexplored routes.

Out of the combined traditions of the carrack and the cog was to come the true modern sailing ship: the sixteenth century galleon.

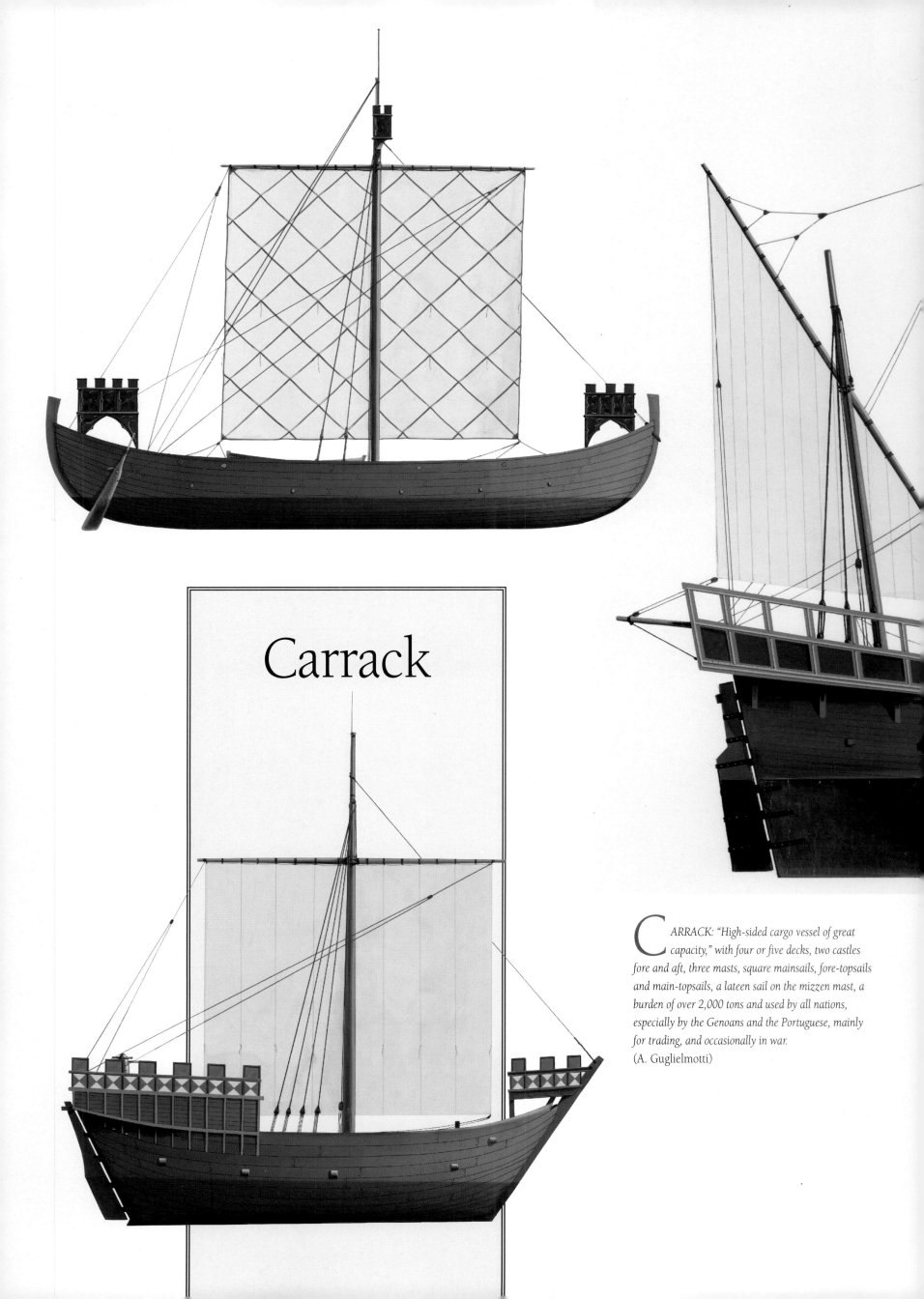

Carrack

C ARRACK: *"High-sided cargo vessel of great capacity,"* with four or five decks, two castles fore and aft, three masts, square mainsails, fore-topsails and main-topsails, a lateen sail on the mizzen mast, a burden of over 2,000 tons and used by all nations, especially by the Genoans and the Portuguese, mainly for trading, and occasionally in war.
(A. Guglielmotti)

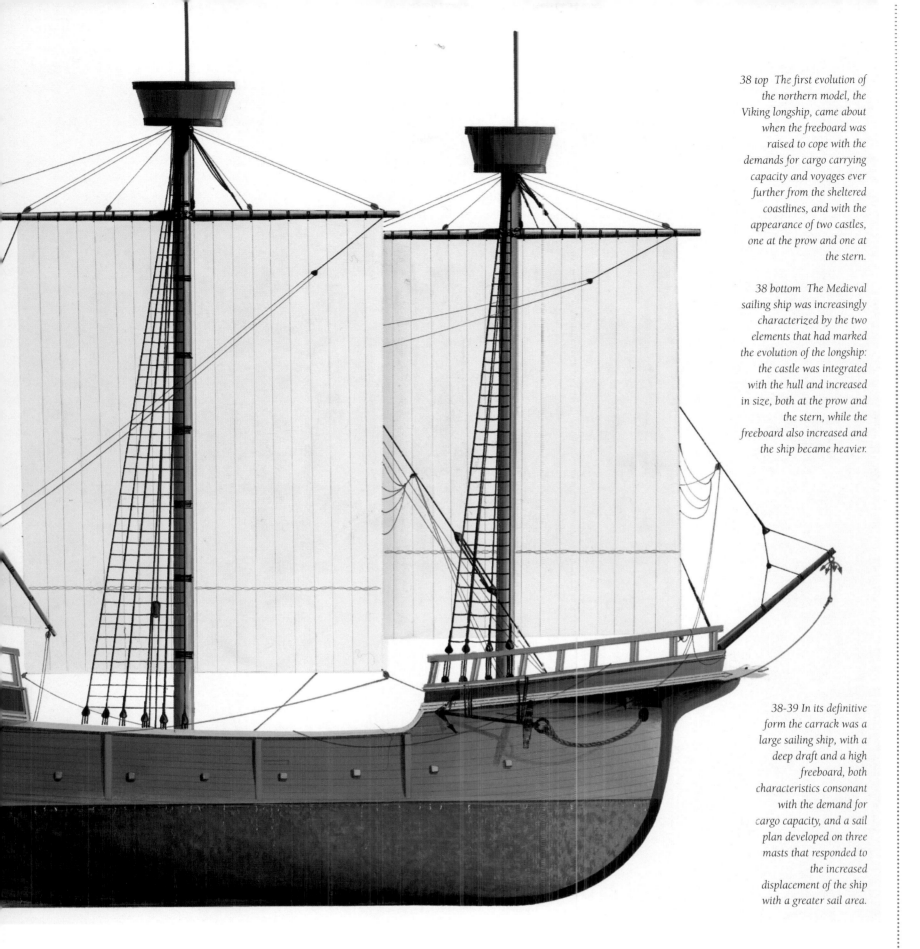

In the "Pizigani Charter," a document dating from
the late fourteenth century, a two-masted ship is
depicted with a square sail rigged on the mainmast
and a lateen sail on the mizzen. This vessel displays all
the historical features of the typical ships of the
Mediterranean, the round ship and the galley, and the
northern seas, the cog.

This is, in fact, the first representation of a carrack,
the sailing ship that for two hundred years, up to the
advent of its direct descendant the galleon, was to be
the archetypal merchant ship. Carracks were operated
in the Mediterranean, above all by Venetians and
Genoans, and used by the Spanish and the Portuguese
on their voyages of exploration and trade in the
Atlantic.

The carrack was the last development in naval

architecture of that period. It had a rounded stern
with the center rudder hinged on the sternpost,
against which the planking butted. The castles fore
and aft were lighter superstructures, simple
platforms surrounded by rails or even a netting so as
not to overload the extremities of the ship and to
allow more rapid run-off of water. As shown in the
drawing from the document mentioned above, the
rig was originally two-masted, with main and mizzen
masts, but the classic three-masted layout rig was
subsequently adopted.

The triumph of sail over oar as a means of
propulsion was now complete and sailing techniques
had, in the wake of Nordic examples, reached levels
that were not to be significantly improved upon until
the clipper and windjammer era. Motive power was

provided by the large square sail rigged on the
mainmast, whilst maneuverability depended on the
two small, agile sails rigged on the mizzen mast at
the stern and the foremast at the bow, the first to luff
the ship and the second to bring her round.

The need to increase performance subsequently
led to an increase in the number of sails: forward of
the bows, a square sail, the true spritsail, was bent to
a yard rigged from the bowsprit, while the main mast
was extended by a topmast setting a square topsail.

The square mainsail was fitted with bonnets, the
bands of canvas added to the foot of the sail to
increase its surface area. This was a Nordic system
that by then had replaced the old system of
shortening the sail in use since antiquity.

This was the rig fitted to the *Santa Maria*, the

40 top The carrack was the typical ship of the late Medieval period, used by all the nations involved in maritime traffic as well as the major maritime powers of the Mediterranean such as Venice and Genoa. This painting by Vittore Carpaccio illustrates the technical features of the model: sternpost rudder, mizzen mast rigged with a lateen sail, main mast with a square sail and, although hidden here, a short foremast on the forecastle. The two castles characterize the lines of the ship.

flagship of the small fleet with which Christopher Columbus crossed the Atlantic and discovered the American continent at the end of the fourteenth century.

The *Santa Maria* was called a nao by Columbus. But *nao* simply means "ship," and was just used to mean a large sailing vessel.

Although we have no images that actually confirm the thesis, the *Santa Maria* would undoubtedly have been a carrack. Columbus provides detailed descriptions of the rig and her construction in his accounts of the voyage.

She was by no means a large example of the type and her hull dimensions have been reconstructed to approximately 78 feet 6" in length,

with a beam of just over 26 feet. We know the dimensions of other carracks of the era of greater tonnages. In a treatise on naval construction conserved in the British Museum, the vital statistics of a large carrack are reported as 124 feet 8" long (85 feet 4" at the keel) and 34 feet 2" beam.

The Venetian carrack represented in a view of the city by the fourteenth century painter Jacopo De Barbari must have been even larger. The sailing ship depicted also features a significant technical innovation: she is rigged with four masts. Set right at the stern, in fact, is a second mizzen which was to become known as the bonaventure and which balanced the sail plan and allowed the ship to luff.

40 center and bottom The Santa Maria, the flagship of the small fleet with which Columbus undertook his voyage of discovery westwards, was a modern interpretation of the carrack.

There are actually no surviving images available of this particular vessel, but the descriptions provided by the Genoese admiral make her easily identifiable, despite differences in interpretation, as a Portuguese nao, a generic name attributed to a large ship and thus to the carrack form. The high castles had been lost, evidence of a trend that was eventually to lead to the development of the full-rigged ship.

40-41 The Portuguese used the carrack for their voyages of discovery, developing the highest expression of the form. As the ship itself increased in size so did the proportions of the castles, while the sail plan saw an interesting increase in the number of masts with the appearance of the bonaventure at the stern and the number of sails with the introduction of topsails.

Caravel

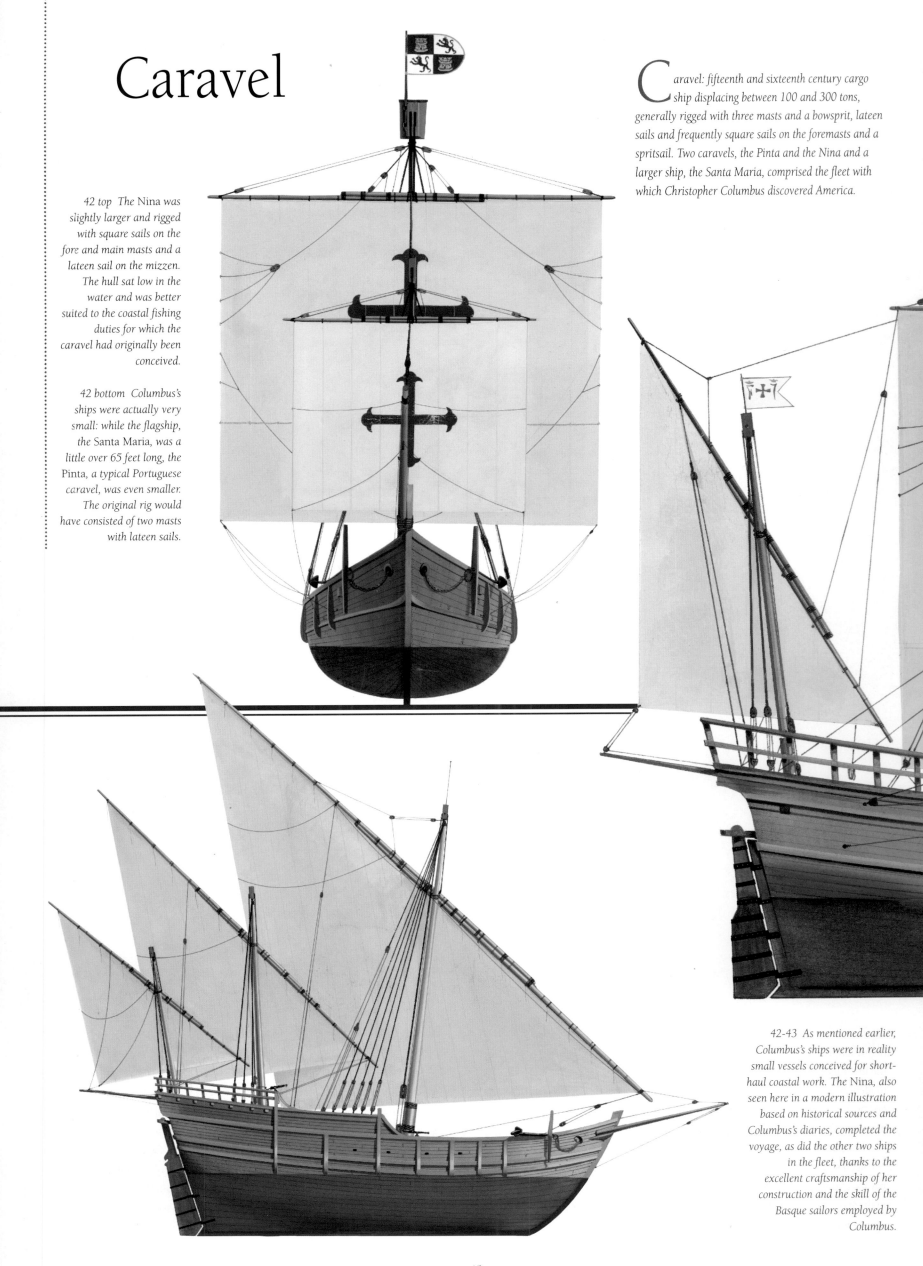

Caravel: fifteenth and sixteenth century cargo ship displacing between 100 and 300 tons, generally rigged with three masts and a bowsprit, lateen sails and frequently square sails on the foremasts and a spritsail. Two caravels, the Pinta and the Nina and a larger ship, the Santa Maria, comprised the fleet with which Christopher Columbus discovered America.

42 top The Nina was slightly larger and rigged with square sails on the fore and main masts and a lateen sail on the mizzen. The hull sat low in the water and was better suited to the coastal fishing duties for which the caravel had originally been conceived.

42 bottom Columbus's ships were actually very small: while the flagship, the Santa Maria, was a little over 65 feet long, the Pinta, a typical Portuguese caravel, was even smaller. The original rig would have consisted of two masts with lateen sails.

42-43 As mentioned earlier, Columbus's ships were in reality small vessels conceived for short-haul coastal work. The Nina, also seen here in a modern illustration based on historical sources and Columbus's diaries, completed the voyage, as did the other two ships in the fleet, thanks to the excellent craftsmanship of her construction and the skill of the Basque sailors employed by Columbus.

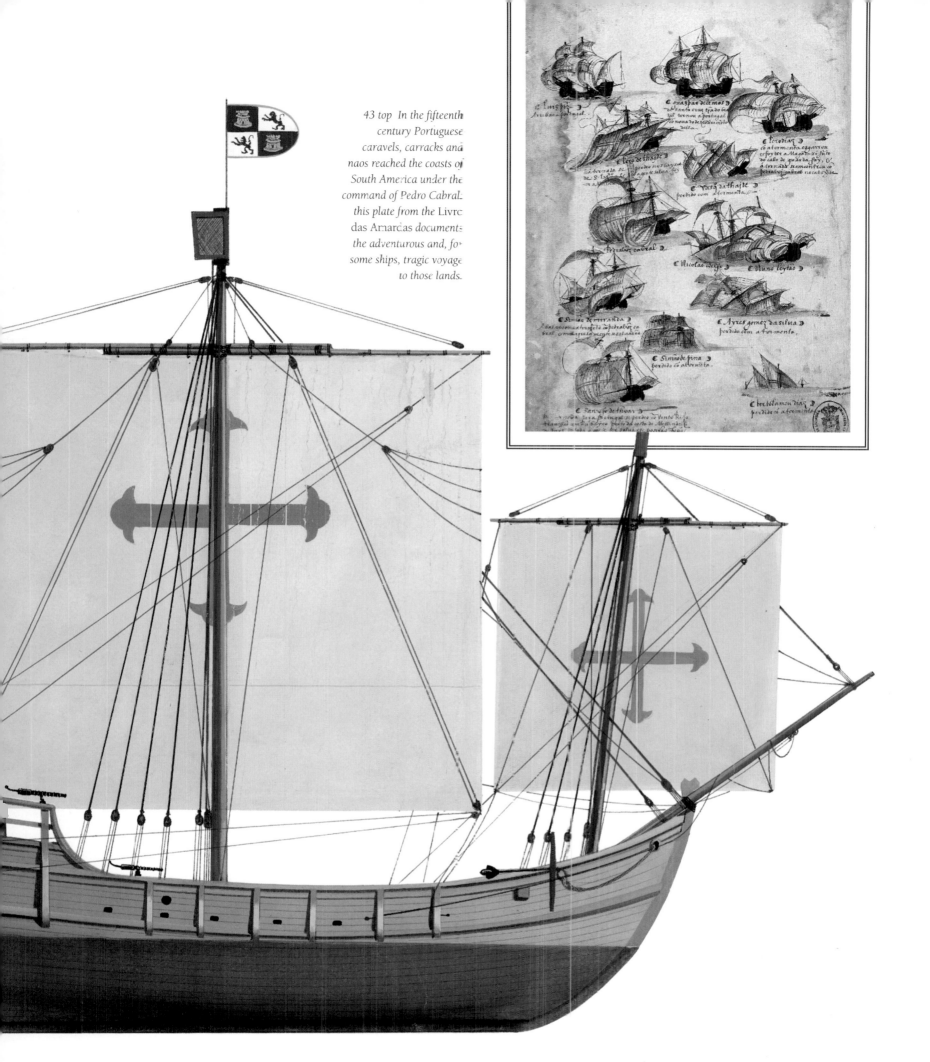

The definition of the caravel has always been highly ambiguous. The term would seem to appear for the first time in the "Charter of Alfonso III" from 1255, to identify a fishing boat used in the Atlantic waters of Portugal. Subsequently it was used to define small merchant ships rigged with two masts and lateen sails

The caravel owes its fame to Columbus who used two such ships, the *Pinta* and the *Nina*, on his first voyage of discovery "following the course of the sun" to the Indies. For the maritime historians, the term caravel is also significant because a variant spelling,

carvel, has been used since the sixteenth century to distinguish a type of construction in which, in contrast with clinker-built vessels, the planking does not overlap but is set flush.

Throughout the fifteenth century, the naval architecture of the northern European countries, albeit advanced in the introduction of the center rudder and initiating the transition from structural planking to a load-bearing framing, was still tied to traditional clinker planking, with the frames inserted after the planking had been set.

An account from the late fifteenth century reports that *craveischepen*, or carvel-built caravels along the lines of the Portuguese model, were built in Holland and Denmark for the first time between 1459 and 1460. This type of construction allowed on the one hand, greater thickness and therefore increased stiffness of the planking itself, while on the other permitting it to be fastened over the framing. However, it should be pointed out that in order to build the framing first, and subsequently fix the planking to it, it is indispensable to start out with a

drawing that allows the correct curvature to be applied to the frames, which in turn ensures that the planking is aligned correctly. However the technique of scale drawing only appeared from the seventeenth century onwards and it is thus improbable that, two hundred years earlier, anyone would have been capable of building a ship frame first. Some credit should, nonetheless, be given to the Dutch chroniclers: it is probable that those *cravelschepen* were built by taking the forms of an existing ship, or by setting up only a few guide ribs rather than the entire transverse frame.

In any case, thanks to Colombus and the tradition of carvel-building, this type of ship has remained one of the best known in the history of navigation.

The caravel was undoubtedly of Portuguese origin: Prince Henry the Navigator used caravels for his expeditions along the coasts of Africa. While having no precise data, we know that they were smaller than the already small *Santa Maria*, and thus less than 65 feet 6" on deck. They did, however, have particularly interesting technical features, being low-sided, having a shallow draft, being fairly narrow and with light displacement, with very fine and actually concave waterlines at the bows, and having a transom stern. Rigged with two masts, and on rare occasions three, with a mizzen-mast stepped on the transom, with the mizzen sheeted to a boomkin, caravels were rigged with lateen sails. These were all features that made the

caravels fast and, especially in comparison with other ships of the era, weatherly, capable of sailing reasonably close to the wind. This was a quality prized by Henry the Navigator who knew that the prevailing winds he would encounter on his return voyage after exploring the African coastline would mainly be against him. Moreover, the Portuguese fishermen were well aware that after leaving port with favorable winds, they would frequently have to beat home.

Large lateen-rigged boats can still be seen on the River Tagus, in Portugal, today, the frigatas. Their hulls, even more than their rigs, resemble those of the old caravels, with their high, arching stems and slim lines.

45 top A stylized representation of a caravel, or rather a Portuguese nao sailing off Nagasaki in Japan. There is no doubt that the Portuguese ships reached these waters, though what is surprising here is the apparent use of clinker construction when the Portuguese had developed carvel planking, a feature in turn refined by the Dutch.

45 bottom In recent times Columbus's ships have had the honor of multiple, albeit frequently unreliable, representations. This nineteenth century ceramic piece conserved in the Madrid naval museum nonetheless provides us with a reasonable impression: the Santa Maria, in the center, undoubtedly has the characteristics of a carrack, while the Nina and the Pinta are smaller and rigged with lateen sails.

44-45 For a certain period the Portuguese enjoyed a monopoly over the great voyages of discovery. Vasco da Gama took his carracks to the Far East where he loaded exotic goods of all kinds before turning for home where he was greeted with fame and honors, as shown in this Flemish tapestry from the sixteenth century, conserved in the Museo de Caramulo in Lisbon.

46-47 and 47 bottom
In the Mediterranean, the
fast, oar-driven galley
was still the principal
component of the fleets,
especially that of the
Turkish empire. Their
demise came about as a
result of the introduction
of guns which were better
suited to the heavy, tall
and stable ships of
northern Europe.

46 bottom In spite of its
name, the galleon was not
a larger version of the
galley. The galley in fact
developed into the
galeazza, or galeass, a
larger, heavier and better
armed vessel. The galleon
was instead an armed
version of the round ship,
of the northern carrack.
Both types, however,
decreed the end of the
galley.

47 bottom In the
eighteenth century
Chapman collected
drawings of all the types of
ships then existing, at least
in the memories of the
local shipbuilders. We are
obliged to him for these
beautiful, technically
impeccable drawings of
Venetian galleys.

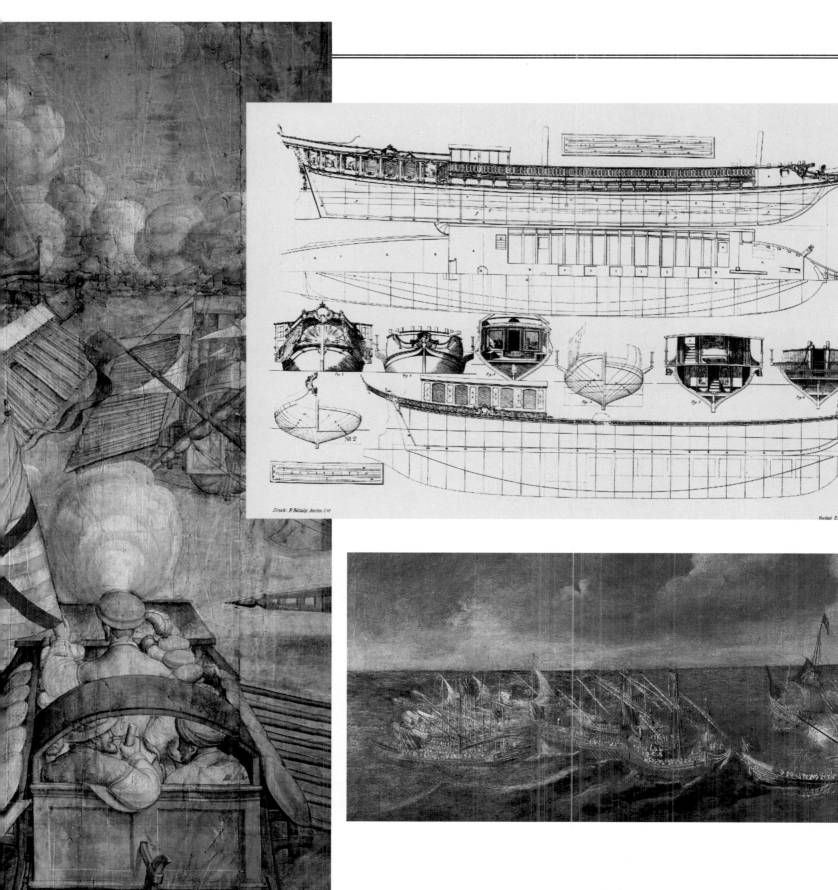

Galley

GALLEY: *Kind of long, slim boat with lateen sails and stepped tiers of oars, principally used as ships of the line in past centuries.*
(Dizionario della Crusca)

....

While the Mediterranean ship derived from the Greek, Phoenician and later Roman triremes, which relied on oars for propulsion and used sails as an auxiliary system, was in difficulties once beyond the calm waters and light winds of the Latin peoples' inland sea, it is equally true that that the heavy Nordic round ship, rigged exclusively with a square sail, fared badly in light and variable winds. Thus, for some

centuries after the turn of the millenrium, the naval ship par excellence continued to be the galley.

Light, long and slim, this type of vessel moved with agility and adequate speed on the relatively short Mediterranean routes. Its lateen rig allowed it to sail close to the wind without having to wait for it blow in a more favorable direction.

The Genoans, the Venetians, the French and the Spanish all had fleets composed largely of galleys. This is to say nothing of the Turks and the Arabs from whose coasts the galley originated, a direct descendant of the Byzantine dromon.

The hull of the later galley was long and low in the

water like that of antiquity, but it had lost the ram. In truth, there was a long protruding structure at the bow, the beakhead, but it was completely above the waterline and appears to have been more of use when boarding rather than ramming another vessel.

There was, in contrast no rear overhang, but the stern was rounded, at least in the fifteenth century model, with the original steering oars that were fixed to the sides of the sterncastle being replaced by the more modern centerline rudder hinged on the sternpost. Above this would be erected a light castle little more than a slightly cantilevered platform with a rail and a light framework supporting an awning to

48 top As late as the seventeenth century, the Turks and the Venetians fought naval battles with fleets composed of large numbers of galleys. In restricted waters, with variable winds, the maneuverability of this type of vessel, the origins of which long predate Christianity, was a valuable characteristic.

48 bottom The Arsenale at Venice was for many centuries the greatest European shipbuilding center. The yards provided all the ships that allowed the Serenissima Republic to dominate the Mediterranean.

48-49 In the period and area in which it was predominant the galley was flanked by the round ship used for trading and transportation. The convoys of these vessels that carried pilgrims to the Holy Land and returned with cargoes of precious goods had to be escorted by galleys to protect them from Saracen pirates and the Turkish fleets.

FRANᶜᵒ MOROˢⁱ CAPⁿ GNᾹLE INSEGVISCE L'ARMATA TVRCA, CHE FVGGE SEBENE PIV' NVMEROSA ASSAI DELLA VENETA, ARRIVA DVE DELLE PIV' GROSSE GALERE, E LE PRENDE. APRILE 1659.

FV FATTO LANNO 1517 SOTTO MISIER ZACHARIA D'ANTONIO GASTALDO DE MARANGONI D'NAVE D'L ARSENAL FV RINOVATO D'LANNO 1753 SOTTO LA GASTALDIA DI FRANCESCO ZANOTTO GASTALDO E COMPAGNI

shelter the captain and helmsman in bad weather.

Like the caravel, the galley was rigged with two or three masts (the smallest would have just a single mast), with lateen sails bent to a long yard made of two spars lashed together. A feature of the galley, especially the Venetian version, was the long flagpole that leaned over the bows.

The military version of the galley, the most common, had no decks, only a long catwalk running along the centerline from the poop to the bows, above the banks of rowers. There were, however, also galleys used for commercial traffic and in these cases, while retaining oars and rowers, they lost the beakhead or rostrum and had slightly fuller lines.

Variants on the standard model of the galley were identified according to the disposition and number of rowers: a galea fusta had paired oars while a galea sottile had oars grouped in threes. The galea grossa was built for mercantile use and was generally larger

and, above all, had a ratio between length and breadth of 6:1 against the 8:1 of the galea sottile. Lastly, there was the galeazza, or galleasse, introduced in the sixteenth century as a last attempt to oppose the predominance of the galleon which relied on an imposing sail plan for its performance and cannons for its military might.

There are numerous documents that provide information regarding the dimensions of the galleys. In a manuscript which can still be read in the Biblioteca Marciana in Venice, the Venetian constructor, Theodoro de Nicolò, defines the dimensions for every type of galley: the fusta was 75 feet 4" long, with a maximum beam of 13 feet and a maximum freeboard of 4 feet 6". The sottile had a length of 152 feet 6", a beam of 15 feet 6" and a freeboard of 5 feet 6", and the galea grossa 150 feet 10", 24 feet 6" and 9 feet 10" respectively.

Another source of detailed information is a

document issued by Charles I d'Anjou in 1275 when ordering the construction of galleys of 92 feet 6" in length at the waterline and 130 feet 10" overall, 12 feet 2" in breadth and with a draft of 6 feet 9". They were to be fitted with two masts, the mainmast being 59 feet high with a diameter of 11 8/10" and a 87-foot 8" yard. The mizzen was 36 feet high with a maximum diameter of 9 8/10" and a yard of 55 feet 6".

Late in the sixteenth century the guns of the Christian galeazze, the Mediterranean constructors' first step in the direction of the galleon, or rather the swan-song of the galley, destroyed the Turkish galleys at Lepanto. In the same period, the British galleons at Calais and the Dutch versions in their home waters easily defeated the Spanish fleets still composed of galleys.

Two battles marked the end for this kind of ship and, above all, confirmed the supremacy of the sailing ship over those that still relied on the labors of oarsmen for their speed and maneuverability.

Chapter 2

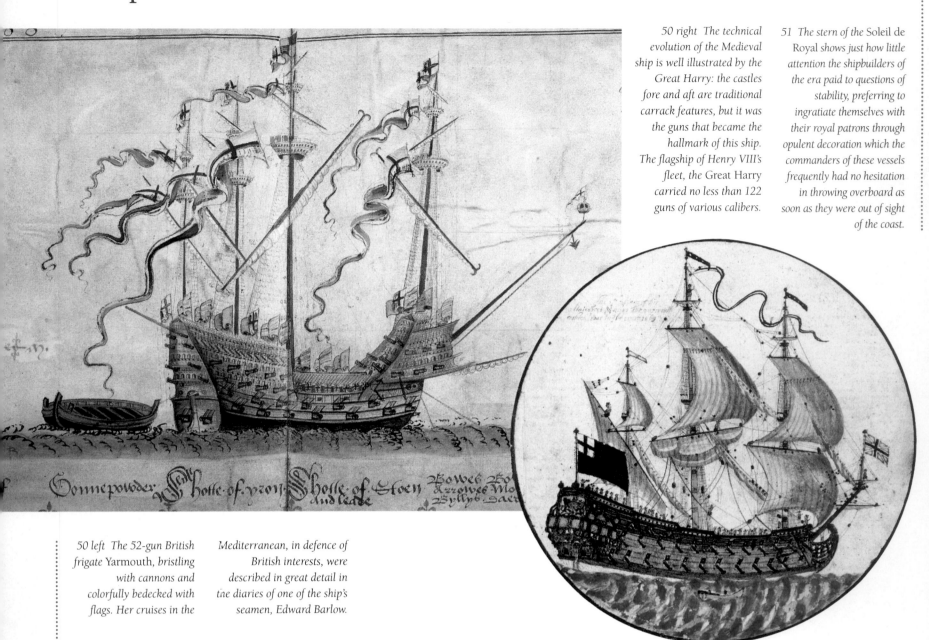

50 right The technical evolution of the Medieval ship is well illustrated by the Great Harry: the castles fore and aft are traditional carrack features, but it was the guns that became the hallmark of this ship. The flagship of Henry VIII's fleet, the Great Harry carried no less than 122 guns of various calibers.

51 The stern of the Soleil de Royal shows just how little attention the shipbuilders of the era paid to questions of stability, preferring to ingratiate themselves with their royal patrons through opulent decoration which the commanders of these vessels frequently had no hesitation in throwing overboard as soon as they were out of sight of the coast.

Gonnepowder hotte of yron hotte of Stoen Bowes arrowee Byllys and lede

50 left The 52-gun British frigate Yarmouth, bristling with cannons and colorfully bedecked with flags. Her cruises in the Mediterranean, in defence of British interests, were described in great detail in the diaries of one of the ship's seamen, Edward Barlow.

From the Galleon to the Ships of the Line

Thanks above all to the progressive tendencies and the voyages of discovery peculiar to the new maritime powers of northern Europe, early in the sixteenth century the sailing ship had reached such technical sophistication that the renowned maritime historian A. Lane was able to write, "while its rig [that of the sailing ship] may have appeared highly unusual to a sailor of antiquity... the captains of the ships of the era of the great discoveries, or even those of a generation earlier, would have had little to learn before taking command of a ship in the era of Nelson."

What was the innovation that made redundant Medieval models such as the cog, slow, wallowing and not dissimilar to a gigantic walnut shell, the galley, so unsuited to heavy seas with its intricate forest of oars, and even the carrack that, while awkwardly high in the water had allowed significant steps to be taken in the direction of the New World? In reality, nothing particularly radical separates those types of ship from the vessels of the following centuries. Rather, it was a

case of refining structural systems and rigs, adapting naval architecture to meet demands that were instead new and innovative. Two above all: the need to modify methods and strategies of naval warfare in the light of the introduction of guns aboard ships and the hunger for new territories, or rather the goods and wealth of those territories, which European society, free from the obscure apprehensions of the Medieval climate, was experiencing once again. The two were, of course, not wholly unrelated.

Guns had appeared on the deck of a sailing ship as early as the beginning of the fourteenth century: French ships used them in the siege of Antwerp in 1336 and Genoan galleys used them against the barbarian pirates two years later.

It was immediately clear that guns on the decks of unstable ships were more of a liability than an efficient instrument of warfare. Moreover, for such weapons to be used to hit an adversary that was moving, as an enemy ship generally was, the vessel it was installed upon had to be reasonably agile. A lack of stability and

maneuverability were instead characteristics, for one reason or another, of late Mediaeval ships.

Things improved with the carrack: it was more stable than both the cog and the galley, which could only fire guns located along its longitudinal axis if it wanted to avoid capsizing, and a little more agile than the first and more seaworthy than the second.

At the same time, that is to say in the fifteenth century, the most advanced European nations, firstly Portugal and Spain and then France, England and the Hanseatic states, were training their commercial sights on ever more distant territories separated by oceans as vast as they were tempestuous. Hence the demand for fast sailing ships to reduce the duration of voyages and seaworthy ships that were easily handled by small crews. These ships, moreover, had to be capacious enough to bring profitable cargoes home.

Another, new factor then entered the equation. While Roman cargo ships sailing in the relatively small Mediterranean could be escorted by naval triremes to protect their cargoes, this would have been impractical

LE
SOLEIL
ROYAL

52 top The historical heir to the cog was the Dutch merchantman with its high, tapering stern castle set above a typical fluted transom. These two East Indiamen are taking advantage of the low tide to allow the caulkers to recaulk the seams on the left, and to coat the hull with tar on the right.

52 bottom and center In the eighteenth century, shipbuilding still made little use of true design drawings, although in that era a number of treatises on naval architecture began to circulate that attempted to catalogue the existing types of ships and the construction techniques employed in the yards. A form of design process in reverse that started from the finished product rather than as an initial idea. This trend did however make a contribution to the technical evolution of the ship, allowing practical experience to be documented and disseminated, thus encouraging progress. In these two drawings the cruciform structures are of particular interest, perhaps introduced to transmit the forces produced by the firing of the guns to the structure of the ship's bottom.

53 The full-rigged ship marks the final separation from Medieval models: the high castles have disappeared both forward and at the stern and sail plan has become lofty with an increasing number of sails, features of tall ships through to the last days of sail.

in the case of a merchant ship venturing as far as the distant West or East Indies. The merchant sailing ships of the fifteenth century thus began to be armed.

For the first time in the history of navigation, the demarcation between naval and merchant vessels was blurred. Responding to similar demands, both had the same shape, more or less complying with the carrack model, and the same armament in the form of guns. In fact, purportedly mercantile expeditions were actually missions of conquest during the initial phase and subsequently the theft and defence of treasures from those who had arrived first.

The response to this basic specification for the ship of the sixteenth century was a progressive mutation of the fourteenth century carrack: the sailing ship of the next century was to be a little larger so as to enable it to be faster, better suited to the high seas and displacing sufficient water to carry an adequate cargo and guns. It was also to have more masts and new sails to improve both its maneuverability and, of course, its performance.

The center rudder having been universally adopted, the best hull shape available, and thus the model to be adopted for the wetted area, appeared to that of the caravel with its finer lines at the prow and its transom stern.

This was, in fact, to become the generally model for all European shipping. It was no coincidence that the caravel originated in Portugal and was therefore suited to the stormy waters of the Atlantic that were so different to the Mediterranean and even the relatively land-locked seas of northern Europe. Oars as a means of propulsion disappeared, their demise being sanctioned by the great battles of the late sixteenth century.

Even the Arsenale of Venice (in the Venetian dialect, *arzanà* derives from the Arabic word dar-as-sinàa meaning "the house of industry"), the symbol of the Mediterranean city's maritime power, a power founded on and supported by the oars of its galleys, fell into decline: it had been the greatest center of maritime production in the whole of Europe, but now the models and shipyards of other nations were rapidly usurping its position.

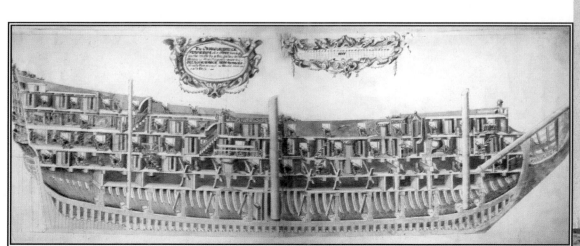

The Galleon

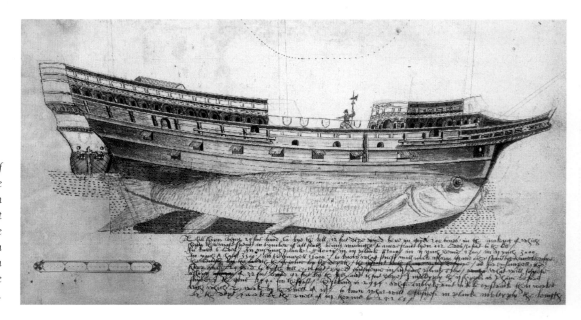

54 top In the second half of the sixteenth century, Matthew Baker, son of James, illustrated the techniques of naval architecture of the period in a series of plates. This plate illustrates a "law" of hydrodynamics that was one of the cardinal points of naval architecture up to the mid-nineteenth century. In order to provide the greatest efficiency in the water, the hull had to present a form similar to that of a fish with the head of a cod and the tail of a mackerel.

The origin of the term galleon is uncertain: from a historical point of view, it identifies a ship that was, in effect, a refined version of the fifteenth century carrack, with slimmer lines and much lower castles, especially at the prow. At the same time, from an etymological perspective, the term undoubtedly derives from galley, and thus from a specifically Mediterranean type of ship.

In terms of architecture, however, the galleon had nothing in common with the galley, except for the fact that it was slim in comparison with the carrack: if one of the two models is related to the galleon, then it has to be the carrack.

The galleon was born in England and was designed to cope with the installation of a new form of naval armament, the gun, which was to dictate the shapes and appearance of sailing ships for three centuries.

Once the carrack was armed, it began to be enlarged, with the guns being located on the deck and on the castles, to the great detriment of what was already precarious stability due to the very shape of the ship.

The solution that allowed effective guns to be embarked, the lateral gun port, was introduced early in the sixteenth century. The Englishman James Baker came up with the brilliantly simple idea of locating the guns on the lower decks with ports in the hull sides being cut to allow them to fire. When not in use the gun ports were closed by hinged lids.

The first ship to adopt Baker's invention was the *Great Harry*, or *Henry Grâce à Dieu* as she was officially named, built in 1514 as the flagship of Henry VIII's English fleet. The Great Harry was a giant of over 1,000 tons but still based on Medieval models: she was rigged with four masts, a foremast and mainmast with square sails, a mizzen and a bonaventure with fore-and-aft sails. The most eye-catching elements of her design were of course the castles fore and aft.

The ship's armament as a whole betrayed the legacy of past eras: apart from the large number of guns, 122 (or 128 according to some authorities) fire-spitting mouths gaping threateningly from their ports, the ship carried archers, with a reserve of 1,200 strings for their bows and 750 quivers of arrows.

A few years later, however, Queen Elizabeth of England, having succeeded Henry VIII, commissioned the treasurer of the royal fleet, Sir John Hankins, to develop a design for a new ship that drew on the experience of Baker's *Great Harry* but eliminated its faults. The galleon was born.

Sir John firstly lowered the towering castles, the forecastle actually being eliminated, and built longer, narrower hulls, the classic 3:1 ratio being extended to 4:1.

The Elizabethan sailing vessel was said to be a "race-built ship," race referring not to its performance (which was nonetheless superior to any other ships of the time), but deriving from the French term *ras* meaning smooth, or flat. Hankins also introduced multiple-section masts, a rigging feature that was subsequently used on all sailing ships until their eventual replacement by steam.

In practice, the ships of Hankins's era were much faster and more agile, capable of circling the enemy

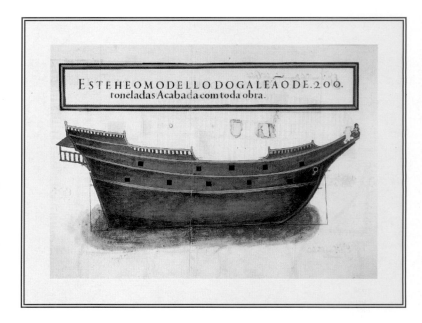

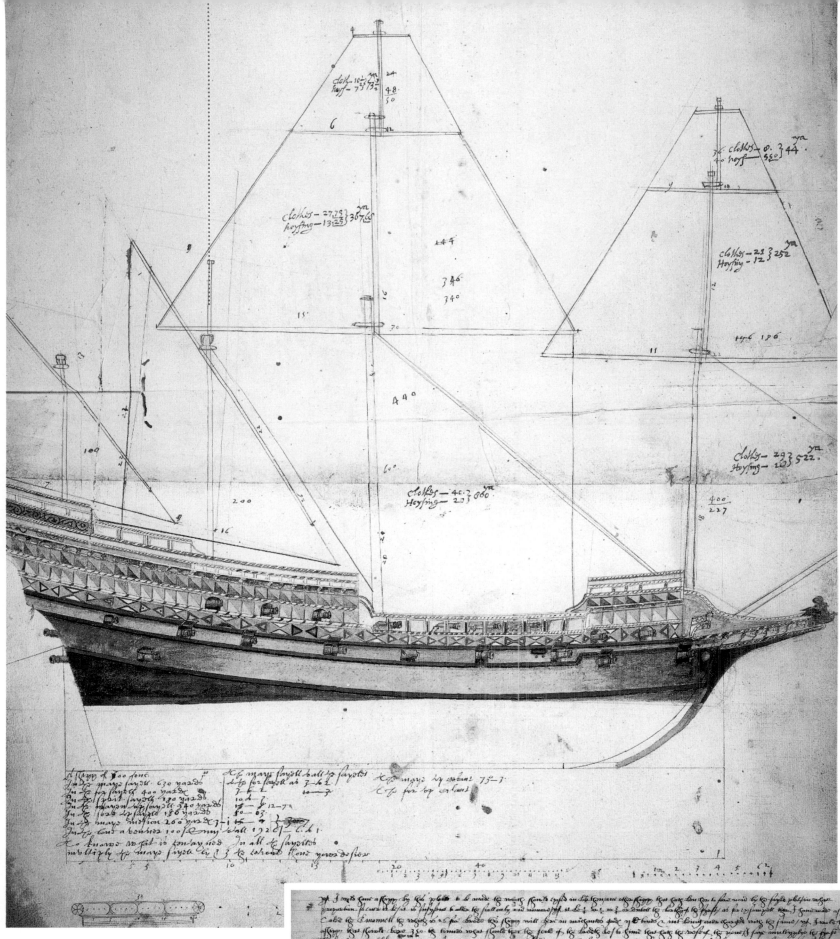

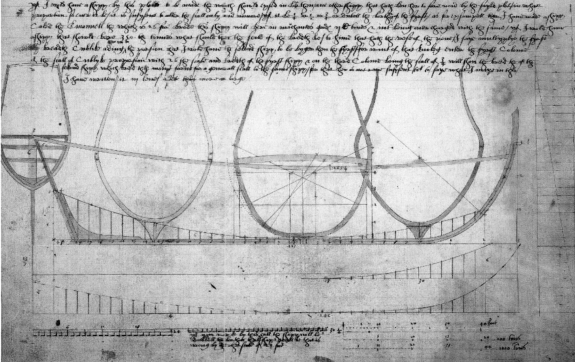

54 center In this plate Baker depicts a master boatbuilder communicating to his assistant the data taken from the drawing of the hull with a compass.

54 bottom The Livro de traças de carpintaria from 1616 was one of the first texts to illustrate, again after the fact, aspects of ship construction. The work was compiled by the Portuguese Manuel Fernandes and included these images of a galleon clearly illustrating its descent from the sixteenth century nao.

55 top Compiled by Baker, this is one of the first drawings of a sail plan. The ship is rigged with a bonaventure and still has a single order of top sails on the main and foremasts.

55 bottom Thus does Baker illustrate the main structural elements: ribs, beams, floor timbers, with indications as to the woods to be used and the geometry of the various components.

ships and taking up the ideal position to fire a deadly broadside.

Ever aware of the crucial role of a navy in the development and security of a nation, the British concentrated their efforts on the perfecting of naval vessels, making a serious attempt at scientific study at the drawing board rather than experimenting empirically in the shipyard.

James Baker was succeeded by Matthew Baker (possibly his son) who for the first time was granted the title of Master Shipwright. He can rightly be considered as the father of the craftsman boatbuilders.

Baker was himself succeeded by Phineas Pett, the founder of a dynasty of shipbuilder-designers who for two centuries enjoyed the patronage of the English royal family. Early in the seventeenth century Phineas Pett wrote, "I have begun to build a diverse model [of a ship - in that period the practice was adopted of presenting the newly founded Admiralty with models of English ships with elaborate forms and constructional details] made in part by my own hand; elegantly adorned with sculptures and paintings and placed on a support covered with crimson taffeta, I presented it to the Lord First Admiral in his Whitehall residence."

Pett's model, in reality, differed with respects to the Elizabethan galleon only in terms of its size: it was almost one and half times longer, with a far greater drafts. Its greater displacement allowed the guns to be arranged on three decks.

The admiralty approved the model and in 1610 the shipyards at Woolwich launched the Prince Royal, a galleon that apart from her four-masted rig, had broken away from earlier concepts.

Even though during the sixteenth century the Spanish, the French and the Dutch all built large sailing ships armed with guns firing through ports in the hull sides, the galleon remained an English preserve and determined the nation's maritime supremacy. As mentioned above, it was only the rig that was not subjected to significant modifications in

56-57 The marine paintings of the era frequently depicted scenes of surreal drama: the crowding here would appear to be excessive and the sea conditions are undoubtedly heightened by the terror that storms induced in those times. However, sailing in close ranks inevitably led to similar confusion and the broken mast suffered by the ship in the center was a frequent occurrence.

56 bottom The gun revolutionized warfare at sea. With oars having been abandoned as inadequate for moving the weight of a heavily armed ship, the ram was also eliminated and the ships now presented their "broad" sides when attacking.

57 top Peter Pett was the shipbuilder responsible for the Sovereign of the Seas, the ship that represents hinge point in the evolution from the Medieval model to the modern full-rigged ship. As was the normal practice for the period, Pett, seen here in a contemporary painting, designed the ship on the basis of a scale model.

greyhounds, the lion, unicorn and roses of England, the thistle of Scotland, the French fleur-de-lys, the Irish harp and other heraldic symbols. Carved on the prow bow were Cupid riding a lion, two satyrs and six divinities, on the sides there were coats of arms, helmets, armour, musical instruments and the signs of the zodiac, the stern galleries with their cupolas and fenestration were covered with mythological images and the transom was dominated by the statue of the goddess Victory, with Neptune, Jupiter, Jason and Hercules. Such was the extensive use of gold-leaf on this decoration that at sea the galleon was known as the "Golden Devil."

While in appearance she was a ship of her time, the *Sovereign of the Seas*' true significance lay in her sail plan which finally took on the appearance that was to be consolidated in the centuries to come. The spritsail and spritsail topsail were both large, while on the fore- and mainmasts further sails appeared above the topsails: topgallants and royals.

The bonaventure was definitively abandoned and the mizzen-mast carried two square sails above the lateen mizzen: the mizzen topsail and topgallant.

Above all, the Sovereign of the Seas had one particular feature in the design of her hull that was to distinguish all of His Majesty's ships that came after her with respects to those of other nations: the stern was now rounded rather than a squared off transom.

This ship, despite her fine gilding, participated in numerous battles from which she always emerged victorious. Ironically it was a candle, knocked over in the officers' quarters in 1696, that led to the fire that destroyed her.

the development of the galleon. Apart from the multiple-section masts. A small vertical mast was stepped at the tip of the bowsprit, carrying a small square sail, the spitsail topsail. Lastly, the bonaventure was actually eliminated in late seventeenth century galleons. The growing skills of the captains and, to an even greater extent, the increased efficiency of the hulls, rendered the use of the bonaventure's auxiliary sail superfluous.

In the sixteenth century the fleets of other nations began to follow the English lead. At the turn of the century, France had no ships capable of competing with the English galleon and so turned to the Dutch shipbuilders, with Richelieu ordering 5 ships in 1624. They were all decidedly modern vessels, with three decks, three masts with a fore-spritsail on the bowsprit, and a square mizzen topsail.

Sweden saw the construction and launch of the majestic Vasa of which more later, while throughout Europe studies flourished and treatises dealing with naval architecture were published: the Portuguese, Manuel Fernandes collected his stories and drawings in *Livro de tracas de Carpintaria*, while the German, Joseph Furtenbach, published his *Architectura Navalis*.

The primacy remained with the English, however. In 1637, Phineas Pett constructed the *Sovereign of the Seas*. With a keel length of 127 feet, a beam of almost 46 feet 6" and a drafts of around 19 feet 4", she was a ship at least a hundred years ahead of her time. She also boasted an unheard of wealth of ornamentation and decoration: the figurehead represented a king on horseback trampling enemy troops, the flanks of the cutwater (the structure extending the bows beneath the bowsprit) featured sculptures of the king's

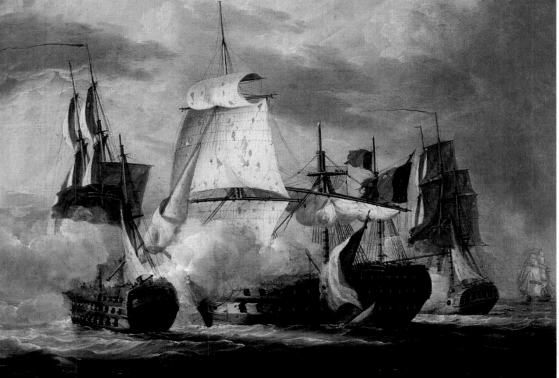

Full-Rigged Ships

I n the era of the galleon, the sailing ship was generally identified in terms of both its form and its sail plan. The presence of guns determined a slow evolution towards larger dimensions as their efficacy in battle was confirmed: the English built ever larger sailing ships to the sole end of embarking an ever greater number of guns.

This length increase was only halted because the material in which the ships were built, wood, has a well defined structural limitation: wooden ships are restricted to a maximum length of around 200 feet

before the rigidity of the structure would be compromised (beyond a certain point any increase in size would be penalized by the sheer weight of the amount of wood required; a new material was needed, such as the steel introduced in the late nineteenth century, firstly in the structural elements and then to clad the hull; this was the only way ships could be built with lengths of over 215 feet).

In contrast, the French, the last to arrive on the scene, and as such the beneficiaries of the errors committed by others, built ships that were a little

smaller, but beamier, with fewer guns but installed on an inherently more stable platform allowing more precise aiming. The French also realised that, in order to load their guns, the English always placed the lower gun deck close to the waterline with the result that, be it due to the movement of the waves, heeling under sail or the roll of the ship, the guns located there could hardly ever be used Thus the French sacrificed one of the gun decks and its battery, obtaining in exchange, ships that were lighter and therefore faster and more maneuverable in battle.

58 top A painting of the time shows the Battle of Quiberon Bay The demands of war at sea, and in the era of sail-power even mercantile activities which had to take into account the presence of the naval cannon,

contributed greatly to the development of seafaring skills. Maneuvering galleons or full-rigged ships in line ahead required skills that would subsequently allow sailing ships to fight the encroaching hegemony of steam to the bitter end.

58 center The French ship is exposed to the broadsides of two smaller British vessels, a position that in earlier periods, when the seas were dominated by galleys, would have been one of great advantage. Instead, in the era of the naval cannon it was perilous.

58-59 The Battle of the Dogger Bank in a painting of the time. Cannonballs were frequently ineffective against the thick oak sides of ships: but guns could be loaded with

chain or bar shot and aimed at the enemy's rigging: with sails reduced to ribbons, severed shrouds and shattered yards, a crippled ship became an easy, defenseless prey.

59 bottom The Rock of Gibraltar, seen here in a work from the eighteenth century, represented the gateway to the Mediterranean and Levantine markets. Small merchant vessels, some with the lateen sails that denote their Mediterranean origins, criss-cross amongst the British ships of the line.

60 bottom Merchant
ships trading to distant
seas had to be
powerfully armed with
guns on account of the
insecurity caused by
pirates and ships from
rival nations. Thus they
ended up being very
similar to contemporary
men-o'-war, and such is
the case of the British
East Indiaman Princess
Royal seen here.

*60 bottom Merchant
ships trading to distant
seas had to be
powerfully armed with
guns on account of the
insecurity caused by
pirates and ships from
rival nations. Thus they
ended up being very
similar to contemporary
men-o'-war, and such is
the case of the British
East Indiaman* Princess
Royal *seen here.*

*60-61 The great ship of
the line, with three
decks if a first- or
second-rater, or two if a
third-rater, was the
battleship of the
eighteenth and
nineteenth centuries; the
vessels destined to fight
in line ahead formation.
The fourth-, fifth- and
sixth-raters instead had
escort duties or were
used as fast raiders.*

However, apart from these basic differences, which
moreover tended to be annulled given that the two
adversaries (on the eighteenth century scene there
were no others) actually copied each other's designs,
the subsequent evolution of the galleon was a question
of fine-tuning.

There was a progressive tendency from the
sixteenth century to lower the castles. Soon, the rich
decoration was also subjected to radical pruning: it
had reached the point where, as the decorators, true
professional artists, outdid themselves to satisfy the
vanity of their sovereigns, the commanders of the
ships objected to the inconvenience, not to say the
danger such ornamentation posed once under sail.
The famous Pierre Puyet, a master decorator of many
French ships, was unaware that at least part of his
laborious and ostentatious work finished up at the
bottom of the sea as soon as the ship was out of sight
of the coast!

A number of significant modifications were, it is
true, made to the rig. Reef points reappeared on the
square sails: used on Roman ships they had been
abandoned in the Medieval period in favor of bonnets.
They had briefly returned on a number of smaller
fifteenth century before making their comeback on
large topsails in the seventeenth century.

With the bonnets having thus been discarded, the
sail area was increased in light winds lateral studding
sails sheeted to booms extending the yardarms.
Particular attention was paid to the fore-and-aft sails.
The spritsail topsail was soon replaced by jibs, while
staysails were rigged between the masts; the mizzen-
mast lost its traditional lateen sail in favor of a fore-and-
aft spanker, firstly with a gaff only and then with a gaff

and boom. The whole sail system was modified to increase the efficiency when sailing into the wind, and thus the ship's ability to maneuver.

With her imposing size emphasized by the threatening rows of guns, with much reduced superstructures at the extremities above a flush upper gun deck and with a lofty and complex full-rigged sail plan, the large fighting ship of the eighteenth century, now sailed the world's oceans. She had progressively evolved from the galleon into the ship of the line, so called because such ships sailed and fought in fleets sailing in line ahead, each ship protecting the vulnerable and poorly armed stern of the ship ahead and the bows of the ship astern.

The ships of the line had two or three continuous gun decks extending the length of the ship and were rated according to the number of the guns they carried. The first-raters were armed with at least 90 guns. The second and third raters had fewer guns.

Smilar in hull shape and rig, but smaller and with only one gun deck, the frigates were classed as fourth raters and the corvettes as fifth raters; they were too small to be part of the line of battle but sailed as "the eyes of the fleet" or on solitary missions; they were powerful enough to fight faster ships and to capture slower ships, and fast enough to evade ennemy ships carrying more guns. The navies of the day also employed sixth-raters, auxiliary vessels of various types and rigs such as supply ships and despatch boats, not intendend for fighting and carrying only a very light defensive armament.

This strict rating system may appear to be somewhat rigid, albeit undoubtedly convenient from a naval point of view. Then again, the difficulty of identifying a particular type of ship with precise terminology is one which we face rather than one that occurred at the time. Back in the seventeenth and eighteenth centuries, local terminology would have been used, especially in the case of the smaller vessels. In any case, a sailing vessel destined for the open sea was always a ship of one kind or another.

Other Vessels

The eighteenth century was an era of order. In all fields of human knowledge there was a perceptible urge to arrange and classify the great mass of information, discoveries and innovations that were gradually becoming available to modern man.

The maritime field was no exception, and the leading figure in this respect was an English naval architect called to work in Sweden for the royal family in an attempt to modernise local shipbuilding, one Frederik Henrik af Chapman.

Af Chapman compiled the *Architectura Navalis Mercatoria*, a vast work in which on the one hand he expounded upon all the current theory of naval architecture (some of which is actually still in use today), while on the other he collected drawings of all the types of ships present in the seas of eighteenth century Europe, classifying them by name.

In particular, Chapman identified five specific categories based on hull characteristics. The first three comprised the ships that terminated with a beakhead at the prow: the frigate with a transom stern, the hagboat with a rounded stern and the pink, derived from the Dutch model, again with a rounded but overhanging stern. The other two categories comprised the brigantine and the cat, both with fuller bows and no beakhead. In their

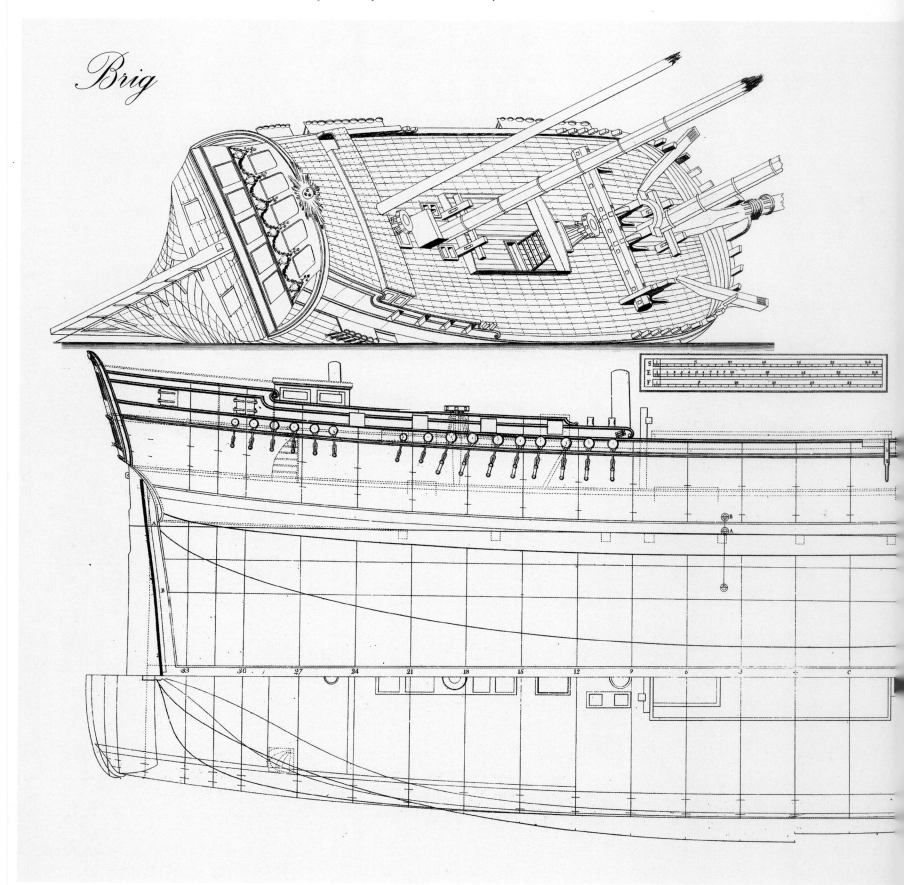

Brig

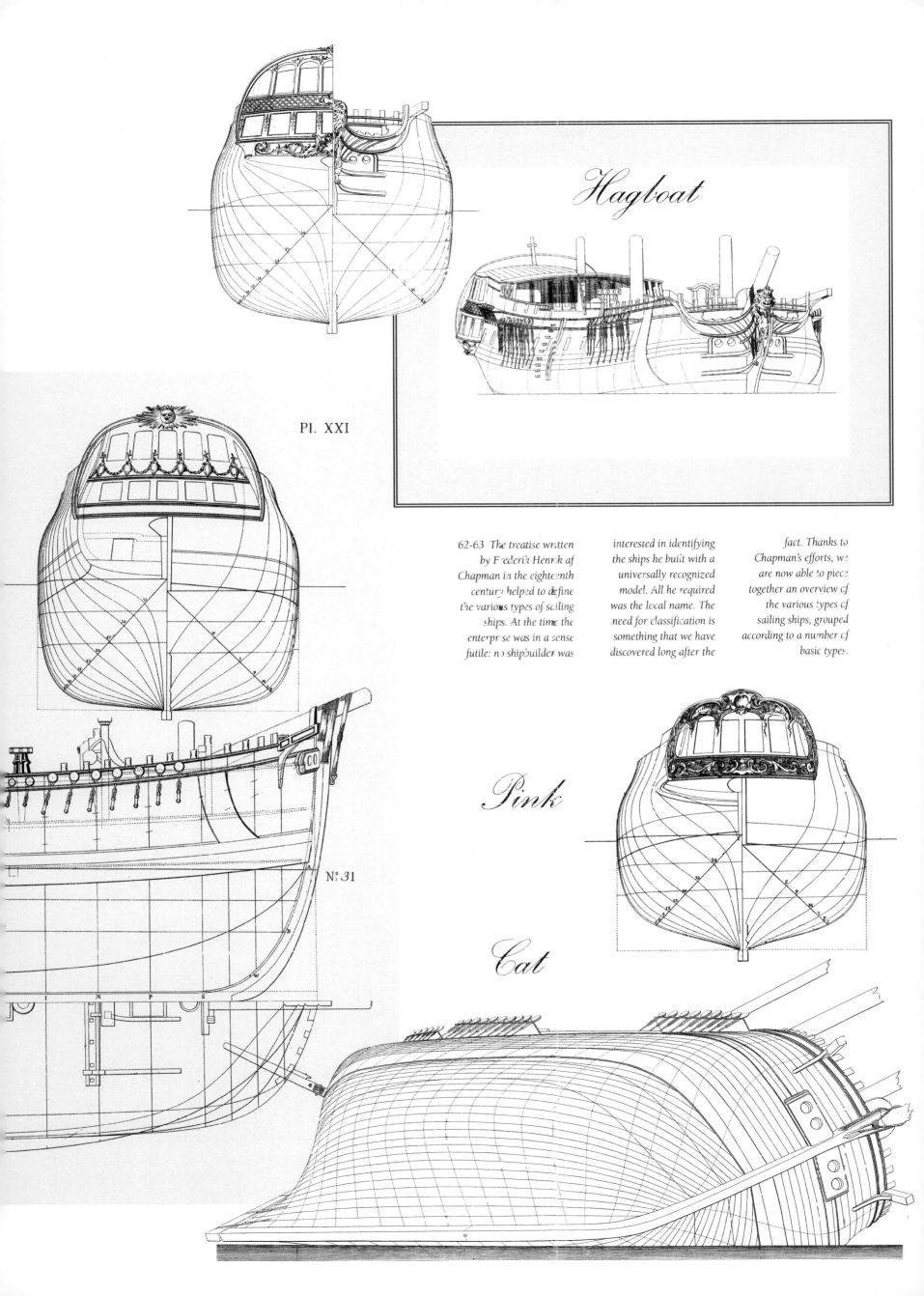

Hagboat

Pl. XXI

N° 31

62-63 The treatise written by Frederik Henrik af Chapman in the eighteenth century helped to define the various types of sailing ships. At the time the enterprise was in a sense futile: no shipbuilder was interested in identifying the ships he built with a universally recognized model. All he required was the local name. The need for classification is something that we have discovered long after the fact. Thanks to Chapman's efforts, we are now able to piece together an overview of the various types of sailing ships, grouped according to a number of basic types.

Pink

Cat

turn, the five categories were subdivided according to the type of rig. In the following century, the larger sailing vessels tended to be named on the basis of their rigs alone.

Despite Chapman's worthy efforts, the seas of the era were in reality plied by innumerable types of sailing ships, above all smaller vessels, the names of which had a purely local derivation. This leads to a series of problems for those who, after the fact, wish to define correctly each type on the basis of presumed universal criteria. This approach, as mentioned earlier, is destined for failure and therefore futile.

During the eighteenth century, Holland in particular developed numerous types which were then, with more or less substantial modifications,

exported to the Dutch colonies established in various parts of the world.

The bezaan jacht, for example, could be seen as the origin of the American schooner, given that it originally had fore- and mainmasts; both the English cutter and the bezaan jacht were also to be found rigged with a single mast.

One type of sailing vessel, two-masted, that was very common from the late seventeenth century was defined by Chapman as a "hermaphrodite brig" and had square sails on both masts. Chapman himself, however, also refers to a similar rig, but with a fore-and-aft spanker on the mainmast which he called snow. Then again, in its most common form the hermaphrodite brig had a bowsprit and a fore-and-aft spanker just like the snow and was

known as the trysail brig. The two types soon fused as the brig.

The frigate was rather better defined. A component of all the European navies, the frigate, like its smaller sister the corvette, was used for exploration and escort duties. The frigate, the hagboat and the pink, to adopt Chapman's classification, replaced those ships that had become, in the seas of northern Europe, the heirs to the Medieval cog, the pinnace (not to be confused with the Mediterranean pinco, a very different breed) and the Dutch fluyt or flute.

Both were three-masted vessels, with square sails on the fore- and mainmasts and lateen sails on the mizzen. They were lightly armed and had at most two through decks. The pinnace had a

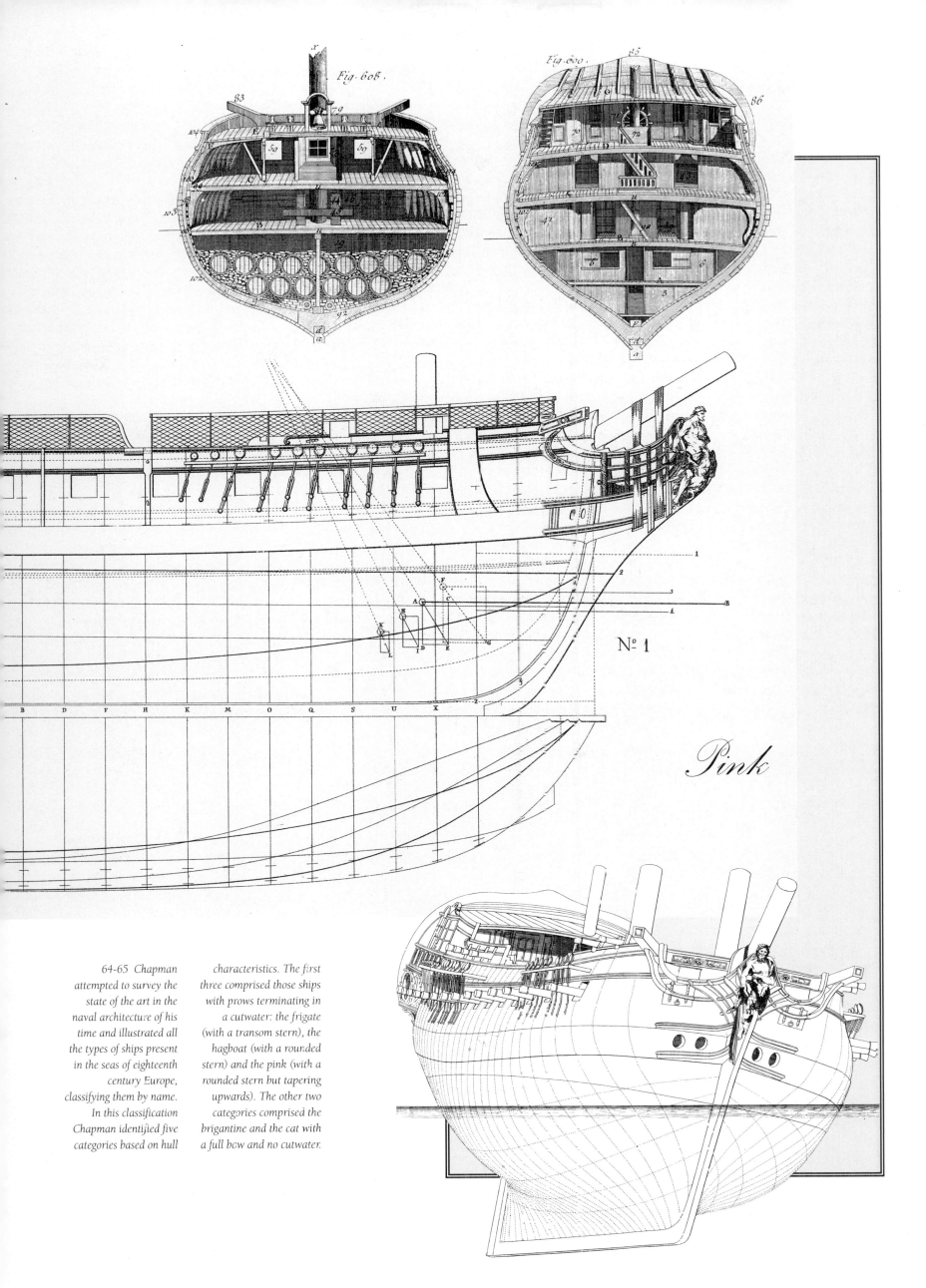

Fig. 608.

Fig. 600.

No. 1

Pink

64-65 Chapman attempted to survey the state of the art in the naval architecture of his time and illustrated all the types of ships present in the seas of eighteenth century Europe, classifying them by name.
In this classification Chapman identified five categories based on hull characteristics. The first three comprised those ships with prows terminating in a cutwater: the frigate (with a transom stern), the hagboat (with a rounded stern) and the pink (with a rounded stern but tapering upwards). The other two categories comprised the brigantine and the cat with a full bow and no cutwater.

66 top Cook's bark
Endeavour is anchored at
the entrance to one of the
Channel ports: a pilot
cutter is alongside the
ship, another is setting sail
in the light breeze.

66 center The launch of
an East Indiaman, one of
the many ships built in
Britain and devoted to the
trade with the East Indies
where wealthy colonies
permitted the importation
of goods crucial to the
economy of the empire.
The East Indiamen
provided what was to all
intents and purposes a
regular service to the
countries of the Far East.

66-67 top The Bark Earl
of Pembroke would be
called Endeavour by
explorer James Cook who
used it for his voyages of
discovery in the Pacific.
The bark was a very
common type of ship,
prized for its versatility.

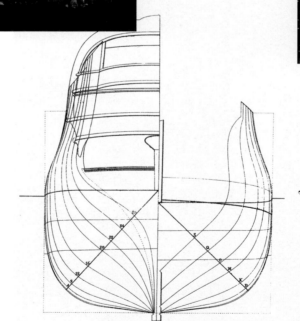

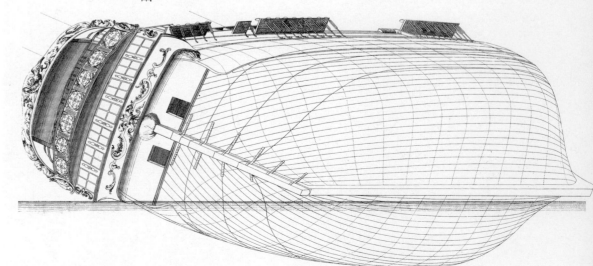

British East Indiaman

transom stern while the flute was characterized by an
unusual rounded and overhanging stern imposed by
the rating formula according to which Dutch
merchantmen were measured.

In general, all mercantile shipping was relatively
small in size. Even the ships that headed into distant
and unexplored waters rarely exceeded 130 feet
LOA. James Cook's famous Endeavour, which from
England sailed to the islands of the Pacific, was a
bark less than 97 feet 6" long from stem to stern,
with a keel length of 81 feet 4" and a maximum
beam of 12 feet 3", half the size of the Victory.

Size apart, the merchantmen of the eighteenth
century, especially if designed to sail towards the
colonies, owed much in terms of form, rig and
armament to the warship.

All the ships of the various East Indies
companies, the east-indiamen, were true warships. In
that period the conquest of new markets and the
defence of goods was, after all, a question of
firepower.

66-67 bottom In these
three views Chapman
illustrates a typical British
East Indiaman, a
longitudinal view on the
right, cross-sections to the

top left and an unusual
view of the heeled hull
to the bottom left.
The ship represented has a
length between the
perpendiculars of 135 feet,

a drafts of 19 feet, a
tonnage of 314 lasts, a unit
of measurement
corresponding to just over 2
tons, and a displacement of
52,333 cubic feet.

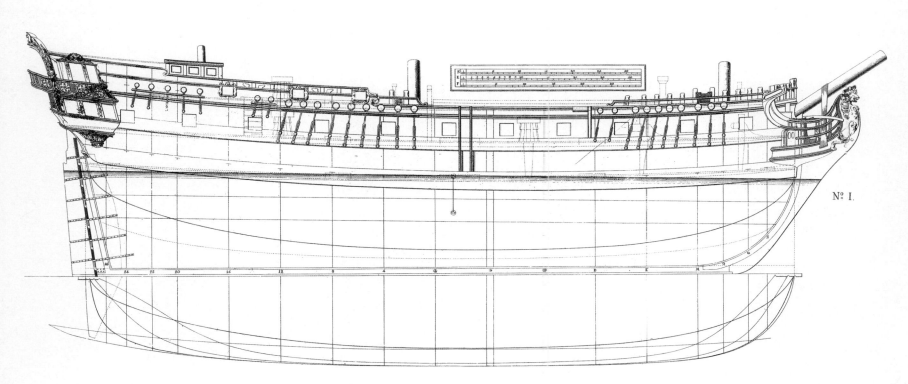

N.º I.

The Vasa

68 top The wreck of the Vasa, the great seventeenth century Swedish galleon, restored following its recovery from the seabed that cradled her for three hundred and fifty years, can be admired and visited in the purpose-built hall within the Statens Sjohhistoriska Museum in Stockholm.

GALLEON: "A type of very large ship similar in length to the galleys and galeazze, but high-sided, with heavy planking, a high prow and stern, like the Quarteron della Luna, fourteen gun ports on the lower deck and the same on the upper gun deck, capable of embarking thirty great guns and thirty smaller ones. Sailed with four masts, two square-rigged and two lateen, used for both warfare and commercial traffic."

The most important and intact wreck of a galleon, precious testimony to sixteenth- and seventeenth-century shipbuilding, was the result of a tragic accident at sea.

The Vasa, the flagship of the Swedish fleet, set out on her maiden voyage in the persistent light of the Nordic dusk on the 10th of August, 1628. Leaving the port of Stockholm, propelled by a favorable light breeze that filled the sails of her fore- and mizzen-masts, the first to be unfurled to allow the galleon to maneuver, her whole crew was on deck ready to set the sails. Two topsails were already in place but the ship had yet to make headway when a transverse gust caused her to heel, first to one side and, rolling back as the gust died, to the other.

As was customary during such maneuvers, the Vasa's lower deck gun ports, barely three feet from the waterline, were still open and water flooded through them. In a ship whose stability was rendered precarious by the weight of the guns she carried and, even more so, the Baroque decoration of her towering superstructures, this was all it took to cause her to capsize and sink.

Despite this tragic event, which actually concluded with the rescue of almost the entire crew, the Vasa represented the highest expression of the galleon form. She was designed in Holland, the nation that had best

68 center The Vasa sank during her maiden voyage, taking with her to the bottom of the sea a multitude of objects belonging to her crew such as these coins, photographed on their discovery.

69 top left A representation of the Vasa under sail, probably the fruit of the artist's imagination given that the galleon was only ever at sea for a matter of hours before a sudden cross wind caught her with her sails set but before there was the opportunity to take her through her paces.

69 top right This drawing
shows the transom stern of
the Vasa, laden as was
customary at the time, with
stucco-work, plinths, statues
and ornamentation, all
intended to glorify the
sovereign rather than induce
terror in an adversary.

68-69 and 69 bottom
The Swedish galleon's
great beakhead, a relic of
the ram of antuiquity and
still external to hull's
body.

developed the technical characteristics of a type of ship introduced by the English. She was intended to be particularly fast and for this reason her three masts rose as high as 130 feet above the main deck and carried a total of 12,900 square feet of canvas. The fore- and mainmasts were square-rigged with topsails while the mizzen featured the traditional lateen sail. A spritsail was rigged from the bowsprit. It is reasonably estimated, given her sail area and presumed displacement, that the *Vasa* would have been capable of a maximum speed exceeding ten knots.

The Vasa had three decks running from stem

70 top left A lion's muzzle carved in the wood of the Vasa's planking, a sculptural exercise for the craftsmen who worked on the construction of the ship.

70 center An uninterrupted sequence of high relief sculptures decorated the galleon's stern. Excessive weight that was, moreover, located high up, thus penalizing the handling of this type of vessel.

70 bottom Tankards, plates, lamps, a whole range of objects recovered from the wreck of the Vasa; today a precious resource that provides us with an idea of what life was like aboard this type of ship.

71 The stunning stern of the Swedish vessel, of which only the upper part is seen here, with the windows providing light for the officers' quarters, separated by grotesques carvings and surmounted by the royal coat of arms supported by two rampant lions.

to stern, heavily sloping on the longitudinal axis and slightly bowed. Sixty-four guns were installed on the two upper decks, the upper gun deck and the main gun deck, while the lowest level, the orlop deck, below the waterline, was devoted to the crew accommodation, magazines, and stores, more of which were carried in the hold below.

At the stern, an extremely high poop-deck, a relic of Medieval models, housed the officers' quarters. Rich decoration, great wooden statues representing classical deities, human and grotesque statues in the style of the era, covered every available surface, interrupted only by the windows supported by carved wooden frames that provided a little light in the cabins.

72-73 The quarterdeck looking aft; the doors in the poop blukhead lead to the officers' quarters. The massive timbers contrasts with the fine web of the rigging. The planking of the deck was reconstructed as the original wood had decayed during the long centuries spent underwater

73 top The gun ports, an English invention of the previous century, open along the sides of the ship and were as convenient from a gunnery point of view as they were a danger to the hull's integrity. The Vasa was in fact lost because water flooded through the lower lee gun ports which were still open.

73 center The gun carriages below decks, a dark, cramped area that would immediately fill with gases from the exploding gunpowder: with all the flames, deafening noise and acrid smoke it must have been an inferno for the gun crews of the time, the first to perish, moreover, should the ship founder.

On the transom stern, at least 40 feet above the waterline, two gigantic lions, sculpted in the round from solid wood, carried the heraldic arms of the Swedish royal family. All this decoration was generally covered in gold-leaf which lent the great war machine a somewhat voluptuous rather than threatening air. This was, however, imposed by the customs of the day, in part a reaction to the obscurantism of earlier periods.

The poop "castle" and its decoration, leaving aside its role in the display of status, actually represented one of the weaknesses, perhaps the principal one, of the galleon architecture and of the Vasa in particular. Faster and more maneuverable than the carrack, with armament that was now efficient in attack and a structure that provided solid defence, the galleon was still particularly unstable: the fact that the forecastle had been lowered did not improve matters in this respect, given that the poop was now bloated with ornamentation as vacuous as it was heavy.

In structural terms, the Vasa was an example of modern practice: the longitudinal frame was based on the keel timbers and the master planks or wales, while the transverse elements were composed of a closely-spaced series of ribs or "frames," linked to the longitudinal elements by floor timbers and beams. The waterlines had also taken on modern patterns. The ratio between length and breadth was far from the 3:1 of the cogs and carracks: in the Vasa it was closer to

5:1 which conferred upon the hull a performance potential previously the prerogative of the galley, a type of ship that had been restricted in terms of outright speed by its propulsion by oars.

In the meantime, the draft of the galleon had also been increased, due in part to the greater displacement deriving from the guns and munitions on the one hand, and the increased weight of the structure for defensive motives on the other. In the case of the Vasa it had reached a ratio of 2.5:1 against the 4:1 of the ships of one or two centuries earlier.

Throughout the Vasa her design was already speaking a different language: the bow had a greater overhang and was almost as fine as that of a caravel, the stern with its center rudder, hardly a new feature sanctioned as it was by almost three hundred years of use, was a sharply cut-off transom. These were, in fact, to be the forms of the last generation of wooden sailing vessels, the full-rigged ships.

74 left and top right The
Vasa's sculptures were
inspired by mythology,
folklore and national
history: the ship thus
constituted a kind of
"summation" of the nation
entrusted to the seamen and
their officers so that they
could act as ambassadors of
the power and prestige of
their homeland.

74 bottom right
A container with a
terracotta lid, found like
many other objects inside
a sea chest, the sailor's
traditional luggage.

75 The Vasa's sculptures: no
drawing and no painting of
this type of ship that has
survived to the present day
illustrates so well the
significance of the great
sailing ships of this era. A
means of promotion rather
than transport, a symbol
rather than a functional
response to a demand.

76-77 The Victory and other ships of the line anchored at the mouth of the River Thames. A salvo of guns salutes the embarking captain or admiral, perhaps Nelson himself. The guns peer from the imposing flanks of the ships, those of the lower deck dangerously close to the waterline. When underway and not in battle, however, the gun ports would be kept carefully closed.

76 bottom left Sir Horatio Nelson was born at Burnham Thorpe on the 29th of September, 1758, the son of Edmund, a modest English country rector, and Catherine Walpole, a relative of Sir Robert Walpole, an illustrious former prime minister. At fifteen years of age Nelson was already at sea and participated as helmsman in an expedition to the Arctic region.

FULL-RIGGED SHIP: *a definition generally given by a seaman to the first-rater with which he sailed the oceans. Among those with little familiarity with naval definitions, this term is very vague and indiscriminate: at times even sailors agree with this general idea. In naval parlance, however, it is more specifically applied to a ship with three masts, each of which composed of lower mast, topmast and topgallant mast with the usual system to keep it in place.* (Falconer)

From the late seventeenth century onwards, the already powerful and predominant English fleet had become a perfect offensive and defensive machine. Naval architecture had progressed with the introduction of the wheel in place of the whipstaff, the copper sheathing of the bottom and a sail plan that was very effective when sailing against the wind, helped by the fore-and-aft staysails and spanker, and with a sail area increased in light favorable winds by the lateral studdings sail.

In the meantime, the British admiralty had issued

The Victory

78-79 The British fleet's great ships of the line, evolved from the armed galleons, were the first true battleships capable of attacking with their guns while being sufficiently seaworthy to cope with ocean crossings. A first-rater like the Victory carried over a hundred guns and almost a thousand men, including sailors and marines.

79 In battle, the opposing ships of the line fought at close quarters: the guns of the era were in fact only had a short range and the cannonball, which was not explosive; frequently did little damage to the massive wooden sides of the enemy vessels. Rather more effective were chain shot, bar shot and grape shopt aimed at the rigging: stripped of its masts and sails, a ship was lost.

its "Fighting Instructions" that codified a series of maneuvers and tactics to be applied in battle, first and foremost, the "line ahead."

Given that the battleships of the era carried their guns arranged along the sides in superimposed batteries, it was clear that the greatest destructive effect could be achieved by presenting the flanks of the ships to the enemy. A fleet of warships, sailing one behind the other past the opposing formation developed formidable fire-power: a 200-foot ship with 100 guns could fire half a ton of cannon balls in a broadside!

Clearly, only the largest ships were destined for this line-ahead battle formation, the first, second and

third raters. Those known historically as "ships of the line." HMS Victory is ship of the line, a first-rater, built at Chatham, England, to the designs of Sir Thomas Slade between 1759 and 1765. Today, dry-docked in the Portsmouth naval base, she is the oldest ship still officially commissioned by the Royal Navy. In reality, she is a living museum, a symbol of British maritime power, a monument to Trafalgar and her admiral, Lord Nelson.

In a career spanning forty years, prior to her last battle which was to assure her of a place in history and lead to the death of her commander, she had been substantially modified without ever losing the typical appearance of the full-rigged ship of the

golden age of the great ships of the line.

The dimensions of the Victory are close to the maximum permissible for a wooden structure: 227 feet long from stem to stern, with a keel of 151 feet 3" and a maximum beam of 51 10" feet.

The construction of the hull required over 2,500 prime quality oak trunks for the double-skinned planking and the transversal floor timbers and frames of which the reinforced ones had a thickness of almost 2 feet.

The keel was constructed of elm and the entire underside of the ship was sheathed in copper laid over oil-soaked linen canvas and nailed to the planking, a system designed to protect the wooden hull against shipworms. A similar system had been used by the carpenters who built the ships of Rome 1,500 years earlier (at that time lead was used rather than copper, but the concept and procedure were analogous).

The rudder blade was 5 feet 8" wide at the base and was over 36 feet long. It was actuated via a 28 feet 6" long tiller that entered the hull through the transom stern, just above the lower gun deck. In its turn the tiller was connected to the twin wheels on the quarter-deck by tiller ropes and tackles.

The Victory has four full-length decks. Provisions, ship's stores, water and powder were carried on the orlop (the lowest deck) and in the hold below. The surgeon's cabin and the senior midshipmen's accommodation, the after cockpit, were on the orlop. That cockpit served as operating theatre during action. The lower, middle and upper gun decks carried thirty guns each, respectively

80 A cutaway of the Victory, showing how the various decks were used: stores and powder in kegs were carried in the hold; the orlop with the magazines, surgeon's and warrant officer's cabins and the senior midshipmens' "cockpit" aft; the lower gun deck with the gunroom (junior midshimpen's quarters) aft; the middle gun deck with the lieutenants' wardroom aft; the upper gun deck with the admiral's quarters aft; the captain's quarters aft of the quartedeck and its double-steering wheel, below the poop deck. The ratings and marines slung their hammocks on the gun decks; the upper gun deck is open to the sky in the waist. The beakhead is no longer ram-like as was the case for earlier galleons, but is still outside the hull.

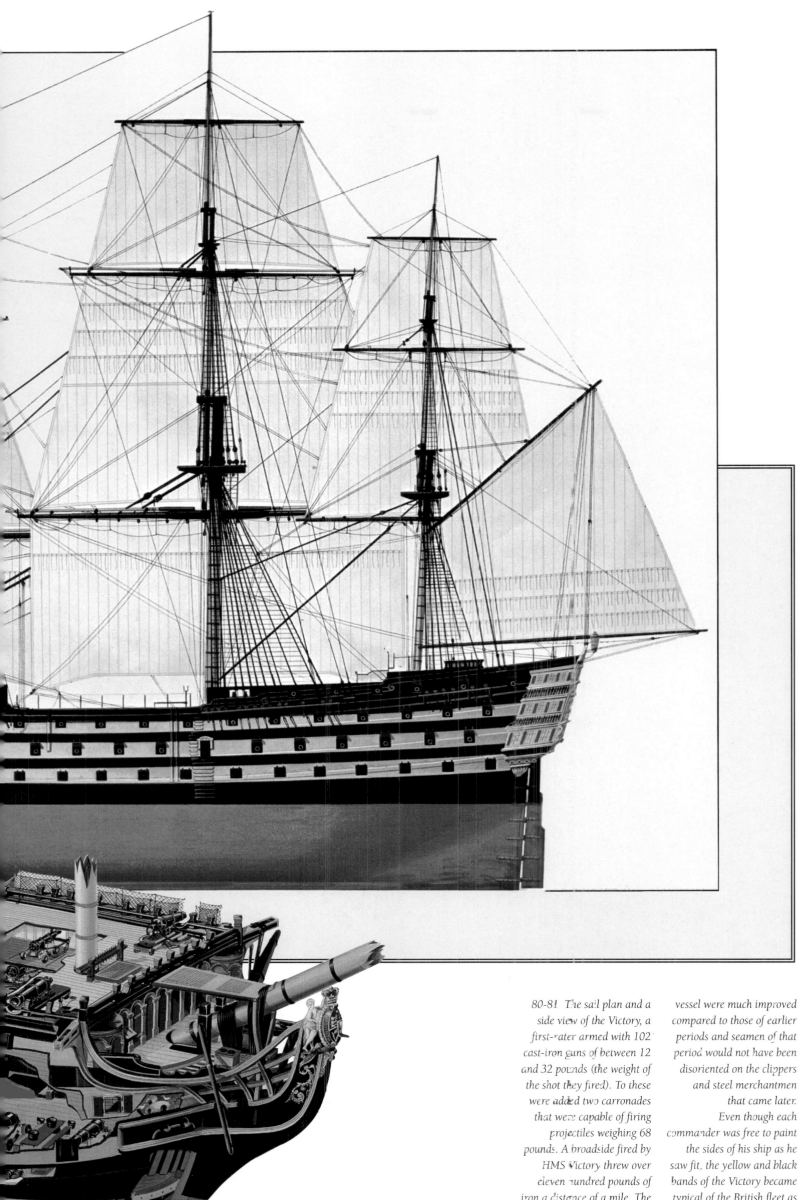

80-81 The sail plan and a side view of the Victory, a first-rater armed with 102 cast-iron guns of between 12 and 32 pounds (the weight of the shot they fired). To these were added two carronades that were capable of firing projectiles weighing 68 pounds. A broadside fired by HMS Victory threw over eleven hundred pounds of iron a distance of a mile. The sail plan and sailing efficiency of this type of vessel were much improved compared to those of earlier periods and seamen of that period would not have been disoriented on the clippers and steel merchantmen that came later.

Even though each commander was free to paint the sides of his ship as he saw fit, the yellow and black bands of the Victory became typical of the British fleet as a whole, such was the influence of Lord Nelson.

and was armed with two carronades.

The Victory's three masts and bowsprit could spread 59,000 square feet of canvas, in a highly divided sail plan of 32 sails allowing the sophisticated sailing techniques of the day. In particular, the staysails and the mizzen mast's large fore-and-aft spanker gave the ship excellent pointing characteristics. Like all ships of the line weighed down by guns and double planking, however, speeds rarely exceeded 6 knots, with a maximum of 11.

Today, approached from the sea, the *Victory* appears like an enormous floating palace, with three yellow ochre lines in which open, like windows, the gun ports. She is an effective symbol of what was once called the "wooden walls of England," an insuperable bastion defending the heart of an empire that had been consolidated on every continent.

32, 24 and 12-pounders. The galley and sick bay were in the fore part of the middle gun deck. Most of the crew and marines slung their hammocks in the lower and middle gun decks.

The admiral's quarters are in the after part of the upper gun deck, under the quarter deck. The central area of the upper gun deck is open to the sky, with beams spanning across it to support the boats and spare spars. The quarter deck has a double steering wheel and six 12-pounders, with the captain's quarters aft, under the poop deck. The latter was armed with two 12-pounders and two carronades. The fore part of the upper gun deck is covered by the forecastle deck on the same level as the quarter deck,

82 top HMS Victory in the roadstead off Portsmouth, the Solent town that was to become the great ship of the line's last and definitive home. The ship has yet to gain her definitive livery of yellow and black.

82 center left Nelson's dining-room and, in the background with the broad windows across the transom stern, the admiral's day cabin.

82 bottom left Nelson's quarters aboard HMS Victory comprised the day cabin, photographed here, a large dining-room where the admiral received his officers and guests, and his personal cabin, actually a very modest room with a simple swinging cot.

82 center right A view of the British ship's stern, with its sober decoration, a dutiful tribute to the prestige of the commanders and officers of the Royal Navy and in clear contrast with the Baroque gingerbread of the galleons of the previous century.

83 The Victory has an escutcheon with the royal coat of arms in place of the traditional figurehead displayed on British merchantmen of the period. Above, the entire masting of the ship, from the bowsprit to the three masts, supported by an intricate web of shrouds and stays.

Chapter 3
The nineteenth century - The era of the Clippers

I n the eighteenth century, the full-rigged sailing
ship was still first and foremost an instrument
of warfare. Great clouds of smoke and reddish glows
distinguished the paintings of maritime artists rather
than the billowing sails and foaming waves that were
to characterize the images of ships produced in the
following century.

It was always armament that dictated the form of
the sailing ship of the time. In truth, going to sea was,
even in an eighteenth century illuminated by scientific
progress, akin to venturing out into the unknown:
maps and charts had vast blank areas in which it was
easy to imagine the presence of men, animals and
nature that was hostile rather than benign. Of the
many who departed, relatively few returned: the
disappearances fed the terrifying legends, which the
survivors tended to confirm rather than deny, perhaps

basking in the reflected glory. And in effect the new
lands were often inhabited by people who did not take
readily to the "civilizing" intentions of their
conquerors, and thus frequently reacted with violence.
The very seas themselves beyond the Pillars of
Hercules and the dark waters of northern Europe,
were inhabited by great whales and the long tentacles
of monstrous giant squid. Tales of the latter were
perhaps not so far from the truth as one may imagine,
given that these creatures can apparently attain lengths
of up to 65 feet, while the ships of the time were
themselves little longer. Cook's Endeavour, as
mentioned earlier, explored unknown oceans with a
keel of less than 82 feet in length. This is to say
nothing of how such hulls reacted to oceanic waves
that were far larger and far more powerful than those
of the Mediterranean which had determined their

original form and structural concepts.

Faced with these conditions, the sailing ship had
evolved, and notably so, in terms of the design and
handling of its rig, while its dimensions had been
increased to the practical maximum for wooden hulls.
It remained, however, essentially a warship, to the
extent that well into the next century even the
painting and thus the aesthetics of the topsides
continued to be bound by the dictates of the admirals
rather than the specifications of the builders. The
choice of colors for a ship was, in effect, left up to the
personal taste of its commander, and thus galleons
and full-rigged ships presented sometimes bizarre
combinations: while the majority of British vessels
combined black and yellow, at the battle of the Nile,
one member of the fleet was painted in red and yellow
stripes and another red and black. At Trafalgar, the

84-85 The best known
English frigates were those
built at Blackwall, in a
yard on the Thames. Even
though the gingerbread and

the statues of the earlier
full-rigged ships had been
abandoned, these modern
frigates still displayed a
degree of decoration

Spanish Santísima Trinidad was purple with white
stripes while another Spanish ship was painted all
black.

In this field too, the victors laid down the law:
Nelson ordered his ships to be painted in black and
white and thus, in the nineteenth century, both naval
and mercantile vessels were painted Nelson-fashion.
The merchantmen may have lost their guns, but gun
ports painted in a contrasting color remained!

The British fleet's most important battle was
fought on the 21st of October, 1805, off Cape
Trafalgar, with the ships of Admiral Horatio Nelson
taking on the combined Franco-Spanish fleet. While
the Napoleonic wars still raged on for another ten
years, mostly on land, Trafalgar was a turning point
and confirmed Britain's maritime supremacy which
was to remain unchallenged for a century. Under the
Pax Britannica most sea lanes were clear of hostile
naval ships, corsairs and pirates, and sea trade
flourished. Under those conditions scheduled sailings
appeared, as well as merchant ship designs freed from
the constraints of having to carry guns for self-defense.

In the meantime, apart from the evidence of the
clearly naval color schemes now adopted on at least
the major vessels of all fleets, only slight modifications
had been introduced to the actual architecture of the

85 bottom left Maneuvers
on a small eighteenth
century frigate were
entrusted to just a few
seamen: two men aloft on
the topsail yards had to
suffice to brail up the sails;
with a further two for each
mast on deck to handle the
halyards.

85 bottom right With the
intention of setting all
available canvas, this
frigate from the British
fleet leaves the Cape
Town anchorage, a fine
sight with her hull
painted in the classic
alternating black and
white bands.

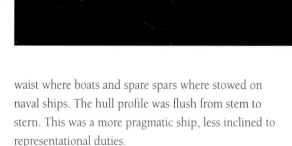

had been introduced to the actual architecture of the ships. The beakhead, a relic of the original Greek ram that had evolved with the galley into the galleon, lost its form and function and became merged with the hull proper, the cutwater, stem and side planking sweeping forward to enclose and replace it. The beakhead rails however survived as ornamental trailboards which are still seen on today's tall ships.

At the stern, the transom lost its ornate decoration, windows and balconies, although there was a reluctance to adopt the solidly planked round stern, as used in certain English ships, until the desire to ensure better protection from raking enemy broadsides over-ruled the officers' vanities and desire for comfort. The upper deck became continuous: even though the stern area continued to be known as the quarter-deck and the forward part of the deck as the forecastle, the geometry of the ship lost those distinctive raised structures which, like the cutwater, were relics of ancient naval traditions. The new sailing ship of the eighteenth and nineteenth centuries was to be the frigate.

In reality, merchantmen were actually the first ships to adopt the new forms. While still armed with guns in batteries on the main deck, they had a continuous upper deck without that well deck in the waist where boats and spare spars where stowed on naval ships. The hull profile was flush from stem to stern. This was a more pragmatic ship, less inclined to representational duties.

This new type of merchantman was still a good fighting ship, a quality still required in order to establish and safeguard traffic and cargoes in colonial regions that were frequently turbulent if not openly hostile. It also handled better than the ships of the line thanks to its lower freeboard and a simplified rig, and actually increased in size.

The British East Indiaman of the eighteenth century was a ship of between 500 and 800 tons (by the end of the century this had risen to up to 1,200 tons), with a length of 165 feet, a beam of around 40 and a draft of 16 and a half.

The sailing ship that instead plied the westwards route towards the New World, the West Indiaman, was smaller, rarely exceeding 500 tons, and built with at most two decks.

Similarly, the ships that operated in the European seas on traditional routes were also smaller. Generally no more than 100 feet in length, initially they were still being rigged with three masts and the classic six to eight sails, but gradually variations on the two-masted theme with various local names and forms began to dominate: thus was born the brig or brigantine, the most common type of smaller ship.

86 center This small
French cutter, probably a
smugglers' vessel, is
attempting to out-run an
English frigate by
exploiting its superior
windward qualities.
Frequently, however, the
great speed and
maneuverability of the
frigate would annul this
advantage.

86-87 Small boats rigged
with lateen sails represent
the traditional
Mediterranean sailing
vessel, especially on the
eastern coasts where the
Turkish galleys and those
of the Italian fleets once
dominated: the great
square-rigged ship of the
line underlines their
decline.

87 bottom The American
shipbuilders, despite their
relative lack of tradition in
the field, managed to
create ships, above all
frigates, that were superior
to their French and English
counterparts, previously
considered to be invincible.
The American frigate was
larger, faster and had a
heavier broadside than
European frigates of the
same gun rating; the
American 44s would
however have been no
match against ships of the
line but they could outsail
them.

86 top An unusual image
of the English frigate Zion,
seen from two different
points of view. Paintings
and engravings were long
the only records of naval
architecture before design
drawings began to be used.

By the end of the eighteenth century, the navies of all the advanced maritime nations had more or less unified the terminology identifying the various types of ships. Thus the term frigate, of somewhat obscure and remote origin (to my knowledge it appeared for the first time in the fourteenth century to describe one of the many variants of the Mediterranean galley, and was subsequently used to define any type of sailing ship of medium size that was lightly armed and fast), also became synonymous with a particular type: the frigate was a long, with a low freeboard, armed with no more than 40 guns installed on the main gun deck and with an open weather deck at the center, a feature of the larger ships of the line.

The frigate, the equivalent of the modern-day cruiser, was designed for scouting and raiding and was particularly fast: a frigate could reach twelve knots and was capable of pointing to 60°. According to Joshua Humphreys, a Philadelphia shipbuilder specializing in these vessels, it was "a ship capable of outclassing the two-deckers in strong winds and able to withdraw from a fight in the case of light winds…"

The Frigate

88 center The frame of this ship is complete and a number of perhaps provisional planking strakes has already been laid to allow the shoring which supports the ship on the slipway to be installed. A full-length roof facilitates the building of the Danish frigate Jylland.

88 bottom The early nineteenth century packet is reminiscent in hull shape and rig of the frigates of the previous century. Its hull is not pierced for guns but false black gunports are painted on by tradition on the white band.

The frigate developed in parallel with the great ship of the line and, even more so than the latter which was considerably more onerous to construct and operate, was built for most of the world's navies. It was eventually identified with the ships used for trading with the Far East, the British East Indiaman being substantially the mercantile version of the frigate.

The type was initially developed by French shipbuilders who, in order to improve the stability of the fully-rigged ship, especially in battle, eliminated the upper deck and slightly increased the beam while maintaining the same structure. The result was a ship that was, in fact, more stable when firing its own guns, as defensively strong as the ship of the line but faster thanks to its lighter weight.

Naturally, the British were not slow to adopt the French design, their frigates sharing the same characteristics as the originals. The model was also exported to the Americas where there was no need for the

ship of the line, but where a reasonably agile warship would be of great use. It was thus that the frigate became the typical American warship as soon as the nascent United States perceived the need to have a navy.

The American shipbuilders immediately recognized that the model was open to improvement: the frigate was, in effect, a fully-rigged ship minus the upper deck, the hull not having otherwise been modified. It was thus slower than it needed to be, even though faster than the ship, and nor was it particularly maneuverable. The waterlines were thus refined and, in order to cope with the coastal shallows, the draft was reduced, displacement being recovered through an increased beam. The result was that the American frigate was faster and more agile thanks to more efficient waterlines, and also a better fighting ship because its increased beam provided a more stable platform for gunnery. In head-to-head conflict, the new American frigates proved to be faster than their British counterparts and also

defeated the best of the French vessels.

The American constructors developed their models in the late eighteenth century and built the largest examples of the type seen in that era. The largest American frigates, rated as 44-gun frigates, were big, with hulls just over 200 feet, and a maximum beam of just under 44 feet; they were 23 feet longer and over 3 feet wider than the contemporary improved English 44s, and 13 feet longer and a foot wider than the French 44s.

The rating was nominal; the actual armamement carried on board could and did vary. A typical armament was a main on the gun deck battery of thirty 24-pounder long guns, sixteen 32-pounder carronades on the quarterdeck, and, on the forecastle, six 32-pounder carronades, and two 24-pdr and one 16-pdr bow chasers.

The extra length and beam, added to the heavier scantlings and lenghtened quarterdeck and forecastle, allowed the significant batteries on those upper decks. In

90-91 top The early American frigates such as the Essex seen in this painting, despite a number of improvements, still have traditional eighteenth century features such a beakhead external to the hull and numerous large stern windows.

90-91 bottom The characteristics of the new sailing ship in this modern reconstruction by J. Batchelor: the profile is low and sleek, and the upper deck is flush. While the stern and bow decorations remain, the appearance of the frigate is nonetheless already far removed from that of the earlier men-o'war.

91 top Crew quarters forward, officers' quarters aft, the upper decks carring batteries of guns, supplies of shot and powder, provisions and stores carried in the hold and some on the orlop deck. A fine cross-section of a late eighteenth century naval vessel illustrates its internal layout.

91 center This drawing by Chapelle shows the increase in sail area that characterized the American frigates developed from the original British model. The President has a loftier rig than the Essex in the painting reproduced on this page.

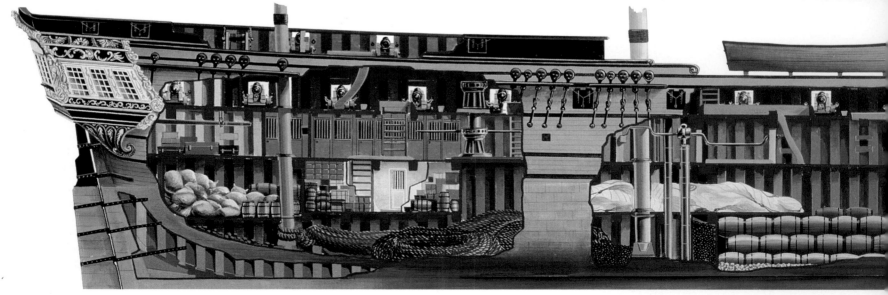

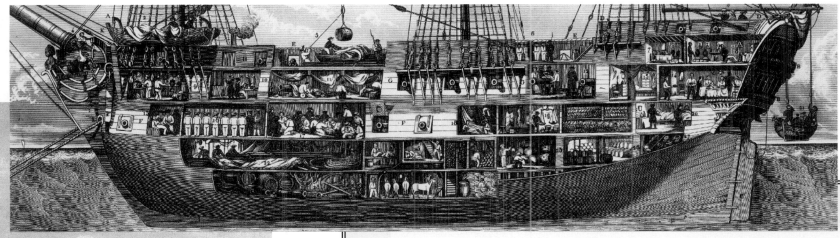

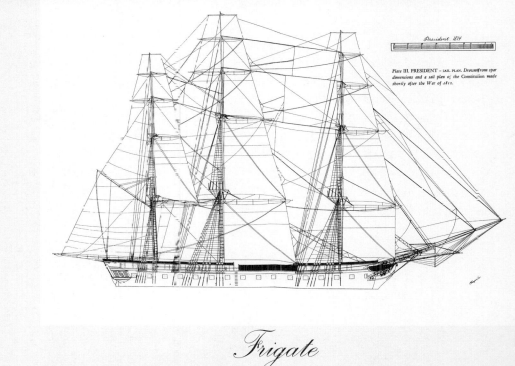

Plate III. PRESIDENT – SAIL PLAN. Drawn from spar dimensions and a sail plan of the Constitution made shortly after the War of 1812.

Frigate

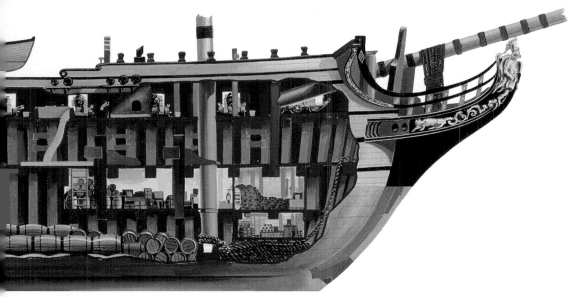

addition the lateral gangways linking those two decks at their level were widened to point of almost merging, creating a flush upper deck level from stem to stern much more convenient for sail handling and boarding. That was the appearance of the spardeck, so called because spare spars and boats were still carried there.

Another feature of the American frigates was the enormous sail they were able to carry, carrying royals on all three masts and, on occasion, setting studding sails and sending up flying skysails. The President, the fastest of the American 44s, achieved peaks of 14 knots!

The British, on the other hand, with the continental wars over and the conflict with the former colonies having cooled, had no motivation for seeking to improve their frigates.

They thus began to specialize in merchant shipping, a sector which, as already mentioned, continued to draw on the naval experience. At the beginning of the nineteenth century, the demand for ships destined for trading with the Far East, Australia and South America increased enormously: the era of the monopolies enjoyed by the so-called "companies" (often state-funded) was over, and numerous private enterprises began to compete to carry emigrants and goods to the New World and colonial products home to Britain.

The builders of frigates simply converted the models they were accustomed to building: the oceanic routes were plied by sailing ships that differed from the frigates of the Royal Navy only in terms of the number of guns they carried and the uniforms of their crews and officers.

Among these vessels, the most celebrated were the so-called "Blackwall frigates," named after a famous yard on the Thames. They were large ships, albeit still smaller than the American frigates, weighing up to 1,400 tons, with hulls around 180 feet with a beam of just under 40 feet.

With these vessels drew to an end the era of sailing ships with hulls painted in black and white bands, ranks of gunports, stern windows and beakhead.

New influences on naval architecture were to arrive, appropriately enough from the New World.

The West Indies, which soon became known as the Americas, already had maritime genes in the era of their discovery: while it may be banal to remark that their discovery was actually made via water, it is undoubtedly of interest to recall that this took place thanks to a Portuguese ship of oceanic traditions, Basque sailors with the sea in their blood, and a commander from Genoa. It is even more significant that the first colonists to settle in the new territories were British and Dutch. New Amsterdam, the future New York, was founded by the latter, while the former established more widespread settlements along the whole Atlantic seaboard and soon ousted the Dutch (hence the change of name to New York!). Both the British and the Dutch brought with them long established maritime customs and technology.

While the attention of the colonists was initially concentrated on the problems relating to settlement, in daily conflict with the Native Americans, less than a century was all that passed before the opportunity of exploiting communications along the coast, which

The New World

Rattlesnake

92 bottom While on the Old Continent most ships belonged to the state, in the relatively young America, sailing ships operated by private companies or individuals had been common since the dawn of the nation. They were armed with guns and, while destined for mercantile traffic, were ready to aid the United States navy should the need arise: these were the privateer ships such as the Rattlesnake seen in this drawing.

generally offered natural harbors and sheltered waters, and the urge to establish return voyages to the distant homelands, generated intensive maritime traffic.

When the colonies decided to affirm their independence from Great Britain, the new-born navy of the United States of America proved to be a match for what was then considered to be the world's greatest naval power.

What had happened was that the last to arrive on the scene had been able to draw on a rich technical heritage while at the same time rejecting the stagnancy and rejection of innovation typical of established constructors. Cultural curiosity and a desire to experiment are, in fact, virtues of the profane.

Moreover, the new American nation benefited from the fact that the experience of British, French and Dutch shipbuilders could be poured into the creation of a single new hull.

Among the first American sailing ships were the Virginia of around 50 feet, built by the British colonists of Maine in 1607, the Onrust of 45 feet built by the Dutch of New Amsterdam along the lines of the jagt of their homeland, and the Chaleur, in reality a French ship, captured by the British in the Channel and sent to the colonies where she was rerigged as a schooner.

All the original models were subjected to the pragmatism of the New World in the meeting of local demands and conditions shallow coastal waters. irregular winds and above all the need for speed, a factor that was of particular importance in a country where life was precarious at best.

For this reason, from the very outset the Americans developed broader hulls in order to recover the volume lost as a result of the reduced draft they were obliged to introduce. They also favored fore-and-aft rigs rather than square sails so as to facilitate sailing against such variable winds and reach ports that were located on broad, deep estuaries. Lighter hulls were also built, thanks in part to the abundance of resinous wood with a low specific density, which made the ships easy to handle with small crews and favored speed.

Despite the different countries of origin of the colonists, along the American coasts there was never a wide variety of types of ships, due mainly to this adaptation to local conditions rather than a reliance on consolidated theories. It was generally specifically functional concerns that differentiated one ship from another. Shipping was born in that country for commercial ends—the urge for conquest being directed inland—or defence given that the peoples on the other side of the ocean were still relations.

Thus the first privateers were made, sailing ships destined for coastal trading and operated by private individuals, itself a novelty compared with the Old World where the fleets were generally operated by the state or monopoly companies closely linked to the state.

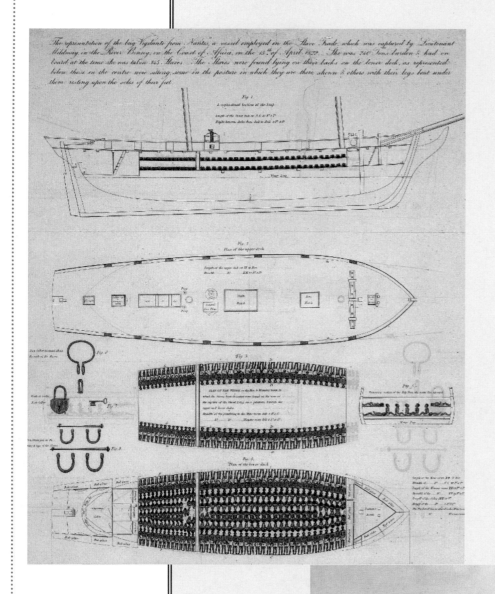

94 bottom The English frigate Electra heaves-to across the bows of the slaver Carolina: after a long chase the guns of the British vessel prevailed over the greater speed of the schooner with her pathetic cargo. Following her capture, the Carolina was renamed as the HMS Fawn.

94-95 The American shipbuilders' first original sail plan, albeit one with undeniable Dutch roots, was the schooner, developed and used for its characteristics of speed and maneuverability with small crews.

94 top An unusual drawing, if only for the drama of theme, illustrating how to load slaves aboard a slaver so as to make optimum use of the available cargo space. The plate records the specifications of the schooner Vigilante.

94 center Speed and maneuverability made the schooner particularly suitable for the transport of slaves from the African coasts to those of America. This lucrative trade brought notoriety to L'Antonio seen in this plate.

In an era in which their respective homelands were in a state of quasi-permanent conflict, the privateers were not above piracy at the expense of the ships of other nations. For this reason they were armed with guns on the main deck, protected by high gunwales with gun ports through which they could fire.

The Rattlesnake, built at Boston by John Peck, was a typical example of the mid-eighteenth century privateer: 88 feet 6" long, 21 feet 4" broad and with a draft of just 8 feet 3", she was rigged with three masts, three jibs on the bowsprit, and a spanker on the mizzen, had a single deck with raised quarter-deck and forecastle, and a capacious hold for cargo.

Slave ships or "slavers," while similar in appearance were destined for a far grimmer purpose, the slave trade. Those ships were designed for crossing the Atlantic, but built to be as fast and to pack in the "cargo" as economically as possible.

The principal quality required of a slaver was, in fact, speed: hence the adoption of what was to become the emblem of American sailing ships, the

schooner rig, one that required a bare bones crew and was extremely versatile and efficient.

Another typical American craft, again defined by the use to which it was put rather than technical features or dimensions, was the revenue cutter, a sailing ship employed by the customs service to combat smuggling. The Revenue Marine was later to spawn the Coast Guard, one of the greatest and most efficient of the many maritime institutions operating around the world.

The first revenue cutters were commissioned towards the end of the eighteenth century and had to meet the following specifications: keel length of between 36 and 40 feet, 6 pivoting guns of the main deck, and a crew made of a captain, a mate and 6 seamen.

Those vessels were generally rigged as schooners, with masts stepped well astern and fore-and-aft sails on both the fore- and mainmasts. They were designed to outrun and out-maneuver the smugglers, thus triggering the race for performance that was to result in the American schooners and clippers being world-beaters.

The diffusion of the schooner, that most typical of American rigs, was thus once again due to a specific purpose. Long distance traffic was logically based on the exploitation of prevailing winds for which square-rigged ships were ideal as they allowed a great area of canvas to be set without the need for excessively tall masts. Coastal traffic, in contrast had to take into account the variability of the winds: a day's wait for a favorable wind is significant when the voyage only lasted a few days. Moreover, coastal waters generally obliged ships to change course frequently so as to follow the shoreline or to enter bays and channels.

The schooner, of Dutch origin, dates from the first half of the eighteenth century and rapidly spread along the whole Atlantic seaboard of North America, finding its spiritual home at Baltimore, Virginia, where a great number of privateers, slavers and revenue cutters were built with this rig. The Baltimore schooner established itself as a distinct type, giving rise to a model that achieved, and still enjoys, great fame, the fisherman schooner.

The first schooners were two-masted, with the mainmast being the after one, and had a gaff foresail and a gaff mainsail. Topsails, not always present, were gaff topsails although the foremasts frequently had one or two square topsails instead. The American two-masted schooners had strongly raked (backward-leaning) masts. In America, schooners were very popular on account of their handiness, weatherliness, speed and low crew requirements and schooner hulls of increasing length were built during the nineteenth and early twentieth century, leading to "multimasted" schooners with three to six masts (with very little rake) and hull sizes reaching the limit for wooden construction, a type of construction that long remained predominant in North America. In 1902 the Americans even launched a steel seven-masted schooner, the only one of that rig and one of the largest sailing vessels ever built, but her sails were so big they were difficult to control. The last big multimasted schooners were built for the timber, coal and guano trades, but this is another story, and for merchant sail, the last.

The Clipper

At the beginning of the nineteenth century, continental Europe abandoned the bellicose posturing generated by the violent conflicts between the various states on land and sea.

During that period, regular traffic was established with the former colonies of the New World which were now displaying unmatched potential for economic development. What were once adventurous crossings, despite the persistent inadequacy of the means of transport, the sailing ship, in the face of the wind and sea conditions encountered, gradually took on the form of a scheduled service. Shipping lines were established to this end and goods and passengers were embarked according to pre-established routes and dates of departure and arrival.

A decisive technical development supported this development in scheduled navigation. In the naval archives in Washington, hundreds of documents had accumulated: ships' logbooks and sailing reports, surveys of coastlines and geographical features, currents and prevailing winds, all collected during the previous century without a precise motive.

The naval Lieutenant Matthew Fontaine Maury immersed himself in that mass of information after being confined to a desk job for reasons of health. Maury's patient and competent sifting of the immense archive resulted in the publication in 1844 of the Wind and Current Charts, the first systematic work in history to identify the routes with the most favorable meteorological conditions, noting the strength of winds and currents for each area.

Sailing was no longer a matter of trusting in the benevolence of Aeolus or the adventurous intuition of the ships' captains. True routes had been plotted around the globe and on these a new generation of sailing ships was ready to set sail.

The small West Indiamen were transformed into packet ships, the Atlantic postal delivery and passenger vessels, the larger East Indiamen instead developed a little later into the clippers.

In the mid-nineteenth century, the packet ship was still a recognizable development of the frigate, maintaining the same forms and rig. The most obvious modification concerned the internal fittings: rather than goods, the packet ship tended to carry passengers who

96 left The great evolution in the design of the sailing ship in the nineteenth century is represented above all by the clipper: a ship with lines of a sleekness never previously seen, setting an expanse of canvas unthinkable only fifty years earlier, and ever more suited to ocean passages.

96-97 The lucrative Far-Eastern trades encouraged British shipbuilders of the nineteenth century to abandon the traditional model based on the frigate, and to follow the American lead: slimmer ships with a greater sail area that were at last stripped of ornamentation and embellishments.

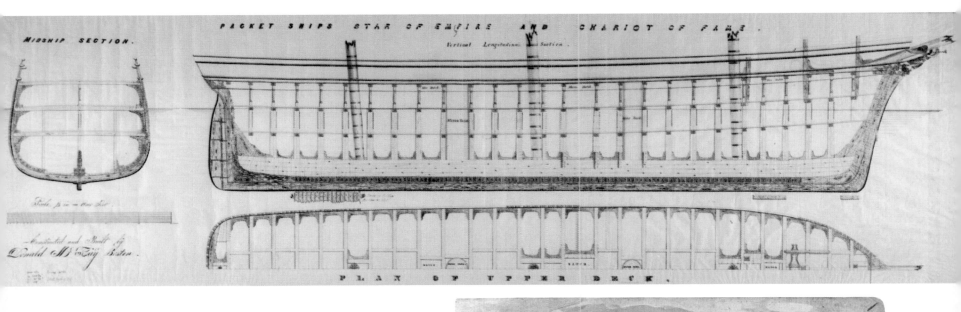

MIDSHIP SECTION.

Vertical Longitudinal and Section.

PLAN OF UPPER DECK.

97 top This attractive drawing, a lines plan of the Chariot of Fame, one of MacKay's famous packet ships, well illustrates the technical capabilities of the renowned Boston clipper constructor. His ships were famed for their speed, but their constructional qualities were perhaps of even greater significance.

97 bottom On the outward voyages from England to China on the tea routes, or to Australia for wool, the clipper carried passengers, emigrants heading for the lands of rosy promise. The Withers, Alfred and his wife Madge, were two such passengers who sailed aboard the James Baines from Liverpool to Australia and kept a delightful illustrated diary of their voyage. The page reproduced here shows the "ship portrait" of the James Baines leaving Liverpool, with the tug returning to port.

demanded decent personal accommodation for the duration of the voyage. The passenger cabins were not dissimilar to those of the commander and were panelled in painted wood, equipped with washstands, desks and bookshelves, and had bunks enclosed by damask curtains. The saloons had mahogany tables and with further wood panelling on the walls and silk upholstery. Furnishings comparable with those of a London club, in fact. In order to meet the changing demands of passengers, the size of the vessels was also increased: while the original West Indiamen rarely exceeded 500 tons, by the early 1840s packets of up to 1,000 tons were being built in Britain. And while the race for the new territories led the increasingly demanding Europeans to cross the Atlantic, the eastern seaboard of the United States was alive with the excitement of competition of a different kind.

When the gold rush in the unexplored western territories demanded new and faster communications, the pioneers were offered a route that was longer in terms of distance but infinitely safer, being far removed from the threat of Indian arrows. The sea route from New England to San Francisco in golden California, despite the heavy toll exacted by the tempestuous Cape Horn, contributed to the

characterized by the specific ability to cover great distances very quickly.

The clipper thus originated in the United States and the first great clipper designer was John Willis Griffith of Portsmouth, Virginia. When he began working at the Smith & Dimon yard in New York, Griffith was able to draw on the technical background that, starting out with mathematical theories applied to hydrodynamics, had led him to be a fervent supporter of the slim bow. Griffith rightly claimed that the ancient and never questioned "cod's head-mackerel's tail" theory prevented the creation of fast hulls, despite the fallacious impression of movement deriving from the spray produced by a voluminous prow striking a wave.

He also wholeheartedly endorsed the assumption that speed was a function of length, and thus argued for ships with very sharp bows that were as long in relation to their

development of decisively faster and safer ships. Out of the Baltimore schooner, appreciated for its speed and agility, was born a three-masted sailing ship, rigged once again with square sails to explore the preferential routes indicated in the Wind and Current Charts, but featuring bow lines so fine as to be concave. This was the clipper.

The etymology of the term is unclear, it was undoubtedly first used in the American shipyards to describe a fast sailing ship, whatever its size and rig, a ship capable of travelling at a good "clip" or pace. An alternative theory suggests that the word derives from clip in the sense of cut, referring to this particular type's ability to cut through the waves with its sharp bow. In any case, the clipper is a sailing ship

98 top The sailings of the clippers, and in general those of the packet ships of the second half of the nineteenth century, were announced via posters

displayed in the ports and advertisements published in the newspapers. This was evidence that sail-powered navigation, made reliable in terms of rig and

hull design, now ran to schedules that could be respected. The speed of passage was always given great emphasis thanks to this new-found reliability.

98 center The Red Rose under sail. A small English packet, the type of ship derived from the frigate which, having lost all bellicose

connotations during peaceful nineteenth century, was used to ferry passengers across the Atlantic to the New World.

volume as possible, rather than short and wide.

Griffith's Rainbow aroused considerable perplexity during her construction but amazement after her first voyages: from New York to Hong Kong and return, with a precious cargo of tea, she set record after record, frequently achieving speeds of 14 knots. Her commander was moved to declare, "we encountered not a single vessel that did not see our stern. There will never be a ship capable of beating us." The second part of this claim soon proved to be ill-founded. The Rainbow was only the beginning.

In the meantime, in fact, the New York-San Francisco route had achieved an importance more or

less equivalent to those heading to the Far East: the riches of California, gold above all, stimulated passenger traffic westwards, with goods being carried on the return voyage. The cargo of the Sea Witch, another of Griffith's clippers which completed the voyage in the record time of 97 days, had been acquired for $ 84,626 prior to the departure and was sold on arrival for $ 275,000, a profit margin that paid the costs of the ship's construction threefold!

The shipyards of New England were soon submerged with new orders for clippers and, by the mid-nineteenth century, no less than ten thousand men were employed on the construction of these ships.

98 bottom Donald MacKay's Great Repubblic: this was intended to be the fastest of the ships launched by the American constructor. However, she was never particularly successful and was in fact dogged by that ill-fortune which seemed to strike many ships and reinforced the superstitions of the sailors.

98-99 The Red Rose again, on the high seas in bad weather, her topsails and flying jib furled. Meteorological conditions still had a great influence on these early oceanic crossings: the efforts of the shipping companies to maintain their promises and sailing schedules were frequently frustrated by adverse winds and seas.

Donald McKay was one of the best known and most prolific constructors of American clippers. His first, the Stag Hound, left his yard at East Boston, Massachusetts, in 1850, and was at the time the largest mercantile ship ever built. Her maiden voyage to the East by way of California was sufficient for her owners, two Boston merchants, to recover the costs of her construction.

The Stag Hound was joined the following year by the Flying Cloud, an even larger ship of no less than 1,750 tons, 230 feet LOA hull length and beam of 41 feet. On her maiden voyage from New York to San Francisco, she knocked a week off the previous record belonging to Surprise, completing the trip in 89 days, achieving peaks of 18 knots and covering 374 miles in a single day. No other sailing ship had ever been so fast. The clipper era had begun in earnest.

Every designer was trying to hone his designs. Every shipbuilder was updating the techniques and technology employed in his yard. Above all, the owners were clamoring for ever faster ships and the captains were doing their utmost to shave days and hours off their sailing times.

The second half of the nineteenth century was to be the era of fantastic, epic duels between clippers, on the American routes and the classic tea and wool routes between China and England and Australia and England respectively.

There was more at stake than mere glory. This was important to the commanders and the constructors, but the true prize was represented by the valuation of

100 top A forest of masts and spars obscures the horizon in the port of New York, and the long bowsprit of a clipper looms over the East River Dock quayside crowded with goods. It is difficult to imagine the maneuvers that these sailing ships had to effect to enter and leave their mooring places.

100 center Precarious scaffolding and improvised shoring: the workforce of the A. Hall & Sons shipyard pose with appropriate pride in front of their "archaic" equipment.

100 bottom The interior of a clipper under construction: a serried rank of frames with doubled knees creates a large hold for the stowage of goods.

101 In the late nineteenth century, the port of New York no longer had the appearance of an albeit busy bay. A multitude of sailing ships are berthed along well organised quays for the loading and unloading of goods and passengers. Down easters, which were also fast and reliable ships, can be seen tied-up next to the majestic clippers.

the cargo: the first ship to land its cargo received a higher price for the goods carried. On the London market, the first load of tea to be landed was worth up to twice that of the second ship into port.

Naturally, the pride of the commanders played a major role in these remarkable contests. In 1851 there were no less than 45 clippers working the route between New York and California: the record was set by the Flying Cloud at 89 days. The following year 15

clippers set sail within three days of each other, all determined to beat the Flying Cloud's time.

Three ships, the Wild Pigeon of 996 tons, the Flying Fish, of 1,505, and the John Gilpin of 1089, "sailed at their maximum speed for three months, practically within hailing distance of each other, over a distance of 15,000 miles" as Matthew Maury Fontaine reports in his careful account of that race. First home was the McKay-built Flying Fish in 92 days, followed

by the John Gilpin thirty-six hours later. The Wild Pigeon reached San Francisco six days later after being left becalmed off the coast of California.

While in 1850 the American yards had launched only 16 clippers, the following year the number rose to 24. The true boom years for this type of ship were still to come, however: 61 clippers were launched in '52 and 125 in '53, which was also the year in which the largest clipper ever built left McKay's yard: the Great Republic was over 320 feet long (the aforementioned 200-foot limit for wooden ships had been overcome thanks to the use of iron structural elements and more modern construction techniques: steam engines had been introduced to the shipyards allowing joints to be sawed and drilled more precisely and larger structural elements to be constructed), she was fitted with four masts carrying almost 140,000 square feet of canvas, and had a burden of almost 6,000 tons.

Even before her maiden voyage, the Great Republic caught fire after a blaze broke out in a building adjacent to the port of New York. The ship was salvaged and rebuilt a few years later, but with shorter masts and a reduced burden.

McKay went on to build a further 38 sailing ships during the remaining 27 years of his career, the end of which coincided with the close of the clipper era.

The "down easter," something of a poor relation to the legendary clipper was to take its place and carry the last cargoes of the age of sail.

102-103 The Cutty
Sark under full sail as
she attempts to beat
another clipper in the
oceanic race for

commercial primacy.
In reality, the Cutty Sark
was never particularly fast,
in fact she owes her fame to
her longevity.

102 top After her record-
braking passage between
Sydney and London in
1885, an anonymous
admirer presented the

commander of the Cutty
Sark with this pennant, cut
in the shape of a small
camisole, or "cutty sark" in
Scottish.

103 top The Scottish clipper anchored in the southern seas where her commander, Captain Richard Woodget, intended to load wool for the London markets and, in the meantime, seek glory in epic oceanic races under sail.

On the 3rd of December, 1850, the American clipper Oriental tied up at the West India Quay in the Port of London. She was carrying a cargo of tea loaded in Hong Kong just 97 days earlier. The British East Indiamen were still at sea.

A reporter in London noted in the newspapers of the following days that the fact "provoked in the country a concern and an excitation like those caused by the memorable Tea Party which took place in the port of Boston in 1773, the spark for the American Revolution..."

In effect, a revolution was what was underway in the maritime world. The British had only the previous year repealed the Navigation Acts which rendered trade with the colonies of the Empire a monopoly enjoyed by the ships of His Majesty: in order to avoid a commercial isolation that in the long term would have undoubtedly harmed the nation's economy, the British had opened their shipyards to progress. Away with the swollen hull and stubby masts for the sailing ships destined for the high seas, the American lesson was to have uprooted the theories that had stagnated

103 bottom The Cutty Sark's figurehead represents the attractive young witch Nannie, her camisole in audacious disarray, grasping the tail of the horse who fled with peeping Tam she was chasing. The name of this the most famous of the clippers derives from Robert Burns' famous poem Tam O'Shanter.

on the designers' drawing boards for centuries (it should be noted that no more than a year later, in 1851, the United States' schooner America was to beat the Royal Yacht Squadron's entire fleet in a race in British waters: America had the same slim lines as the clippers, in contrast with the British yachts that were still influenced by eighteenth century thinking!).

While the Oriental was unloading its eagerly awaited cargo, the Admiralty asked her commander permission to inspect the design of the hull. Once towed into dock, the American clipper revealed her forms to the eyes of the British shipbuilders.

In Britain too, the shipyards began to construct the new type of ship, subsequently taking advantage of the

The Clipper Cutty Sark

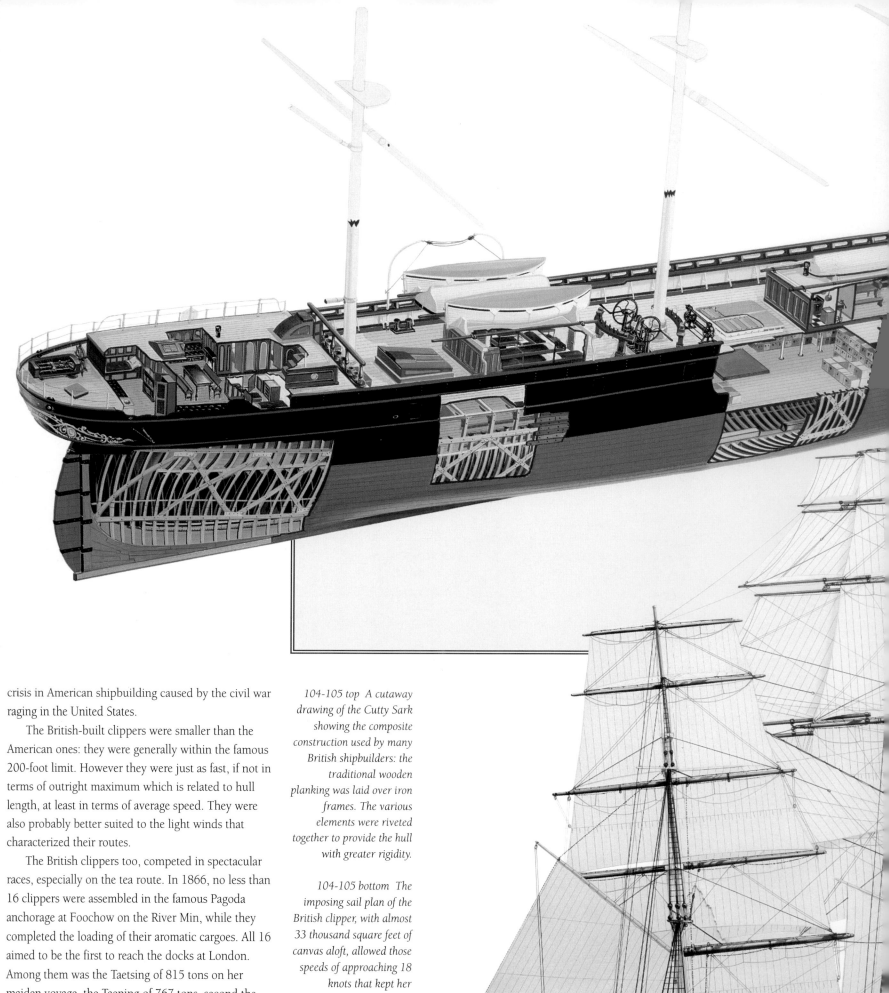

crisis in American shipbuilding caused by the civil war raging in the United States.

The British-built clippers were smaller than the American ones: they were generally within the famous 200-foot limit. However they were just as fast, if not in terms of outright maximum which is related to hull length, at least in terms of average speed. They were also probably better suited to the light winds that characterized their routes.

The British clippers too, competed in spectacular races, especially on the tea route. In 1866, no less than 16 clippers were assembled in the famous Pagoda anchorage at Foochow on the River Min, while they completed the loading of their aromatic cargoes. All 16 aimed to be the first to reach the docks at London. Among them was the Taetsing of 815 tons on her maiden voyage, the Taeping of 767 tons, second the previous year, the Serica of 700 tons, the Fiery Cross, a four-time winner of the race, and the 853-ton Ariel, another ship making her maiden voyage and the great favorite for the race.

After 99 days of sailing the Ariel sailing at 14 knots had just a mile lead over the Taeping. They entered the Thames estuary together, the Taeping managing to tie up first (thanks to a slightly shallower draft that allowed her to move before high tide), just a single hour ahead of Ariel after a 100-day voyage. Third home, the following day, was the Serica followed by the others.

Three years later, the Scott & Linton yard at Dumbarton in Scotland launched the Cutty Sark, rightly or wrongly the most famous of the clippers and

104-105 top A cutaway drawing of the Cutty Sark showing the composite construction used by many British shipbuilders: the traditional wooden planking was laid over iron frames. The various elements were riveted together to provide the hull with greater rigidity.

104-105 bottom The imposing sail plan of the British clipper, with almost 33 thousand square feet of canvas aloft, allowed those speeds of approaching 18 knots that kept her competitive over the decades despite the threat posed by steam. Copper sheathing nailed to the planking protected the hull from ship-worms and other organisms that tended to slow the ship and eat her timbers.

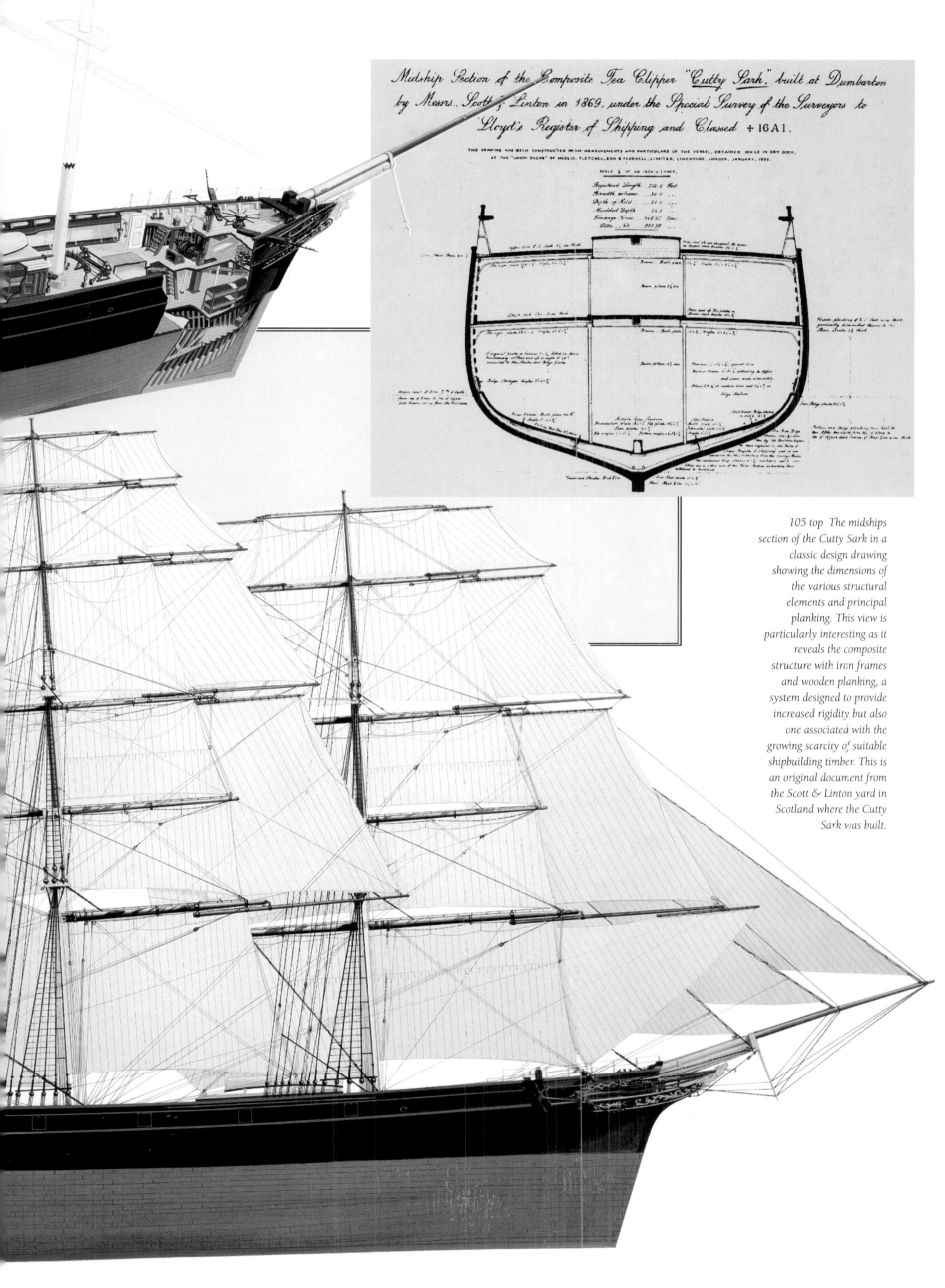

Midship Section of the Composite Tea Clipper "Cutty Sark" built at Dumbarton by Messrs. Scott & Linton in 1869, under the Special Survey of the Surveyors to Lloyd's Register of Shipping and Classed + 16 A1.

THIS DRAWING HAS BEEN CONSTRUCTED FROM MEASUREMENTS AND PARTICULARS OF THE VESSEL, OBTAINED WHILE IN DRY DOCK, AT THE "UNION DOCKS" OF MESSRS. FLETCHER, SON & FEARNELL, LIMITED, LIMEHOUSE, LONDON, JANUARY, 1922.

105 top The midships section of the Cutty Sark in a classic design drawing showing the dimensions of the various structural elements and principal planking. This view is particularly interesting as it reveals the composite structure with iron frames and wooden planking, a system designed to provide increased rigidity but also one associated with the growing scarcity of suitable shipbuilding timber. This is an original document from the Scott & Linton yard in Scotland where the Cutty Sark was built.

106 top The crew stowing the jibs out on the bowsprit. The ship is about to arrive in port and on this occasion the maneuver is not being hampered by the conditions typical of the high seas where the wind and waves frequently put the lives of the sailors involved at risk.

106 bottom left The photographs of the British clipper at sea were taken by her commander, Captain Woodget. This shot was evidently taken by the captain as he drew away from his ship in one of her boats.

106 bottom right Three men from the crew of the Cutty Sark: on the right, the cook, a Chinaman like many of them who worked those routes, an important not to say crucial member of a crew who had to face entire months at sea.

in any case the only restored survivor.

An ancient Scottish legend recounts that a young man, returning home on horseback on a dark and, inevitably, tempestuous night, found himself followed by dreadful witches: terrified, he spurred on his horse until, by the glow of a lamp, he saw a young and beautiful witch wearing a short shirt ("cutty sark" in the Scottish). He stopped suddenly and, turning to the girl, cried "Wonderful, cutty sark." The wind dropped, the lightning stopped and the witches disappeared. The young man managed to find his way home with the image of that "cutty sark" in his eyes.

The only connection between this story and the famous tea clipper is their shared nationality, a Scottish ship and a Scottish legend.

The Cutty Sark was designed by Hercules Linton, of the yard of the same name, for the owner Jock Willis, one of the most important tea importers of London in the second half of the nineteenth century. Most importantly, Willis was a man who knew the sea and a lover of sail in an era in which the snorting steam ships were beginning to exert their inexorable domination.

The Cutty Sark was launched in November, 1869. Three months later she undertook her maiden voyage to China. There she loaded tea and headed for home together with the other British clippers. The Cutty Sark took 110 days to make the return trip to London, five more than the fastest ship Thermopylae.

The following year she succeeded in beating the Ariel but again had to acknowledge the superiority of Thermopylae, a result repeated for a third year running in 1873. In fact, Cutty Sark never managed to set records nor to win races but she was nonetheless, and still is, an undoubtedly fine example of the breed, well built and comfortable in bad weather. Significantly, she was to have a long career.

Converted to the carrying of coal on the Atlantic routes, again without any great success, her period of glory came after eight years on the tea run and five shipping coal, when she was put onto the Australian wool route. Here she won and set those records that were to ensure her eventual restoration and survival.

The Cutty Sark made her first voyage from Sydney to London in 1883, in the record-breaking time of 82 days. The following year she lowered the record to 80 days. Her great adversary, Thermopylae, was constantly at her side, however, ever ready to match her performances. Up to 1885, that is. That year the Cutty

106-107 The Cutty Sark loading large bales of wool in Sydney harbor, Australia. The jibboom extension of the bowsprit has been housed inboard, evidently to avoid interference with the activities on the quay.

107 bottom right No other sailing ship before the clipper carried such a great cloud of canvas and never had masting and rigging been subjected to such strains. Clippers could set many light weather sails such as the Cutty Sark's main skysail.

Sark reached London from Sydney in just 73 days, beating eight clippers including the Thermopylae! Again in Australian waters, the British clipper took sweet revenge on the all-conquering steam when she overtook, under full sail and at a rate of 17 knots, the steam ship Britannia which was also heading for Sydney.

By the end of the century, sail would have been obliged to surrender to steam. Most of the clippers, like all other types of sailing ships, had far shorter life-spans, on average ten years. Some were lost in the frequent accidents at sea, being driven on to rocks or running aground in bad weather or through bad navigation, others suffered the fate of many wooden ships and were destroyed in fires. With the advent of steam many were downgraded to carrying low-freight cargoes such as coal, timber and grain and even slaves. The last survivors ended their days as floating storage hulks or, the supreme insult, as coal tenders for the triumphant steam ships.

The Cutty Sark enjoyed a somewhat different fate. After a number of years' service under the Portuguese flag, she was bought back by a British captain and restored as a training ship. Only in 1952, at the venerable age of 83 did she reach her final berth, a dry dock at Greenwich, as part of the National Maritime Museum.

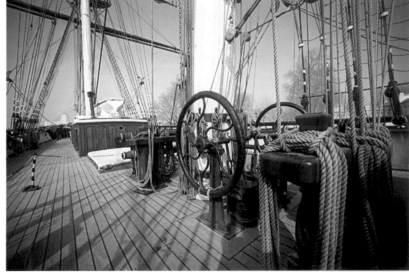

108 top left The rigging and the masts of the Cutty Sark, no longer stressed by the sails and the movement of the ships, are nonetheless kept in perfect working order to the point where, should the need arise, the ship could be put to sea without undue difficulties.

108 bottom left As well as the ship's name, the Cutty Sark's bell carries the date of her launch. The ship's bell sounded the changing watches and when dropping anchor signalled to the helmsman and the commander the lengths of chain lowered by the men at the the bows.

108 top right The compass binnacle, located on the poop deck in front of the ship's wheel.

108 center right The Cutty Sark was equipped with mechanical winches for certain operations. A Scottish captain was later to optimize this invention which would have reduced the number of men needed to handle the sails.

108 bottom right The Cutty Sark's hold, once used to stow tea chests and, later, bales of wool, now houses a collection of figureheads.

110 top and bottom left The Constitution represents the most advanced form of the American frigate, the great speed of which derived not so much from its sail plan as its highly efficient water lines. The American frigate's armament was nearly as powerful as that of the smallest ships of the line and she outclassed European frigates. These two images are akin to a photographic sequence of the battle between the Constitution and the British frigate Guerriere. As they approach one another, the two ships maneuvered to present their flanks to the enemy. As soon as they were within range they both fired a full broadside.

110 bottom right and 110-111 The last sequences of the battle between the American frigate and her English counterpart. The broadside fired by the latter has vainly battered the famous "ironsides" of the Constitution, while the American guns have swept the Guerriere's deck with devastating effects on the masts. The English ships has no choice but to surrender to the superiority of the former colonies' famous frigate. The artist, Michael Corne, informs us that the entire battle sequence lasted just 30 minutes.

FRIGATE - *Technical term of Italian origin, also used by other nations, describing a fast, elegant ship. From the thirteenth to the fifteenth century the frigate was a skiff, smaller than a felucca, with no deck, a single lateen sail and oars, serving larger vessels. With the subsequent prevalence of square-rigged ships and oceanic voyages to the Indies, it began to increase in size: it was fitted with a deck, two and then three masts, eight guns, twelve, twenty-four, thirty-two and up to sixty in two batteries; but always as an auxiliary ship at the service of larger vessels, used for scouting, convoy escort and despatches.*

Continued to be known by the same name, appropriate to its primitive, agile, slim, fast and elegant forms.
(A. Guglielmotti)

Frigate - in the world's navies, a light, agile craft, built for speed. These ships embarked between twenty and thirty-eight guns and were considered to be excellent cruisers.
(Falconer)

In 1813, the British frigates patrolling the Atlantic received a peremptory order from the

The Frigate *Constitution*

Admiralty not to engage in combat with the
American frigates unless they enjoyed numerical
superiority. Such an attitude on the part of those
who considered the domination of the high seas to
be the privilege of its fleet and its sailors would
appear to be somewhat atypical. In fact, the few
skirmishes that had taken place at sea with the
ships of the former colonies had prompted this
uncustomary prudence.

The American frigates, in particular, had
demonstrated their clear superiority in combat:
they were faster, more maneuverable and could
take a heavier pounding. Despite being of
traditional wooden construction, in line with the
technology of the time, they were so robust as to
become known as "ironsides." This nickname had

been coined by a member of the crew of the
American frigate Constitution after seeing a 24-
pound cannonball bounce off the side of his ship
into the sea. The Constitution continued to be
known as "Old Ironsides," even when in 1830,
fifteen years after her last battle and following a
period of flag-flying duties, she was recommended
for demolition.

Such was the fame of the ship and her symbolic
value to the young American nation, that as soon
as she was towed to the port of Boston, a vast
groundswell of public opinion led to the creation
of a subscription fund for her restoration and
recommissioning in the US Navy.

The Constitution was not, of course
subsequently used in combat, but served well as a

flagship in the Pacific, the Mediterranean and
Africa, completing a circumnavigation of the globe
and acting as a cadet training ship. In the 1930s she
was still to be sailing the waters of both the eastern
and western seaboards of the United States, before
finally retiring to the port of Boston where, each
year she completes a short cruise, towed by two
tugs which in a couple of hours take her out of her
berth, turn her around and maneuver her into place
with her opposite flank moored to the quay. A brief
moment of glory with the sole aim of allowing her
to age in a uniform fashion. It is nice to think,
however, that this is actually a gentle tribute, a
short stroll for an old lady of the sea.

The Constitution was built in Boston's Hartt
yard between 1794 and 1797. She was the largest

112 top Bedecked with bunting, her crew positioned on the yards, the Constitution celebrates the birthday of George Washington with a salvo from her guns. This took place on the 22nd of February, 1837, when the United States' warship was paying an official visit to the British naval base on Malta.

112 center The Constitution under construction: planking that in certain areas was up to 20 inches thick, was laid over frames that were over 7.5 inches thick and centerd at 15.5 inch intervals. This is what provided the ship with her renowned strength and earned her the nickname of "Old Ironsides."

vessel in the US navy, along with her virtual sister ships, the President and the United States, all three being 44-gun frigates.

From beakhead to taffrail she was 204 feet long, 23 feet more than comparable English frigates, and she was also over three feet wider. This last factor made her a more stable platform for firing broadsides. At around 2,200 tons, she was also twenty-five percent heavier than her English rivals. Above all, the Constitution, like her sister ships, carried an enormous sail area: her masts, towering 187 feet above the waterline, were made of silver spruce, a wood in which the forests of New England were rich (American pines,

112 bottom After years of glorious service, the Constitution, an unmatched symbol of maritime might, was restored for future generations: long flag-flying cruises awaited her, like the one completed between 1931 and 1934 during which she sailed through the Panama Canal.

113 The Constitution is photographed here in the 1930s, berthed at a quay in the port of Washington.

particularly the silver spruce, are particularly suitable for masts as the trunks are very tall and straight and the wood is light, dense and very even. In contrast, in Europe and in particular, England, where oak predominated and providing excellent timber for the structure of the ship, the pines were generally shorter and curving, more appropriate for planking), and could carry 43,000 square feet of canvas. This sail area compensated for a hull built with planking and frame elements that were oversized with respects to the overall dimensions of the ship. The frames were almost 8 inches thick and were set at spacings of just 15 and a half inches. This was in effect double planking

with a thickness that varied from a minimum of 15 inches to a maximum of 20. Hence the renowned strength of the ironsides!

Despite this massive structure, the Constitution was particularly fast, easily reaching 14 knots, partly thanks to that abundant sail area and partly to the efficiency of her waterlines.

The guns were carried on the covered gun deck and on the unusually long quarterdeck and forecastle. They were spaced further apart than on British ships, making their handling easier. The spardeck linking at a level the quarter deck to the forecastle did not carry guns for reasons of weight, stability and speed, but it provided an improved

space for handling the rig. The crew of four hundred ordinary seamen and officers was housed on the gun deck and orlop, the seamen being accommodated in hammocks strung between the beams. Only the officers had proper, albeit tiny, cabins; the accommodation for the commander and the commodore when aboard, was somewhat roomier.

The layout was similar to that of the European ships, the origins of the type being the same. On the American ships, however, it is more difficult to detect features that were not born out of sheer pragmatism while the European vessels were still conditioned by tradition.

The twentieth century - "Windjammers"

Steam

BRITISH & NORTH AMERICAN ROYAL MAIL STEAM SHIP "PERS

Were it not for the evident advantages of mechanical propulsion in the form of steam engines, ships would still today be propelled by the wind through the action of masts and sails. In reality, the inventors of those snorting, deafening and extremely clumsy, heavy and slow machines encountered considerable resistance from the majestic and increasingly efficient sailing ships.

In the end, of course, the romantic supporters of sail could do nothing in the face of the clear economic advantages the new enjoyed over the old. Thus, after over 5,000 years of universal use, sail was finally defeated by a mechanical means of propulsion, a fact which justifies the inclusion here of a brief historical note regarding steam ships.

The first instances of the steam engine adapted to provide motive power for water-borne transportation date back to the early eighteenth century: tentative trials reserved for small boats with side-mounted paddle wheels that were tested on rivers. The thrust provided by those boilers was minimal and certainly insufficient to cope with the weight of a ship or to counter the movement of the sea. Throughout that century, in fact, the only experiments made in the field of steam navigation were those of inventors and pioneers invested with the enlightened impulse of the time.

By the early nineteenth century, however, thanks largely to the innovative nature of the Americans, steam had begun to take over the bellies of ships. In 1807, Fulton's Clermont inaugurated a regular service on the Hudson River and, just twelve years later, in 1819, the Savannah left the city of the same name in Georgia and docked twenty-five days later in Liverpool, England. For eighteen days during the crossing, she relied on the thrust provided by two huge paddle wheels powered by the steam from her boilers. On the remaining seven days she preferred, or was obliged, to hoist the sails with which she was also equipped.

This was, then, rather more than a mere trial. Steam had demonstrated that it was capable of competing with sail. In reality, however, almost all maritime traffic continued to be the prerogative of sail for at least the next fifty years, and even the Savannah herself, like all the ships of the next few decades, to all intents and purposes still looked like a sailing ship: masts still towered over the main deck and were still rigged with the typical sail plans of the era. The steam engine had yet to inspire absolute faith.

The Savannah was a modest vessel of around 100 feet LOA with a beam of 27 feet. In that period even the "small" West Indiamen were roughly twice the size. And, moreover, all the hull space and displacement could be devoted to cargo. This last fact was to constitute a seemingly insurmountable obstacle to the spread of steam and represented efficient advocacy for sail. In order to have sufficient range to complete an Atlantic crossing, the Savannah had to embark 75 tons of coal and over 1,000 cubic feet of wood to feed her boilers.

In spite of the continuous evolution of steam engines and the introduction of the more efficient propeller in place of the paddle wheel, throughout the nineteenth century the mechanically powered-ship was handicapped by the need to embark the source of energy that the sailing ship instead found freely available more or less everywhere.

The steam ship, penalized by the weight and bulk of its machinery, the former only partially compensated for by a certain reduction in the rig, also had to cope with the problem of refuelling in an era in which ports were few and far between, those with the appropriate infrastructure naturally being even rarer. To say nothing of the scarcity of coal supplies. This was particularly true of the oceanic routes that skirted lands which at that time "civilization" had yet to reach.

Early in the twentieth century, the Russian fleet, sent to engage the Japanese at Tsushima, had to make an exhausting voyage, punctuated by difficulties in finding coal, along the coasts of Africa and the Asian sub-continent.

The Suez Canal was inaugurated in 1869: while it represented a negligible saving for the Russians (in

Chapter 4

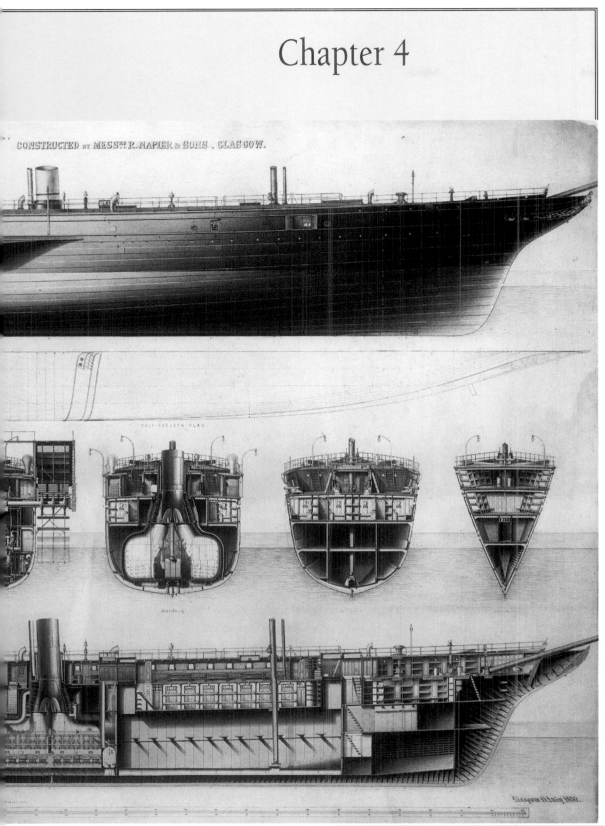

CONSTRUCTED BY MESSRS R. NAPIER & SONS, GLASGOW.

reality the route followed by the fleet was determined by political factors), it was a vital short-cut for the European traffic to and from the East Indies.

The canal was, above all, a bitter blow for the advocates of the technical supremacy of the tea clippers. Thus, by 1890, only 10% of the ships launched by the British yards lacked steam propulsion systems: the majority were in fact equipped with towering funnels between the persistent forest of masts and shrouds.

Few routes remained the preserve of the sailing ships. These included the longest voyages to the most distant and isolated regions such as Australia where the Cutty Sark finally proved her worth, or Chile, the source of a fertilizer of vital importance to the demographic expansion of Europe and North America. Those regions were too remote for the still restricted range of steam ships, too isolated to guarantee adequate facilities for the replenishment of wood and coal. Sailing ships also continued to ply coastal routes carrying cargoes of little value with profit margins that were too slim to support steamers that were still decidedly expensive, at least in terms of construction costs. These were the routes on which the sailing ship was to write the last chapters of its history.

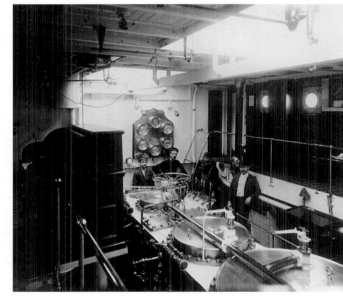

114-115 In the second half of the nineteenth century the large ships, while unchanged in form, felt the impact of the new system of propulsion: among the masts appeared funnels, great paddle wheels followed by the first propellers embellished the hull, enormous boilers filled the interiors.

115 top The engine room of the Manning, 1904, is rich in brass and solid wood fittings. Technology has yet to eliminate the elegance and decoration that was always part of the sailing ship.

The engineer and the stoker were new professional figures, seamen destined to cope with heat and scalding vapors rather than squalls and the drenchings of breaking waves.

115 bottom The opening of the Suez Canal was the first major set-back for sail which at that time still managed to demonstrate its worth by frequently beating the speeds of steam ships which were, above all, penalized by their restricted range.

Technological Evolution

When building the Cutty Sark, the Linton yard had already adopted a material that might appear inappropriate to a vessel intended to float: steel. It had previously seemed only logical to use wood to build ships; wood does after all float naturally.

The Cutty Sark's framing was instead made of steel upon which conventional planking was laid, a building method known as composite contruction. The steel conferred greater rigidity upon a structure that, for a given weight-strength ratio, allowed larger ships to be constructed and the previously mentioned 200-220-foot threshold to be overcome.

Clearly, for the use of this material to become widespread, casting technology and metalworking processes in general had to be improved. Developments in this field relied, in turn, on the availability of a fuel such as coal.

In the second half of the nineteenth century Great Britain was in the happy position of being able to count on abundant supplies of both coal and iron ore, just as the supplies of high quality domestic timber were dwindling as a result of the intensive exploitation of forest resources over the previous centuries. Supplies of timber from the colonies were also restricted by less favorable internal political conditions.

This situation led to notable progress in shipbuilding technology: the yards abandoned materials and shipbuilding methods that had, for better or worse, been employed for at least two thousand years, and adopted steel and its associated technologies. While this was also true of most of Europe, in the United States the situation was somewhat different in that while there was an abundance of suitable timber for shipbuilding, there was a scarcity of coal and iron ore. Wooden shipbuilding thus continued to prevail in the American shipyards, at least until the end of the century.

While the size of the ships increased to degrees unthinkable just a decade earlier (the American seven-masted schooner Thomas W. Lawson, for example, was no less than 393 feet long), rigging evolved at a similar pace. Masts and spars were also made of the new material. Steel allowed stiffer and lighter masts to be stepped (a wooden pole cannot be loaded at the tip as it is extremely sensitive to this kind of stress and thus has to flex— in order to maintain efficiency it has to have a greater diameter and thus weigh more than necessary). Longer single-section masts could be made in steel and, given that timber was inevitably expensive and required costly craftsmanship (one could hardly skimp on the quality of the wood destined for the construction of a mast, a vital part of the ship), they could be made more cheaply.

In the meantime, the old hemp shrouds were also replaced by steel wire: the former was more elastic, to the detriment of the efficiency of the propulsive system, more expensive and deteriorated rapidly. Steel cable was instead well suited to the technical characteristics of a mast made of the same material.

Naturally, the entire rig moved in this direction: the blocks also began to be made from steel, a fact which meant that it was not only from a technical point of view that ships changed. The sound produced by a sailing ship, that symphony of whistles and squeaks produced by the wind blowing through the rigging and the creaking of the wooden structures under stress was transformed into an infernal clatter well described in the prose of W.L.A. Derby, "...under stress some of them [the blocks] emit a deep, echoing note, others a buzz similar to that of telegraph wires. The shrouds produce the same vibrating sounds as the strings of a banjo; while a continuous wail comes from the turnbuckles. The wind roars through the running rigging, the heavy blocks of which dance a madcap rhythm against the steel masts."

Mechanical assistance was introduced to the rigging in the form of the winch, allowing a much smaller crew than would have been carried by the clippers of the early nineteenth century to comfortably handle a large ship.

The installation of winches to the rigging of sails and spars did not lighten the labors of the individual sailor, but it did mean that fewer men were needed, something which was clearly an economic advantage in operational terms and thus contributed to the survival of sail. A maneuver which previously required at least ten seamen could now be entrusted to just two. The winch was developed by the Scottish captain J.C.B. Jarvis and from 1880 became an integral part of the rigging of the great ships of the "last age of sail."

Materials and dimensions apart, the late nineteenth century sailing ship was little different in appearance to its predecessors: the slim hull shape was derived from that of the Baltimore schooner and developed by the builders of the American clippers, while the sail plan was either that of the classic full-rigged ship or the brigantine, although there was a tendency to reduce the height and increase the number of masts. This too was a result of the need to reduce crew sizes for economic motives.

One new element which characterized a certain number of sailing ships built between the nineteenth and twentieth centuries was a superstructure amidships which effectively divided the main deck into two parts. It was wider than the clippers' deckhouse and in some cases actually extended the full width of the ship. This superstructure frequently housed the officers' quarters who thus abandoned their traditional stern cabins. The helmsman was also relocated amidships, thus sparing him from the drenchings to which he was exposed with the wheel located, as it always had been, on the poop deck. The central superstructure was subsequently linked to the quarter-deck and the forecastle by a raised walkway over the main deck. This feature was designed to protect seamen from heavy seas when they had to move from prow to stern.

Built in steel, with a more modern rig and a profile moving in the direction of the shapes that were to become typical of mechanically powered vessels, these last sailing ships tackled ever more arduous voyages with crews that in general never exceeded thirty men. A clipper of half the tonnage would have carried twice as many. As late as 1930 the Grace Harwar was still rounding Cape Horn with a crew of ten!

The era of the armed sailing ship ended with the nineteenth century: the world's navies now relied exclusively on steam, albeit in the form of vessels that retained a residual sailing rig, initially because steam engines were unreliable and also to extend range and limit dependency on bunkering supplies. Merchant shipping, however no longer needed guns for self-protection. While the sailing ship of the twentieth century was exclusively mercantile and extended its useful life up to the Second World War, it could no longer compete with steam for the passenger and high-freight trades. As steam technology improved and became more widespread, the sailing ships found themselves cornered into ever less profitable and limted trades and trade routes.

It could be said the great era of sail ended with the wool and colonial clippers of 1,000-1,500 tons generally built in Scotland, on the Clyde at Leith in particular, or at Aberdeen, and destined above all to carry colonists to the Australian ports and wool and cereals on the return trip.

The wool clippers were direct descendants of the ships that had once loaded tea in China before being replaced by steam ships following the opening of the Suez Canal. They had a brief career, albeit one marked by the glorious duels between the Cutty Sark and Thermopylae mentioned earlier. Sold principally to Finnish and Italian owners, they were destined to continue sailing for a number of decades on the coastal routes: wandering from port to port throughout the world, in search of cargoes. They wrote epic chapters in the history of a type of navigation that had now reached the end of its days, with little support and meager financial resources, associated with great captains, frequently Italian, handled by crews as scarce in number as they were rich in seafaring skills.

Tracing a voyage of one of these vessels, which would frequently have lasted two or three years, during which the crew members would have only the most precarious of contacts with their distant homes, provides us with an overview of a fascinating era that is

Types of Ships

118-119 Loading timber aboard the four-master Australia. This type of ship, along with the multi-masted schooner, put up tenacious opposition to steam ships: cheap to build and run, they continued to work up to the 1940s.

118 top At the threshold of the century, the sailing ship had been relegated to mercantile duties. The insignia and guns having disappeared, the cargoes became ever less profitable and many ships turned to the transportation of immigrants, as was the case with the Voorspoed seen here as she lands British emigrants on the Australian coast.

118 bottom left Captain E. Gates and his wife in their quarters aboard the Lynton. Ever less interesting to the large companies, the sailing ship was operated by her captain who in many cases would end up spending his entire life on board, frequently accompanied by his family, replicating the domestic environment.

118 bottom right In spite of the competition offered by steam, on certain long distance routes and for certain cargoes, the sailing ship was still at work into the twentieth century: large steel-hulled carriers reached the distant ports of Australia, Chile and China.

not only romantic, but also the key to the functioning of various economies through the goods they carried.

As late as 1913, the Yallaroi, one of the last wool clippers, sold to the Genoese operator Drago and captained by Luigi Gazzolo also of Genoa, set sail from Marseilles with a cargo of roof tiles for Dunedin where she would await further orders (that is to say, she would wait for instructions regarding the cargo her owners had managed to arrange. On occasion it was the captain himself who would find a cargo in loco). From there she sailed to Newcastle, Australia, to load coal for Antofagasta in Chile. Antofagasta was one of the large ports, or rather anchorages devoted to nitrate, a substance harvested in the form of guano on the islands of the Chilean coast. This fertilizer was a major source of income for sailing ships at the turn of the century as the Chilean ports were still out of range for steam-powered vessels. The final nail in sail's coffin was perhaps the introduction of chemical fertilizers which

rendered guano uneconomic.

Loaded with nitrate, Yallaroi sailed out of Antofagasta, heading for Genoa by way of Cape Horn: she was to round the Cape with all sails aloft in a fresh breeze, only to encounter a terrible hurricane which placed both ship and crew in serious danger.

Again with the intent of opposing the hegemony of steam by creating ever more economic operational conditions, the British shipbuilders modified the clipper design which was clearly hampered by the slim lines originally intended to privilege speed. Their answer was to build a great number of "carriers," large ships with fuller lines and reduced mast heights. These vessels were capable of carrying large bulk loads but were slow: their economy of construction and operation allowed them to keep steam at bay for a few more decades. The opening of the Panama Canal meant that rounding Cape Horn, a voyage felt to be prohibitive for the steam ships of the day, could be avoided and thus relegated

even the carriers to minor routes and finally to ignominious demolition.

By that time, both the wool clippers and the carriers, mostly British built, were being constructed with steel hulls. They were contemporary to the last of the American sailing ships which, as mentioned earlier, were still built with traditional wooden planking. These last were the so-called Down Easters, large, full-rigged sailing ships of around 1,500-2,000 tons, and launched from the yards of of the Canadian maritime provinces and of New England. Again destined to sail from port to port in search of cargoes, they generally headed towards the capes of the southern oceans and were thus frequently referred to as Cape Horners. They carried above all timber, loaded in the great estuaries of North America and destined for the south. They would make the return voyage northwards laden with various cargoes such as nitrates, cereal and other bulk goods.

Many Down Easters ended their days as coasters in

the Mediterranean, where they were generally known as Nova Scotia after the North American land of their origin.

Again along the American coasts, the multi-masted schooner also enjoyed a period of great popularity. Those were ships evolved from the Baltimore and the Gloucester fishing schooners. In contrast with all other types of fully rigged or brigantine sailing ships to square riggers, those multi-masted schooners had fore-and-aft gaff rigs. Some intendend for coasting trades were of the shallow draft model, fitted with centerboards for ease of access to small ports. Initially most of those schooners were three-masted, but as hull lengths increased to augment carrying capacity and profit margins, versions with four masts began to be constructed from 1880. The following year the first five-master appeared and was joined shortly afterwards by six-masters. The largest of the multi-masted schooner, the 393-foot Thomas W. Lawson, was fitted with no less than seven masts. Clearly she had a steel hull, such dimensions being

impossible using wood. This giant vessel met with a tragic fate, however, as having crossed the Atlantic she was lost on the English coast.

The four-masters were particularly successful with at least 460 examples being constructed, while the five- and six-masters proved to be too weak in relation to their length.

The multi-masted schooners enjoyed an effective monopoly of the North American coastal trade at the expense of steam. They were highly economical vessels that could be handled by very small crews and did not need to be ballasted when sailing unladen.

Used mainly in coastal waters, on occasion they made successful ocean crossings. In 1876, for example, the Island City reached Australia from New York in just one hundred days after having rounded Cape Horn from east to west.

With the building boom in Florida in the period immediately following the First World War, a large number of these ships was still being used to carry

timber and building materials. European operators also commissioned eighteen large, steel-hulled, five-masted schooners of between 1,500 and 2,500 tons from American shipyards. They were built for the Società Navigazione Italo Americana and differed from the classic model only in terms of the square sails rigged on the foremast and their less elegant hull lines: the entire hull volume was in fact devoted to cargo space.

Towards the end of the nineteenth century a final generation of sailing ships proved to be worthy heirs to their glorious forebears, the windjammers. The etymology is uncertain, but the term probably refers to these vessels' ability and willingness to seek out every last breath of wind in an era in which the ominous smoke from the funnels of steam ships was already in sight well over the horizon. It did, on the other hand, have pejorative overtones when used by the sailors aboard steamers to describe those enormous hulls topped by mountains of square sails they still encountered at sea.

The windjammers were huge, steel-hulled, four- and five masted barques with square sails on the fore-, main- and mizzenmasts and a fore-and-aft spanker on the bonaventure. Between the end of the nineteenth century and the First World War, they staged a revival of the clipper era, loading coal and cereals in Australia, timber from the American North West and Canadian Pacific coasts, and the inevitable nitrate in the South American Pacific ports. With hulls well over 300 feet in length and displacing between two and three thousand tons, those ships were as fast as the far smaller clippers and could carry many times the cargo.

Like the clippers, they duelled with one another on the oceanic routes, seeking out the strongest winds, cramming on the canvas, confident that their steel hulls and rigging could withstand the pressure.

As late as 1934, a sign of the continued vitality of sail was provided by the Herzogin Cecilie, built in Germany but by then sailing under Åland (Finland) registry. She was operated on the last of the great sailing routes, carrying Australian grain. In the middle of the South Atlantic, en route from Belfast, Ireland, to Port Lincoln, Australia, she encountered a British steam liner heading for Rio de Janeiro. With a full set of sails aloft, around 45,000 square feet of heavy cotton canvas, propelled by a wind of between 35 and 40 knots, the Herzogin Cecilie overtook the steamer at 18 knots, repeating Cutty Sark's feat of fifty years earlier.

The majority of these vessels were built in Great Britain, France and Germany, countries in which there were shipowners who still believed in the supremacy of sail and deeply rooted traditions.

Many of those windjammers were sunk by the German submarines during the First World War, but the most bloodthirsty executioner was perhaps the southernmost tip of the American continent, Cape Horn. Between 1900 and 1914 no less than 54 Cape Horners were lost while attempting to round that cape which continued to claim victims from among those vessels which had been taken to the seas once again after the war. The Peiho sank there in 1923 while the Pinnas was dismasted and then abandoned by her crew in those waters in 1929.

The Last Age of Sails

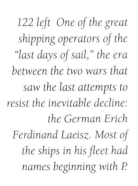

The conclusion to the historical part of this volume is inspired by the title - *Ultima Vela* - of the last paragraph from a Tomasso Gropallo's book, the nostalgic, celebratory tone of which I fully endorse.

By the end of the First World War wooden-built sailing ships had all but disappeared. Most of them had already been pensioned off at the end of the previous century, some had been sunk during the conflict, while the few survivors undoubtedly lay abandoned and forgotten in minor ports.

Numerous steel-hulled sailing ships survived, around 540 of them, the majority European, a few from North America. Within a few years these too were destined for demolition, the world's navies and mercantile fleets all having now embraced steam, very few owners having the means and desire to take them back to sea.

A few big square-riggers belonging to German owners did survive, distributed among the allied nations as war reparations.

Among the first operators to start over again was a German, Erich F. Laeisz, who slowly reacquired what remained of his fleet, including the famous Pamir, and then the Passat, Pinnas, Peiho, Peking, Parma and Pellworm. In 1926, he even commissioned the Padua, a 3,064 ton four-master with a central "island" superstructure, a magnificent example of a windjammer. This was the last great cargo-carrying sailing ship ever to be launched in the world. With these ships Laeisz once again worked the Chilean and Australian routes, carrying nitrate and grain and also embarking cadets for the merchant navy. He was

122 top right The Padua, a typical Laeisz fleet windjammer: four masts, the last rigged fore-and-aft, a large, black-painted steel hull with an island, the raised superstructure housing the steering gear, amidships. Built in 1926, she was the last great sailing ship to be constructed.

122 bottom right Another of the Laeisz fleet ships, the Pamir. As late as 1949, in the period of reconstruction after the war, she was sent to sea again to load grain. She completed two voyages before finally surrendering to her destiny.

122 left One of the great shipping operators of the "last days of sail," the era between the two wars that saw the last attempts to resist the inevitable decline: the German Erich Ferdinand Laeisz. Most of the ships in his fleet had names beginning with P.

Association, based in Almeda, California, was still operating fifteen large square-riggers for the salmon fishery in the freezing waters of Alaska. These vessels took between four and six weeks to sail from the Golden Gate to the fishing grounds where they would remain for up to four months. In 1930 the last of these sailing ships was decommissioned.

In 1924, by which time almost all the world's merchant navies had pensioned off their last sailing ships, a Finnish shipowner, Captain Gustaf Erikson of Marienhamn, in the Åland islands, acquired, one by one, no less than seventeen windjammers which he manned with a few experienced men and numerous youngsters attracted by an adventure that smacked of a glorious past. Erikson was joined by other Swedish and German owners who worked the Australian grain routes to northern Europe.

While steam ships of all shapes and sizes were now to be found throughout the globe, this handful of windjammers restaged some of the great voyages of the past. They usually reached the Pacific coasts loaded with ballast which they replaced with timber and nitrates for Australia. They would then return to Europe via Cape Horn, laden with Australian grain. Thanks to the low maintenance costs of these ships and, above all, their crews, there was a degree of

eventually put out of business by the Second World War.

Another German owner, Vinnen, actually built a new fleet, albeit of motorsailers, the 3,500-ton Magdalene Vinnen and the smaller, 1,800-ton Suzanne, Adolf, Carl, Christel and Werner Vinnen, all rigged with five masts. The Adolf Vinnen was lost off Lizard Point during her maiden voyage, while the others continued to sail into the post-war period, although not commercially.

With the fleets of the shipowners Bordes and Nantes, the French competed with the Germans for the primacy in sail transports up until 1915, but were unable to continue after the First World War. Almost all the French ships had been sunk, with only a few Nantes vessels managing to complete a number of voyages on the Australian grain route.

The United States and Italy created a joint shipping company, the SNIA mentioned earlier, which operated eighteen multi-masted schooners on a charter basis. Poorly designed ships, slow under sail and with an inefficient engine system, they were soon broken up.

In 1919, the South American nitrate trade was briefly revived. The Compania Administradora del Guano of Lima in Peru prepared three ships, war reparations received from the Germans, the 2,360-ton Drumcliff, rebaptised as the Omega, the 1,675-ton Maipo and the Dutch-built Tellus. For around forty years these ships sailed the Pacific routes with cargoes that in the twentieth century few other vessels carried. Among those that did were the British ships, Dovenby and Kilmallie, the Finns Lilloran and Fonape and the Italians Regina Elena and Antonio Padre.

In the post-war period, the Alaska Packers

economic logic to the business. Erikson in fact managed to keep his fleet sailing until the outbreak of the Second World War.

When the world returned to normality after the dramatic events of the war, Erikson's fleet had been dismembered and the captain himself died in 1947. Only Pamir and Passat, proud relics of a bygone age, made two further voyages, in 1949, to Australia to load grain. With them the era of merchant sail drew to a definitive close.

124 left The Caroline has unloaded the timber carried along the West Coast of the United States, from the ports on the Puget Sound in the north to the hot Californian regions. Spankers on the booms and gaff topsails, without spars, on the topmasts. The Caroline is a pure fore-and-aft schooner, setting a gaff sail on each lower mast and gaff topsails on the topmasts.

124 top right The slipways of the Hall Brothers yard at Port Blackely. This photo dates from 1902, the first hull on the left, with the entire framing completed, is that of the Caroline. On the right, the great forests which reached the very gates of the shipyard, an invaluable storehouse of shipbuilding timber.

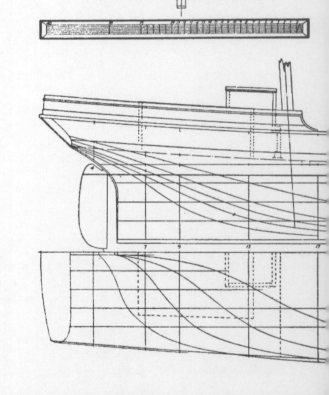

124-125 The sail plan, the sections and the lines of the multi-masted schooner Caroline: an absolutely original rig, conceived to respond with a small crew to the competition posed by steam. The shape of the hull is that of the American schooner, with a shallow draft and stability enhanced by the wide beam. Only the era in the which it was introduced, that is to say coincidental with the terminal decline of sail, prevented the widespread adoption of this model.

The multi-masted schooner
Caroline

The keel of the schooner Caroline, commissioned by a certain Joseph Knowland, was laid in 1902 in the yard run by the Hall brothers at Port Blackely in the state of Washington. The Caroline was a typical four-masted schooner, one of the most successful versions of a type of ship that responded in terms of its easily handled sail plan, to the demand for low running costs (that is to say, small crews). The multi-masted schooners also featured a highly standardized form of construction that utilized cheap materials in the form of the abundant local timber, factors that helped contain the initial capital investment. As has been mentioned earlier, the shipyards tackled the construction of schooners with five, six or even seven masts but these had proved to be

too demanding at sea, while the three-masters were too small in terms of the cargo capacity they offered. The four-masted schooner like the Caroline appeared, in short, to be the ideal compromise. The Halls's yard was founded at Port Blackely on the Puget Sound in the state of Washington, one of the most favorable locations in the world. The Puget Sound is, in fact, overlooked by mountain ranges characterized by immense forests of conifers which provided excellent timber for shipbuilding and other purposes and led to the establishment of shipyards, landings and sawmills, as well as, naturally, intensive mercantile traffic carrying this timber by sea to the rich and flourishing cities of California. Ships such as the Caroline were

ideal for this trade.

The information that follows was taken from H.I. Chapelle's *The History of American Sailing Ships* and is intended as a tribute to this unique and invaluable work by a great popularizer of the maritime history of the United States and, more generally, to the constructors of sailing ships: reading about thicknesses, diameters and lengths, one gains an idea of the difficulties involved in a process that for centuries benefited from little mechanized assistance. The dimensions of the Caroline, first and foremost: six feet above the keel, that is to say at around half her draft, she was 151 feet long. The length at the waterline was little different given that the stern post was vertical and the stem only slightly

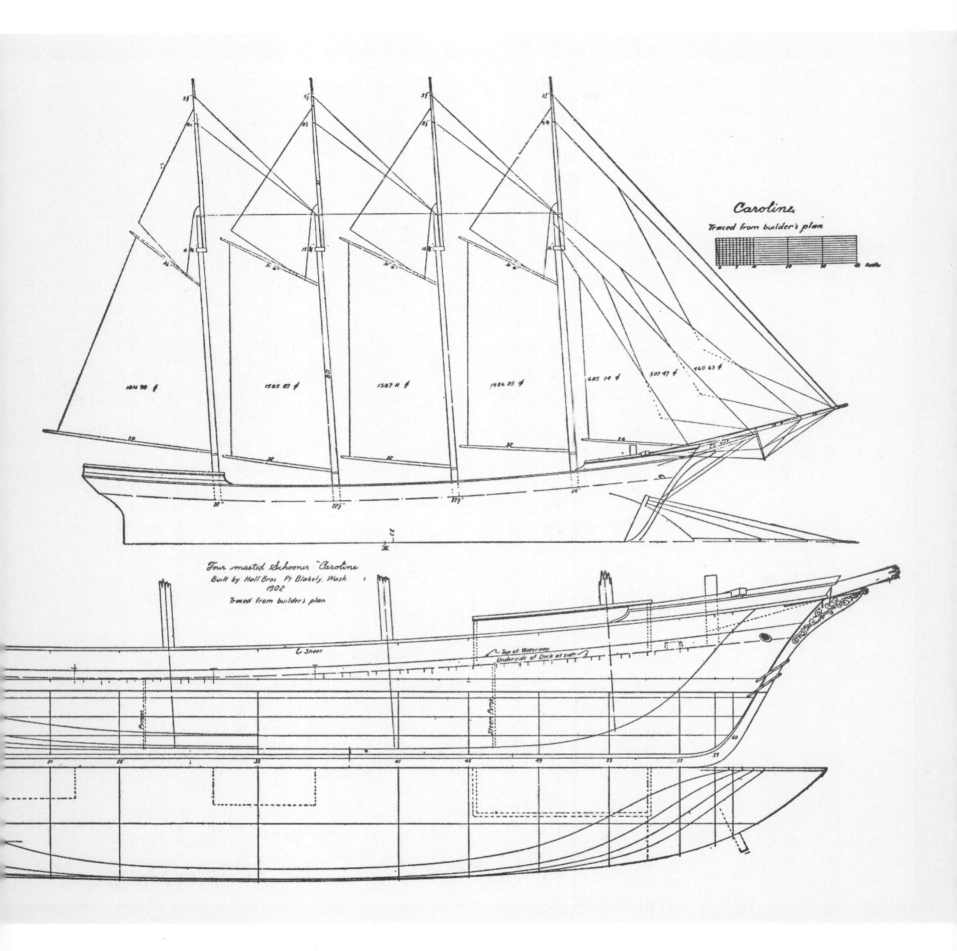

Caroline
Traced from builder's plan

Four masted Schooner "Caroline
Built by Hall Bros. Pt Blakely, Wash
1902
Traced from builder's plan

inclined. On the main deck, however, the ship was 165' 6" long. She had a beam of 38 feet and a draft of just under 11 feet. The planking and frame were constructed in the local yellow pine throughout. The specifications, in fact, contain only generic instructions regarding the manufacture of certain parts of the rig in "hard wood" and mention oak only in relation to the rudder stock. The keel had a cross section of 15.5 by 19.5 inches while the frames were centerd every 31.5 inches, supported longitudinally by a keelson with a cross section of 19.5 by 43.3 inches and by two side keelsons each side of 15.7 by 19.6 and 11.8 by 15.7 inches respectively. The planking had thickness ranging from 7 to 3.9 inches for the hull and from 3.9 to 2.9

inches for the decks. Inside the frames, the ceiling planking had thicknesses varying from 3.9 to 9.8 inches. The ceiling planking and structural elements were linked to one another with iron screws while four iron through-bolts fastened each strake to the frames. The external planking and the keel were instead assembled with galvanized iron nails and robinia trunnels. The ship was equipped with a steering an emergency "Providence" hand-pump and a winch for the halyards. The shrouds were steel wire while Manila ropes were used for the running rigging. Three tanks with a combined capacity of over 1,400 gallons were provided for water while there were three 100-gallon barrels for drinking water. The cabins were supplied

complete with furniture,; galley, heads, lamps, linoleum floors, curtains, sheets, tablecloths and linen in general, all were provided. Two boats were kept on the main deck, one of 19 and one of 15 feet. There follows a list of safety equipment, in truth rather scarce in comparison with modern-day standards, but with precise references to the demands of the U.S. Inspection Laws. Finally, the price: 37,500 dollars, 3,000 payable at the signing of the contract, 5,000 once the keel had been laid and ribs installed, 8,000 on the installation of the ceiling planking, 9,000 on completion of the hull planking and 12,500 on final completion of the ship. The Caroline was launched in June 1902, just as stipulated in the contract.

The windjammer
Preussen

126 left The Preussen: launched in 1902 by the German Tecklenborg yard, she was 438 feet long and could spread around 60,000 square feet of canvas. Under full sail she easily reached speeds of seventeen knots.

In 1900, the German operator Laeisz commissioned the Tecklenborg yard to build what was to be the largest sailing ship ever constructed, undoubtedly the most important vessel in what was then the world's largest fleet of sailing vessels.

Two years later, the yard launched the Preussen. She was intended to be the forerunner of a new generation of windjammers and only historical events prevented her from becoming so.

126-127 The handling of the sails on the yards of the Preussen, the masts of which towered over seventy meters above the level of the sea, required nerves of steel: the men, their feet planted on the footrope, lean on the spar, one hand for the ship, one for themselves.

127 top In terms of aesthetics, the Preussen, built in an era in which sailing ships had lost part of their appeal, earned the title of "Queen of the Seas," an honor which did little to prevent her being rammed by a steam ship in the English Channel.

127 bottom Repairs to the sails on board a great Laeisz windjammer. This was a continuous activity to ensure that the ship's "engine" was always in peak condition. An activity with far more appeal than that of the engineer it was to be replaced by.

was fitted with Jarvis brace winches, two boilers produced the steam required to operate the bilge pump, the power-assisted helm and the four halyard winches. All of the shrouds were in steel wire, while the running rigging's 1,168 blocks were all made of the same material. The Preussen's hull had a central "island" superstructure with the wheelhouse and the captain's and officers' quarters, linked to the forecastle and the poop via a central gangway raised above the level of the main deck. The hull plates were riveted to one another and hot-riveted to the frames. There were five watertight bulkheads and a watertight, cellular double bottom that ensured the ship would remain afloat even if holed. The ship had three cargo decks plus the main deck and was specifically fitted-out to embark sacks of Chilean nitrate.

Despite the fact that she was designed to

126 bottom right The Preussen's aft wheel was generally only used in the event of problems with the principal steering wheel located on the central raised deck and equipped with steam-powered assistance.

optimize cargo carrying capacity, and thus had a particularly full transverse section, the Preussen's hull, the topsides painted black in accordance with Laeisz company traditions, was both powerful and elegant in appearance, earning her the nickname "Queen of the Seas."

Given her technical specification, the Preussen could have provided the profits envisioned by her owner, despite the claims of those who saw sail as being less economic than steam. It was, however, a steam ship that nullified the threat of a dangerous competitor.

Eight years after her launch, on a foggy November night in 1910, the Preussen was sailing through the English Channel, bound for Chile with a cargo of pianos. A modest English steamer, underestimating her speed, cut across her bows rather than affording her the precedence that was hers by right. The collision was inevitable and although the damage to the German sailing ship was not serious it was sufficient to make her difficult to govern in the gale blowing up the Channel from the ocean. The largest and most modern of the windjammers was thus inexorably blown onto the cliffs of Dover.

The ship had hull length of 438 feet, a beam of just over 54 feet and a hull depth of almost 33 feet. She displaced 11,150 tons while her holds could carry 8,000 tons of cargo.

The Preussen was rigged with five masts, all square-rigged, the only five-masted full-rigged ship ever built until the holiday cruise sailiner Royal Clipper put into service in 2000. The Preussen's mainmast soared to 223 feet from foot to truck. Those masts allowed the ship to spread something in the region of 60,000 square feet of canvas!

The steamers of the time could maintain a cruising speed of around 8 knots, something the Preussen could comfortably achieve in moderate winds: when driving hard she was easily capable of peaks of 17 knots. In 1903, in the South Atlantic, she covered a distance of 368 miles in twenty-four hours, an average speed of 15.3 knots. On her fastest crossing the Preussen took 57 days to reach Iquique from the English Channel.

The largest of Laeisz's windjammers was crammed with modern technology. The Preussen

Still sailing
Contents

128 The Norwegian Christian Radich, sailing in a light wind, all her canvas set.

129 A wall of white canvas propels the barque Sagres, a Portuguese training ship with five square sails on the fore and main masts.

Chapter 5

The Ladies of the Sea

While it is difficult, if not impossible to identify the moment in which sail was born, it is no easier to define the point at which its slow decline reached its nadir as, in truth, certain commercial routes in areas bypassed by progress continue to be plied by slow, archaic sailing vessels.

However, to all intents and purposes sail-powered navigation no longer exists except as a recreational or sporting pursuit, or as a memento of past glories.

While it may not be possible to describe a specific event that decreed the end of sail, it can safely be said that after the Second World War it was the black smoke of steam rather than the white canvas of sail that revealed the presence of shipping on the horizon.

A series of motives, some of them technical but the majority associated with the economics of transport which has always been a determinant factor in trading practice, led in the second half of the twentieth century to the disappearance of the last sailing ships. Mechanical propulsion, first and foremost, despite its unreliability even at the dawn of the new century. The problems relating to the initial reliance on external combustion - the space that had to be devoted to boilers and fuel, be it wood or coal, the relatively scarce power outputs, the need for frequent fuelling stops - were largely resolved with the advent of the internal combustion diesel engine, to the invincible advantages of which sail had no answer.

Developed in 1897 by Rudolf Diesel, the new propulsion unit was first installed aboard a ship, the German vessel Seelandia, in 1912, inaugurating a new era for navigation.

The early diesel engines boasted a factor of efficiency of 35% compared with the modest 15% offered by steam, against which sail could still be competitive. Moreover, the diesel engine used a fuel that was less bulky in relation to its yield, more easily embarked (a tanker can actually refuel another ship while underway) and, above all, it did not require the numerous, perilously employed stokers demanded by steam.

In the meantime, while the routes linking the various parts of the world had expanded to cover virtually the entire globe, they benefited from increasingly numerous and well equipped port facilities, thus nullifying the last of the strengths of sail propulsion, its unlimited range. This was also undermined by the opening of the great canals, the nineteenth century Suez Canal avoiding the need to circumnavigate the African continent, the Panama Canal instead eliminating the need to round Cape

Horn, the bane of generations of sailors.

Another technical factor favored the development of the new type of ship: steel construction. The introduction of this material had, of course, allowed the 200-foot restriction on length to be overcome. Applied as plating too, it allowed hulls of any size to be constructed, especially once welded seams had replaced the more expensive, heavier and less rigid riveting after the Second World War. Dimensions were, after all, crucial in the economic viability of shipping. Clearly, a sailing ship, even with all the intelligent rigging of the American multimasted schooners, had to have a larger crew as the length of the hull increased. This was not necessarily true of mechanically propelled ships.

Only two great sailing ships, two windjammers, spectres of past eras, attempted to put up a last desperate fight against destiny and history in the period after the Second World War.

Pamir sailing out of Antwerp under the command of Captain Bjorkfeldt, reached Auckland in New

130 left Pamir and Passat, noble relics of a glorious mercantile past, moored while waiting to be loaded.

130 right Pamir in the port of Montevideo, Uruguay, in the February of 1957: this was the famous ship's last year of life. Launched for the German operator Laeisz in 1905, she was lost in the South Atlantic on the 22nd of September '57.

131 Pamir again, seen here under sail from San Francisco to Auckland, New Zealand, in May, 1942. In the immediate post-war period, together with the Passat, she completed a number of voyages as a commercial training ship.

Zealand in the November of 1948, in order to load grain in what would, in any case, be her last commercial voyage.

Passat, commanded by Captain Hagerstrand, who during his career had rounded Cape Horn no less than thirty-six times, followed in her wake. Both of these ships, all that remained of the great Laeisz fleet recovered and set to work between the two wars by the Finn, Gustaf Erikson, found themselves in New Zealand at the outbreak of the Second World War. They returned to Europe, restored to Erikson's heirs, and completed a further two grain voyages in 1948 and 1949 before being sent to be broken up in Belgium: they were eventually saved by a group of German operators who had them refitted, installing auxiliary engines, and put them to work as cadet training ships.

Pamir and Passat, nonetheless met their inevitable

end at sea. The first was lost in the South Atlantic during a cruise in 1957, only five of the cadets being saved. The second suffered diverse problems after having set sail from Mar de Plata for Europe that same year and was abandoned in South America, from where she was eventually to reach her last anchorage at Travemunde, by then stripped of her rigging.

A sailing ship again rounded Cape Horn in 1967. This was the Regina Pacis, a wooden schooner acquired by operators in Santiago, Chile, after spending years laid up. Sent back to sea once again, flying the Maltese flag given that no other register was willing to accept her, she undertook the voyage down the Pacific coast of Chile, rounding the Cape from west to east and reaching New York, replicating the hundreds of voyages on the same route that she had completed laden with cargo during the course of her century at sea.

The post-war voyages of the two German windjammers and the Regina Pacis, while far from denoting any residual viability of sail, did at least provide material for a notable literary output that made a significant contribution to the historical memory of sail and kept interest in the practice alive.

A New Dawn?

series of reasons with a common economic matrix that went beyond the undeniable technical factors, lay behind the decline of commercial sail-powered shipping.

It was actually an economic motive, the cost of fuel, that led in the 1970s to a revival as sudden as it was ephemeral, of the desires and hopes of the supporters of sail. Political rather than concrete geological factors had led to a sudden revelation of the limitations of crude oil reserves, previously thought to be virtually infinite. The whole of the western world. that is to say, the driving force of the global economy, had to come to terms with the oil crisis, and thus reappraised some of the methods and practices of the past, albeit in an impulsive rather than logical manner.

Along with the concept of energy saving, attempts were made to revive sail-powered navigation. In effect, at that time technological progress had provided a series of innovations, both in terms of materials and equipment, that allowed significant strides to made in terms of the efficiency of sailing ships and an equally significant saving in terms of the size of the crew needed to handle them.

Light alloys such as those based on aluminum and composite materials with glass fibers and synthetic resins, allowed lighter but equally stiff hulls to be constructed, a factor which signified increased speed. The rigs developed for the extremely widespread racing and cruising yachts meant that maneuvers were less demanding than had been the case even in the "last days of sail." A crew numerically identical to one carried by a motor vessel could now handle a sailing ship of the same size.

In particular, there was great interest in combing the two forms of propulsion in ships designed for routes chosen, as in the era of Matthew Fontaine Maury, on the basis of the prevailing winds.

However, this last, doomed attempt to revive past customs soon faded, leaving only minimal traces of its passing. The Arab nations reopened the oil wells and increasingly powerful engines once again appeared to be the only viable means of propulsion for commercial shipping.

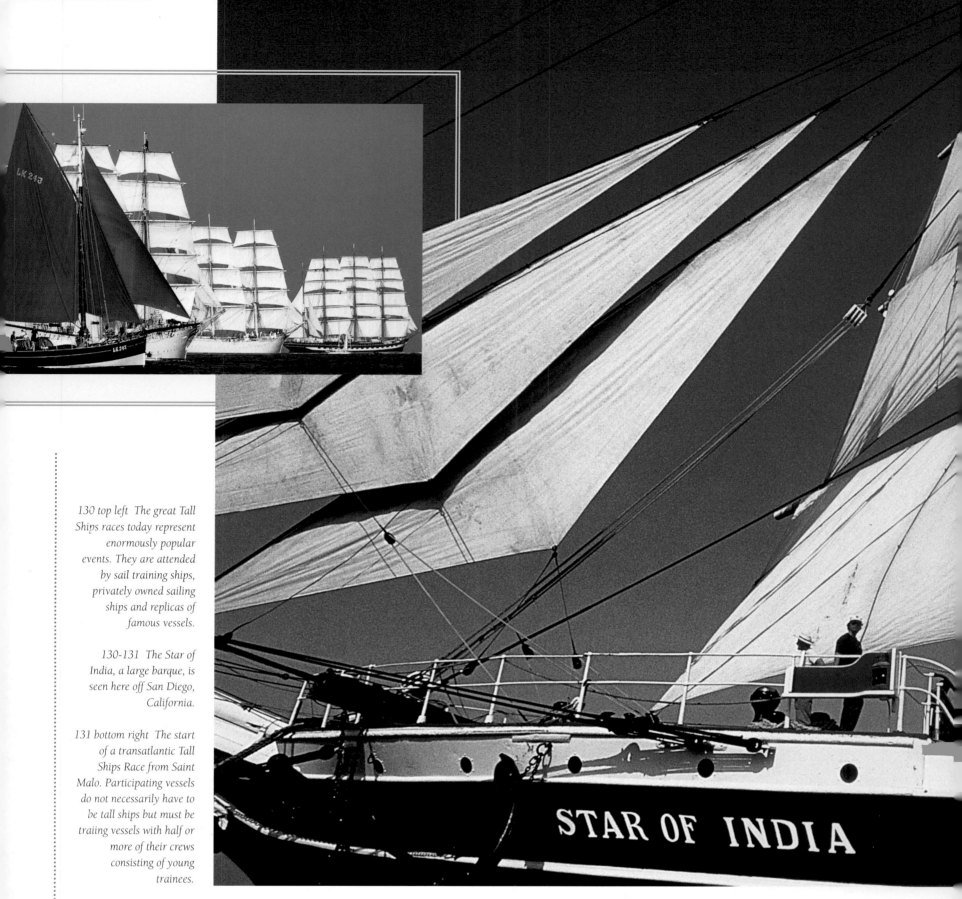

130 top left The great Tall Ships races today represent enormously popular events. They are attended by sail training ships, privately owned sailing ships and replicas of famous vessels.

130-131 The Star of India, a large barque, is seen here off San Diego, California.

131 bottom right The start of a transatlantic Tall Ships Race from Saint Malo. Participating vessels do not necessarily have to be tall ships but must be traiing vessels with half or more of their crews consisting of young trainees.

Sail today

For centuries, sail-powered navigation represented a significant part of human civilization. Men and goods were transported by sea, under sail, discoveries and conquests were made, generally with the aid of sail. Virtually any major journey that was undertaken had to cross a sea and thus sailing was a necessity.

It is only logical, therefore, that after playing such a crucial role, sailing could hardly disappear altogether, could hardly vanish despite the fact that man no longer relied exclusively on the winds to cross the oceans.

In effect, rather more than mere traces of that world do still exist today: a number of sailing ships still take to the

high seas and will be discussed later, others are integral and integrating parts of the maritime museums that most nations with any tradition in the field have founded. The nations of Europe and North America, in particular, are rich in similar relics. The Passat can still be seen at Travemunde as mentioned earlier, while the Fram is conserved in Oslo and the Viking in Gothenberg.

The Pommern can still be seen in Marienhamm, Finland, once the home of Gustaf Erikson's fleet, while again in Finland, at Abo, the Suomen Joutsen and the Sigyn are on display. The Af Chapman, originally a Scottish clipper named the Dunsyre, has now been transformed into a youth hostel in Stockholm.

The most famous of all these museum ships, the glorious Cutty Sark, in perfectly restored condition, is enduring testimony to the clipper era in a dry-dock in Greenwich, the home of the National Maritime Museum.

On the other side of the Atlantic, the Star of India, a ship that once belonged to Alaska Packers, is now

moored at San Diego while the Balclutha, formerly known as the Star of Alaska and belonging to the same company, is today an integral part of the San Francisco Maritime National Historic Park.

Other sailing ships survive in the United States, managed by the Peabody Museum of Salem and the Mystic Seaport Museum on the Atlantic coast.

Many other historic sailing ships are preserved in the United States and in many other coutries.

The traditions of sail-powered navigation are also kept alive by associations dedicated to recording and collating human testimony to bygone times. The International Association of Cape Horners, for example, was founded in 1936 and today has branches in eleven nations. The association brings together those seamen who can boast the experience of rounding Cape Horn, under sail naturally.

The Cape in question is the extreme southern tip of the South American continent, a rocky outcrop of

organization for no less than sixteen national associations of the same name. Founded in England in 1956, it organizes the International Sail Training Races in which merchant and naval schoolships and youth-training vessels from many different countries take part. As many of those vessels are square-riggers and big schooners, those races have been nicknamed "Tall Ship Races."

The I.S.T.A. is responsible for providing young people from all nations with the opportunity to embark on these ships and enjoy the experience of navigation under sail (despite the presence in this day and age of auxiliary engines).

Annual rallies and regattas races are held between the ports of the various nations and the Tall Ships Races are organized periodically. In 2000 the ships assembled at Genoa in Italy and Southampton in England before sailing to Cadiz. From that Spanish port the two combined fleets raced across the Atlantic to Bermuda from where the fleet dispersed to visit various American ports. Most of those tall ships joined others not part of the I.S.T.A. fleet for the July 4 OpSail tall ships parade at New York. The racing fleet regrouped in Boston in the United States and Halifax in Canada before returning to Europe and the finish at Amsterdam, Holland.

Today, therefore, sail survives, albeit in mutated forms. With passenger traffic and cargo carrying having been abandoned and guns left to more deadly modern

sinister appearance that rises four hundred meters above the surface of a continuously agitated sea. A small island, the last outpost of lands battered by the southern winds of the fiftieth parallel, an uninterrupted corridor around the globe along which the winds and waves, generally moving from west to east, find no obstacles to slow their storm force progress.

Rounding the Cape with the wind is a relatively easy proposition for a sailing ship. But arriving from the Atlantic in order to ascend the continent's Pacific coast, the route typically followed by the ships sailing out of New York bound for San Francisco, or those from Europe heading for the South American nitrate ports, was a very different proposition. A sailing ship might take weeks to round the Cape from east to west, and would almost always lose sails, have trouble with spars and masts and frequently lose men overboard. And, of course, there was always the very real risk of the entire ship being lost. In the first fifteen years of the twentieth

century no less than 53 windjammers were lost attempting to round the Cape.

The dreaded headland's last victims were two ships belonging to the Erikson fleet, the Peiho, wrecked on the 23rd of March, 1923, in the Strait of Lemaire, before she even reached Cape Horn, and the Pinnas which began to take on water 25 miles south of Diego Ramirez on the 26th of April, 1929 and was dismasted.

There are still a number of rusting hulls of old windjammers at Port Stanley, in southern Chile, melancholic testimony to these tragic stories of the sea.

In the post-war period associations were founded throughout the world with the aim of stimulating interest in sailing. Among the many, the International Sail Training Association today acts as an umbrella

grey vessels, the ancient sailing ships ply the seas in order to teach something of life itself, adding a touch of adventure to otherwise excessively programmed package cruises, recalling a combination of activities from shipbuilding through to navigation that have signified so much in the history of humanity.

Today navigation under sail signifies training ships, sailing vessels devoted to a particular style of cruising, and replicas of ancient models.

134-135 *The Palinuro, a sail training ship belonging to the Italian navy, under sail and against the light, an image which emphasizes her barquentine rig with square sails on the foremast and fore-and-aft gaff sails on the main and mizzen masts. Three staysails are set between the foremast and mainmast.*

135 left *The barque Kaiwo Maru, under full sail. Her masting consists of a foremast, a mainmast, a mizzen mast and a jigger mast; the latter carries a gaff jigger and jigger-topsail.*

135 right *A seaman working aloft aboard the Palinuro. At one time the men would go aloft with no protection whatsoever, at the mercy of the sharp movements of the rigging and the rolling of the ship. Today, strict safety measures are imposed.*

For many years following the disappearance of the last mercantile sailing vessels, the practice of navigation under sail on the high seas was kept alive by the world's navies.

Every nation with a certain maritime tradition had at least one sailing ship within its naval fleet, generally used for cadet or officer training and for flag-flying duties: the cruises undertaken by these sail training ships visited foreign ports and were considered to be a form of diplomatic mission and as such, were carefully organized to present the best possible image.

There are currently active sailing ships with duties that go far beyond training, but this activity does still remain central to the survival of sail. There may some perplexity as to the propaedeutic value of a cruise on a sailing ship: the naval and mercantile fleets of today are of course exclusively propelled by mechanical means and certainly many of the specific aspects of navigation under sail are foreign to the problematics of modern shipping. There is, however, an undoubted educational value to the practice of sailing. Navigating under sail means coming into direct contact with the sea and simply causing the ship to move forwards involves adapting oneself and the vessel to whatever means nature has to offer. It thus means recognizing one's own limitations and potential and thus learning respect. The sailor has always had to learn these concepts and consequently has contributed to the evolution of a certain behavioral heritage that, while it is undoubtedly of value on dry land too, is indispensable at sea. For these reasons among others the world's navies have continued to integrate academic activities with sail training.

. Certainly, the sailing practices of today are rather different to those of the past: hands are still sent aloft to handle the sails, but personal safety is naturally now a priority.

While once upon a time clinging to a spar, one's feet planted on the possibly icy footrope, one hand for the ship the other for oneself, as the old seafaring saying went, represented an enormously risky wager with life itself, it is now, and rightly so, little more than tiring, adrenaline-pumping exercise.

Since 1993, an annual international conference has been held, the "Sail Training Safety Forum," during which the theme of safety aboard the great sailing ships is discussed. One of the most lively debates is always that concerning the prevention of accidents for the crew members who have to go aloft. In effect, in spite of conditions that have improved radically since the golden age of sail, in 1998 two seamen lost their lives while working aloft. The conference has also considered questions such as the management of watches, meteorological information and the various technical features of hulls and rigging.

Life on board the sailing ships of today has little in common with that of the nineteenth century. While corporal punishment has naturally been eliminated, prompt obedience to commands remains vital to the safety of crew and ship, as anyone with any experience of sailing, even aboard small yachts, knows well.

While the crew members may still sleep in

Sail training ships

hammocks, the conditions of hygiene of the internal accommodation are exemplary and a far cry from the eternally damp, suffocating and disease ridden below decks areas of a clipper or a frigate of centuries past. The clothing and hygiene of today allow a quality of life that once upon a time not even the officers could have hoped for.

Scurvy having been conquered, there is no comparison between the standards of health on board today and those encountered by Dr Scudamore as described in "The True Story of the Pirate Long John

Silver," by Bjorn Larsson: "From Scudamore I learned what little there is to know of the art of medicine, that was conceded to me, and it was not such a great art, at least that which concerned the inside of the body. Sores and wounds were instead the strong suit of men like Scudamore and, with regards arms and legs, they were capable of amputating them blindfold. With needles, sores and cauterizing irons they were as able as we seamen with ropes, lines and boat hooks. But for the rest? Leeches, blood letting, hot and cold poultices, drops of camphor in liquor, or pure liquor, remedies to make one's bowels move, remedies to make them stop; it was no more complicated than this. But did it do any good?"

Sail training ships are not, of course, a modern day phenomenon. They had always existed throughout the era of sail, both civilian and military naval. At one time, however, this function was performed by ships that at the same time kept up their naval or mercantile functions, the cadets being embarked to work with the professional crew.

This practice was taken to the limit during the last days of sail, as a means of cost-cutting by reducing the number of professional seamen required. All of Erikson's ships, for example, carried a commander, a second officer, a boatswain and a sailmaker: the rest of the crew would be composed of young men attracted either by the adventure of sail or the prospect of a career at sea. Without reaching these extremes, the situation had always been similar in all navies. The various captains and officers would all begin their training by embarking as cadets or even cabin boys.

British ships always carried a certain number of cadets or "apprentices," with duties that were different to those of the paid seamen and their own accommodation on the half deck. In 1890 the shipping company Devitt & More embarked around twenty apprentices on its ships. They received hands-on instruction by taking part in the various

maneuvers.

Between the wars many vessels played a dual role as a cargo and training ships. This was the case with the Kobenhaven, built in 1921, the last five-master to be launched by a European yard. She carried five officers, ten seamen and forty-five cadets. Unfortunately she met a tragic end: on the 14th of December, 1928, she left Plata bound for Australia where she was due to load grain: she disappeared with all hands somewhere and nothing was ever heard of her again.

Most nations had their own training ships: apart from the Danish Kobenhaven, subsequently replaced in the role by the Denmark, there were the German Kommodore Johgnsen Johnsen and Admiral Karpfanger (ex-L'Avenir), the Swedish Beatrice, Pedersen and A. Abraham Rydberg, the Finnish Fennia, one of the victims of Cape Horn which today rests, a rusting hulk at Port Stanley, and Favell; the

Belgian L'Avenir and Mercator and the Italian Patria while in Britain the training ships were generally organized along the lines of those of the Devitt & More company. All of these sailing ships participated, part-crewed by cadets, in the Australian grain races.

Today, sail training ships generally survive as naval institutions. This is true of the two Italian vessels, Amerigo Vespucci and Palinuro, two of the best known and most widely admired, the former carrying officer cadets and the latter non-commissioned officers. Their cruises, following different routes and taking in different ports, twice a year, following the courses of the Naval Academy. Each cruise lasts around a hundred days and visits some of the principal Mediterranean and North Sea ports of Europe. The two ships never fail to attend the international events organized by the I.S.T.A and always present sail and the sailing ship in the best possible light.

136 left The Alexander Von Humboldt flies in the face of one of the most deeply rooted maritime superstitions whereby the color green aboard brings bad luck. Nonetheless, the weather is looking good, the wind is blowing and the crossing has got off to a good start.

136-137 The Gloria, a Colombian sail training ship: the foresail and mainsail, the lowest of the square sails are still furled. The practically non-existent wind does not justify the setting of additional canvas. The upper sails are the first to catch a rising breeze.

137 bottom left The barque Nippon Maru, a Japanese sail training ship, one of the latest to join the tall ships circle. Japan did not have particularly strong sailing traditions: the country was a closed world in which the junk with its unusual rig was perfectly suited to the demands of coastal traffic.

137 bottom right The men of the Gloria manning the yards, in the traditional salute of the crews of the naval sailing ships, a demonstration of their familiarity with the basic handling of a square rig.

138 bottom left Even in her days of carrying live mules, cane sugar and cocoa beans, the Belem was often called the "the yacht from Nantes" because of her smart appearance.

138 bottom right and 139 top left The livery and rig are back to original appearance. The deck saloon in the waist and the ornate poop rail stanchions are inherited from her days as a yacht.

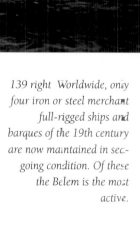

Belem

The Belem was launched in 1896 at the Dubigeon yard of Nantes, France, a yard famed for its big Cape Horners. The Belem was not one of those but a much smaller bark built for the transatlantic trade to the Caribbean and the East Coast of South America: she was a West Indiaman, one of the very last.

Her first owners were Denis Crouan Fils & de Lagotellerie, of Nantes. A typical voyage of the Belem in those days was loading coal at Cardiff for delivery to ports on the River Plate, carrying live mules from Montevideo to the Brazilian port of Belem where she would load cocoa beans for the Menier chocolate factory in France. Those voyages were not all plain sailing; the Belem suffered a fire on board and a collision with a steamer, encountered South American revolutions and was quarantined several times for yellow fever.

However she was very fortunate on 2 May 1902 when she was waiting at a distant anchorage for a vacant berth in the busy Martinique port of St. Pierre and the Mt. Pelée volcano blew its top, obliterating that town and its 40,000 inhabitants.

In 1907 the Belem was sold to Demanges Frères who employed her to deliver food and supplies from France to the notorious prison of Papillon fame in French Guyana. She made ten such voyages before being sold on, still to trade across the Atlantic. After a total of 32 transatlantic voyages she was finally retired from trade in 1914 before the outbreak of war, and sold to Duke of Westminster for conversion to a private yacht.

The Belem spent the war years at the Camper & Nicholsons yard at Gosport, England. Her first twin auxiliary engines were fitted at that time but she retained her barque rig. She cruised in the Mediterranean from 1919 to 1921.

In 1921 she was sold to Lord A.E. Guinness, the brewer, who changed her name to Fantome II and sailed on her round the world

138-139 The Belem, currently largest sailing vessel and the only square-rigger sailing under the French flag, was built over a century ago as a West-Indiaman.

139 right Worldwide, only four iron or steel merchant full-rigged ships and barques of the 19th century are now maintained in sea-going condition. Of these the Belem is the most active.

VESSEL	**BELEM**		
LAUNCHED	1896	BEAM	8.80 m (28.9 ft.)
DESIGNER	Chantiers Dubigeon,	DRAFT	3.50 m (11.7 ft.)
	Nantes, France	TONNAGE	406 grt
BUILDER	Chantiers Dubigeon,	DISPLACEMENT	750 t load
	Nantes, France	SAIL AREA	1,200 mq
OWNER	Fondation Belem,		(12,900 sq. ft.)
	Paris	ENGINES	2 x 300 hp
FLAG	France		Fiat Iveco;
RIG	Barque		twin propellers
TYPE	West Indiaman	USAGE	Sail training and
CONSTRUCTION	Steel		representation
LENGTH EXTREME	58.00 m (190.3 ft.)	COMPLEMENT	54: 16 crew +
LENGTH HULL	50.96 m (167.2 ft)		48 trainees

141 bottom
The Belem is no clipper
but she is descended
from them and her bow
and underwater lines
are more hydrodynamic
than those of ships
before the clipper days.

and to the Arctic and Canada. Guinness died in 1939 and the barque was laid up at Cowes, Isle of Wight.

In 1951 she found a new owner in the person of Vittorio Cini, an Italian count, who presented her the Cini Foundation of Venice, a school for sea orphans.

Re-rigged as a barquentine, she became a schoolship named Giorgio Cini in memory of Count's son. She made short cruises in the Adriatic until 1965 when she was laid up for financial reasons.

The Carabinieri, the Italian State police, were the next owners, with the intention of using her as a cadet ship and for promoting the Service's image. To that end she was taken to a shipyard in Venice for a major refit in 1972 but the funds to pay for the work failed to materialize. The yard kept the ship for unpaid bills and, with the matter still unresolved, put her up for sale in 1974.

Following a campaign for her return to France, the Caisses d'Epargne, France's national savings bank, came forward in 1979 and bought the ship. Renamed Belem once more, she was towed to Brest by the French Navy which was to refit and recommission her for off-season cadet cruises while the owners would have use of her during the summer months for promotional purposes. That did not happen and the Belem narrowly avoided becoming a static museum ship. She was exhibited as such in Paris from 1982 to 1985 but work towards her restoration as a sailing barque was pursued at the same time. The work was completed at Le Havre and Caen in 1985 and she made her sailing trials late that year.

In 1986 she sailed to New York for the centenary re-dedication of the Statue of Liberty. Since then she runs short public training cruises, 3 to 10 days in duration, from March to October, along the Western and Mediterranean coasts of France.

140-141 The short spike bowsprit was a feature of the Belem's original rig. The present sails are Terylene, lighter and more durable than the flax and cotton sails of old.

140 bottom At the break of the poop deck a trainee is taking a compass bearing on a landmark, a buoy or another ship.

141 top A head for heights is required to go aloft on a tall ship. However the great majority of trainees overcome their initial fear, often to their own astonishment.

141 center With the Sørlandet and Statsraad Lehmkuhl of Norway the Belem was third to offer big square-rigger experience to members of the general public.

142-143 As merchant ships grew in size, double topsails replacing the single deep topsails appeared in the mid 1850s, to facilitate handling. When ships grew even larger, in the 1870s onwards, double topgallants were also used on the larger units, as seen here on the Sedov.

142 bottom left A view of the foremast with the billowing fore-course in evidence. The furry covering on the forestay, known as "baggywrinkle," is to prevent the foresail and slack windward fore-topmast-staysail sheet from chafing (wearing through rubbing) on the stay.

142 bottom right From deck to truck the square sails are named course, lower and upper topsail, lower and upper topgallant, and royal. This rig has the same number of sails per mast as found on some earlier clippers that were differently rigged and carried course, (single) topsail, (single) topgallant, royal, skysail and moonraker.

The Sedov is the largest schoolship ever and was the largest square-rigger in service during her lifetime until overtaken in 2000 by the Royal Clipper.

She was built in 1921 at the Germania Werft yard in Kiel for the ship-owning firm of F. A. Vinnen of Bremen. Her original name was Magdalene Vinnen and she was intended for the nitrate trade from Chile to Europe by way of Cape Horn. She was the penultimate square-rigger built for the Cape Horn trades, Chilean nitrates and Australian grain, that were the last stand of deep-sea merchant sail. The economics were already marginal and the Magadelene Vinnen was fitted from the outset with an auxiliary

Sedov

diesel engine in an attempt to make her passages less dependent on the vagaries of wind, and she also carried accommodation for sixty merchant navy cadets who worked as unpaid crew attracting premiums. In effect she was a cargo-carrying schoolship.

In 1936 the ship was sold to the Norddeutscher Lloyd of Bremerhaven and renamed Kommodore Johnsen. Her cadet capacity was increased to 100 by building a spardeck between the poop and the midship "Liverpool house" or "island" (a deckhouse extending to the sides of the hull). She was then switched to the other ultimate sailing trade not yet grabbed by smoke-belchers, the South Australian grain trade. During the war the barque served solely as a cadet ship, conducting summer cruises in the Baltic.

In May 1945 she was given to the Soviet Union as war reparations. She was officially incorporated in the Soviet Baltic feet on the 11 January 1946 under the name of Sedov, after the Russian polar explorer Georgij J. Sedov (1877-1917). She was commissioned as a naval training ship in 1952. In 1957-8 she sailed as a research vessel in the International Geophysical Year, under the auspices of the Soviet Academy of Sciences. She conducted surveys in the Atlantic and the Mediterranean. In 1962-65 she sailed in company

143 top right The lower topsail and lower topgallant yards are fixed in height; when the upper topsails and upper topgallants are not set, their yards are lowered to just above their respective lower yards, as seen on this picture.

143 bottom A large bronze medallion plaque fixed to the facing of the flying bridge forward of the mizzenmast, commemorating the hundredth anniversary of the birth of the Russian polar explorer Georgij Sedov (1877-1917).

with the Kruzenshtern, both barques combining cadet training with hydrographic and oceanographic work.

In 1965 both barques were transferred to the Soviet Ministry of Fisheries which employed them to train future officers and men of the fishing fleet. The Sedov's registered homeport became Riga. She was laid up from 1972 to 1975 pending an overdue refit and was given the latter at Kronstadt from 1975 to 1981. The overhaul included the replacement of her old 500 hp engine by a 1,180 hp one, up-to-date navigational electronics and extensive improvements to the accommodation to raise the cadet capacity to 164. She was put back in service in 1981. In 1983 she called at her old home port of Bremerhaven for the first time in her Soviet days, and the Russians invited aboard many of her former German officers and men, including one of her former masters, 81-year old Captain Gottfried Clausen, last of the German Albatrosses (master mariners who have been in command of a square rigger on a Cape Horn voyage).

The Sedov took part in her first Tall Ships Race in 1986 and has been a frequent participant since then, including the 1992 Columbus Regatta. Since 1989 she has been embarking some Western "adventure" trainees in addition to her own cadets.

144 bottom The Sedov sailing on a close reach. For a sailing ship she was capable of carrying large cargoes of nitrate or grain in bulk and sacs, but compared to modern bulk carriers she is tiny and requires three times the number of hands.

144 top The twin wheel, manned by 2-4 men, is not a luxury on a sailing ship of Sedov's tonnage. The bell and its dolphin brackets are a of a 17th century design.

144 center The decorated crown of a berthing-line bitt. Sailing ships are more than utilitarian constructions; they inspire their owners and crews to spend money or time adorning them.

As Latvia was moving towards independence, the Russians changed the ship's port of registry from Riga to Murmansk in April 1991 and attributed her ownership to the Murmansk State Technical University.

In July 2000 she attended by invitation the international tall ship gathering at Brest and found herself under arrest in that port when served a writ on behalf of a Swiss impex company claiming hundreds of millions of dollars of unpaid debt from the Russian government. The matter became national news in both France and Russia and nearly caused a major diplomatic row. It was fortunately defused when a court in Brest ruled that the ship was not State property but an asset of an autonomous institution that could not be held liable for government debts.

145 The topsails are the first sails to be set when getting under way, the last to be handed when reaching port or anchorage, and the last to be kept set in heavy weather. The horizontal ropes between the shrouds and mast are footropes on which seamen stand and hold on to while handing the mizzen-topgallant staysail.

VESSEL	SEDOV		
LAUNCHED	1921	LENGTH HULL	109.00 m (357.6 ft.)
DESIGNER	-	BEAM	14.66 m (48.1 ft.)
BUILDER	Friedrich Krupp	DRAFT	7.52 m (24.7 ft.)
	Germania Werft, Kiel,	TONNAGE	3,556 grt
	Germany	DISPLACEMENT	7,831 t
OWNER	Murmansk State	SAIL AREA	4,192 mq
	Technical University	ENGINE	1,180 hp VEB SKL
FLAG	Russia		Magdeburg
RIG	Four-masted barque	USAGE	Schoolship (for
TYPE	Cape-Horner		fisheries) and
CONSTRUCTION	Steel		adventure sail training
LENGTH EXTREME	117.50 m (385.5 ft.)	COMPLEMENT	64 crew + 180 cadets
			/ trainees

Behold the last Cape-Horner and the last cargo-carrying square-rigger to be built, the swan song of the Age of Working Sail! For such is the Kruzenshtern, the last of a breed, who has sailed into legend in her own lifetime. For such ships will never be built again.

Built at the yard of J.C. Tecklenborg at Wesermünde, the Kruzenshtern was launched on 24 June 1926 under the name of Padua. She was the last of the famous fleet of "Flying P-liners" of the Hamburg ship-owning firm of Ferdinand Laeisz. The "P-liners" were so called because they had names starting with a P. The Padua had no engine and was a traditional Cape Horn barque except for additional accommodation in the midship Liverpool house for 40 apprentices – cadets.

146 top The last Cape-Horner to be built, the last of her line, Kruzenshtern is nonetheless a thoroughbred and keeps alive the beauty of her breed.

146 center The masts appear to fan out on this aerial picture because it was taken with a semi-wide-angle lens. One can imagine the pressure exerted by a strong wind on such a spread of canvas. It can amount to well over 2,000 hp of motive power without emitting a single molecule of carbon dioxide.

146 bottom Viewed from this angle, from the deck, square-rigged masts give no impression of scale because they all have the same proportions. However when reaching a royal yard on the Kruzenshtern, one is appreciably more winded than when reaching the royal yard on a small brig.

Kruzenshtern

147 The Kruzenshtern has old-fashioned stock anchors that do not lodge in the hawse holes. The stock, with a 90-degree bend, can be seen hanging over the rail just forward of the swivelling crane which is used to lift the anchor's stock and flukes on to the fo'c'sle deck.

She sailed on her maiden voyage on 26 August, loaded a cargo of nitrate at Taltal, Chile, and delivered it to Delfzijl, Holland, on 11 April 1927. She sailed again on 16 June from Hamburg on her second voyage, bound for Talcahuano. In such manner she made a total of eight voyages round the Horn to Chile between 26 August 1926 and 28 February 1932.

The nitrate trade, however, was at an end for a variety of reasons. The Padua was laid up for the remainder of 1932 and most of 1933. She was put back in service with a government subsidy and sailed on 31 October for Wallaroo, South Australia, to load grain consigned to Avonmouth, England. The next voyage was also to South Australia. Voyages 11 to 14 were once more to Chile.

The 15th voyage turned out to be the Padua's last voyage as a cargo ship, fittingly to both Chile and Australia. She left Bremerhaven on 14 October 1938, called at Corral and Valparaiso where she loaded a cargo of nitrate for Port Lincoln where she loaded with wheat for Glasgow, Scotland. She reached Glasgow on 8 July 1939.

The Padua was laid up in Flensburg for the duration of the war. She was towed from Hamburg to Swinemünde in January 1946 to be handed over to the Soviet Navy as a war prize. She was renamed Kruzenshtern after the explorer and navigator Adam Johann von Krusenstern (1770-1846), the first Russian to sail round the world. He was of East Prussian ancestry and the reason for the altered spelling of the ship's name is that it is written phonetically in the Cyrillic alphabet and retransliterated phonetically into the Latin alphabet.

While officially in commission with the Baltic fleet, the Kruzenshtern remained in harbor until 1959. During a refit in 1959-61 she was fitted with her first auxiliary engines. In 1961-65, while training naval cadets, she conducted hydrographic and oceanographic surveys in the Atlantic, West Indies and Mediterranean. In those days her hull was painted white.

In 1965 she was transferred to the USSR Ministry of Fisheries and was homeported at Riga. She trained seamen and officers for the fishing fleet. In 1968-72 she was given a new set of engines and her poop was extended to merge with the midship Liverpool

Vessel	KRUZENSHTERN		
LAUNCHED	1926	LENGTH HULL	104.30 m (342.2 ft.)
DESIGNER	J. C. Tecklenborg	BEAM	14.05 m (46.1 ft.)
BUILDER	J. C. Tecklenborg,	DRAFT	7.17 m (23.5 ft.)
	Swinemünde, Germany	TONNAGE	3,545 grt; 607 nrt.
OWNER	Kaliningrad Marine	DISPLACEMENT	3,760 t light, 5,725 t load
	Academy	SAIL AREA	3,655 mq
FLAG	Russia	ENGINES	2 x 800 hp Russky;
RIG	Four-masted barque		twin propellers
TYPE	Cape-Horner	USAGE	Schoolship for fishing fleet.
CONSTRUCTION	Steel	COMPLEMENT	228: 68 crew, 110 cadets,
LENGTH EXTREME	114.50 m (375.7 ft.)		50 fare-paying trainees

148 left Even though carrying a complement of cadets, the Kruzenshtern was rigged as a conventional Cape-Horner. The great span of her yards can be appreciated on this picture; dedicated schoolships tend to have proportionally shorter yards.

148-149 The great size and fine lines of the Kruzenshtern are well apparent in this aerial picture. Despite the lengthening of her poop and the bridge between the main and mizzen masts, she still evokes her merchant past. The fifth mast is known as the jiggermast.

149 top right
This ship's bell bears both the barque's present name and her original name.

149 bottom left
The Kruzenshtern dressed over all at a harbor tall ships gathering. The Sedov is berthed astern of her.

149 bottom right
The Kruzenshtern does not have a figurehead but an elaborate fiddlehead.

house. The hull was then painted to the current black livery with painted gun ports.

In 1974 the Kruzenshtern was the first Soviet ship to enter a Tall Ships Race, with the Tovarishch. She took part in the American Bicentennial transatlantic race in 1976 and since then is a regular participant in other Tall Ships Races and tall ship events in the West, including the 1992 Columbus Regatta and Tall Ships 2000.

Around 1980 her registered port was changed to Tallinn in Estonia. In April 1991, just before Estonia became independent, it was changed to Kaliningrad, Russia. The stewardship of this splendid barque was transferred in 1992 to the Kaliningrad Marine Academy. Since 1990, while still serving as a professional schoolship for the fisheries, the Kruzensthern also embarks fare-paying "adventure" trainees.

151 A sail is bent to a jackstay, the steel rod running along the top foreside of the yard. For stowing, the sail is gathered up under the yard, by lines manned from the deck, then seamen roll it up and secure it on the top of the yard.

150 top right Cadets manning a capstan. This could be to haul in a course tack or to hoist an upper topsail or upper topgallant yard. The capstan bars fit into holes in the capstan's crown and are removed when not in use and stowed in racks to get them out of the way.

150 center right Cadets stowing a lower topsail. The sail has been gathered up to the yard by its clewlines and buntlines operated from the deck; the cadets aloft must now roll up the sail in a tight bundle above the yard, as has already been done for the upper topsail above.

150 top left The Kruzenshtern clipping along in a strong following wind. Bowsprits are dangerous places in heavy seas; safety netting, a "modern" feature, is now compulsory on all tall ships. Note the anchor chain and stock, outboard of the starboard bow, with the anchor shank and arms resting on the fo'c'sle deck.

150 bottom left This room serves as Kruzenstern's on-board museum, with a glass case display of her trophies, and bulkheads covered with the crests of visited ports and warships and with ropework and other examples of sailors' arts.

150 bottom right The officer's mess, watched over by Russian officers of the Czarist era.

152 bottom The stowage of this stock anchor on the foc's'le deck is similar to that of the Kruzenshtern's bower anchors. But this anchor is only an emergency spare; the port bower anchor lodges in the hawse hole, as shown on the opposite page.

153 Buntlines are used to gather the bunt of a square sail up to the yard. Clewlines gather up the clews. The fore-topgallant shows a typical disposition for these lines. The outer buntlines double-up as leechlines, drawing the leeches inwards. The courses have separate leechlines.

Sørlandet

The Sørlandet was built in 1927 as a merchant navy schoolship for the "Sørlandets Seilende Skoleskibs Institution" of Kristiansand, the capital of the Sørlandet ("Southland") province of Norway. The money for her construction had been bequeathed by shipowner A.O.T. Skjelbred with the proviso that the ship be a real sailing ship, without auxiliary power. She was the first ship to be built at Kristiansand's Høivolds yard. They did a wonderful job.

Until the Second World War she sailed mostly in the North Atlantic and in 1933 she represented her country at Chicago's World Fair. When the German forces occupied Norway, they commandeered the ship and took her to Kirkenes for use as a military prison. While at Kirkenes the ship sank at her moorings after being holed at the waterline during a Russian bombing raid. The Germans refloated her and towed her back to Kristiansand where she was used as accommodation for U-boat personnel.

After the war she was refitted and resumed normal service in 1947. She took part in the first Tall Ships Race in 1956. By the time she was finally fitted with an auxiliary engine, during the 1959-60 refit, she was

152 top The Sørlandet has a very elegant and traditional appearance. Built without an auxiliary engine, she could have been designed and built in the 1890s. She was only motorized in 1960. In 1980 she was the first big square-rigger to offer adventure training cruises to the general public.

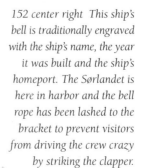

the last of the square-rigged schoolships to have sailed without an engine.

The Sørlandet took part in all the Tall Ships Races from 1960 to 1968; in those years they were only held on even-numbered years.

She was laid-up in 1973 when her institution decided to replace her by a motorvessel. She was bought the following year by the Norwegian shipowner Jan Staubo who had no specific use for her but wanted to prevent her from being sold abroad. In 1977, with the help of Kristian Skjelbred-Knudsen, the grandson of the original benefactor, the ship was donated to the town of Kristiansand which vested her ownership in a specially created foundation, the Stiftelsen Fullriggeren Sørlandet.

The Kristiansanders decided the ship should carry on sailing as an adventure training ship. The ship's recommissioning was financed in part by the municipality, in part by private citizens and local businesses, and many local citizens donated their time and labor. New decking was laid, a new engine installed, a new suit of sails made, and the rigging was completely overhauled. The hammocks in the banjer (berth-deck) were replaced by bunks.

The Sørlandet was the first big square-rigger to offer sailing opportunities to anyone dreaming of crewing on such a vessel, of any age above 14-16, of

152 center right This ship's bell is traditionally engraved with the ship's name, the year it was built and the ship's homeport. The Sørlandet is here in harbor and the bell rope has been lashed to the bracket to prevent visitors from driving the crew crazy by striking the clapper.

152 center left This dining saloon under the poop deck is where the captain, the chief and second engineers, the three mates and the purser take their meals. VIP guests are also entertained here when the ship is in harbor.

154 top left The Sørlandet has neither figurehead nor fiddle head, but she has a pair of elegant trailboards in harmony with the ship's sheer, the profile curve of the main deck.

154 center left Except when running with the wind dead aft, sailing ships always sail with a heel, the angle by which the ship is pushed over by wind pressure. But the same pressure has a dampening effect on rolling, whereas with the wind dead aft rolling can be uncomfortable.

154-155 The feathering of the yards, whereby the lower yards are more braced around than the upper ones, is clearly seen here. The royals will be the first sails to luff (flap) if the helmsman steers too close to the wind. The barque in the distance is the Alexander von Humboldt.

either sex and of any nationality, and no experience required. Her debut as an adventure training ship was in the 1980 Tall Ships Race in the Baltic. She was racing in her class against schoolships manned by cadets who had been on board for several months. She did very well, finishing in mid-league.

After that the Sørlandet stayed away from the Tall Ships Races because her trustees disapproved of a youth event being sponsored by a brand of whisky. She did however take part in other tall ship events. She sailed to Canada in 1981, twice to New York in 1986, and to Iceland in 1991 during a professional training cruise for master mariners. In 1995-6 she

sailed to the West Indies. She took part in the tall ship gatherings at Rouen in 1989 and 1999, and Brest in 1992 and 2000. However most years her "open" cruises (open to all) are a short summer series of 12-day cruises from and to Kristiansand. She also operates "reserved" cruises, sometimes training naval cadets, at other times potential recruits for the seafaring professions, or unemployed youngsters. In 2000 she was at the Brest festival with youngsters from various trouble spots of the world (Balkans, Africa). In 2001 she took part in the Tall Ships Race in the North Sea and Baltic and then sailed to New York as part of the Sea Trek operation.

155 top right
*The Sørlandet proceeding
under power. Note the way
the sails are neatly stowed
above the yards.*

*The neatness and tidiness
of the sails' stowing is one
of the criteria the eye uses
to judge a crew's
professionalism.*

155 bottom
*This magnetic bearing
compass binnacle is above
the after 'tween-deck
companionway.*

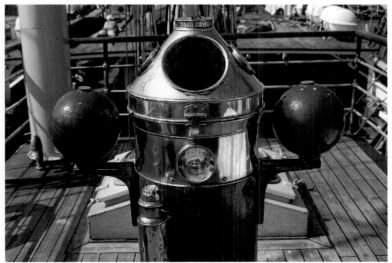

VESSEL	SØRLANDET		
LAUNCHED	1927	LENGTH HULL	56.70 m (186.0 ft.)
DESIGNER	Høivolds Mek. Verksted, Kristiansand, Norway	BEAM	8.87 m (29.1 ft)
		DRAFT	4.42 m (14,5 ft.)
BUILDER	Høivolds Mek. Verksted, Kristiansand, Norway	TONNAGE	499 grt; 153 nrt
		DISPLACEMENT	891 t
OWNER	Stiftelsen Fullriggeren Sørlandet, Kristiansand	SAIL AREA	1,166 mq (12.550 sq. ft.)
FLAG	Norway	ENGINE	564 hp Deutz
RIG	Full-rigged ship	USAGE	Adventure sail training
TYPE	Schoolship		
CONSTRUCTION	Steel	COMPLEMENT	83: 18 crew + 70 trainees
LENGTH EXTREME	65.84 m (216.0 ft.)		

156-157 The Christian Radich, like the other Scandinavian and German tall ships, benefits from a handing-down of skills uninterrupted since the days of merchant sail.

156 bottom left Safety nets under the bowsprits were virtually unknown in the days of merchant sail and only became mandatory on sail training vessels well after the Second World War.

156 bottom right The Christian Radich's wheel, located on the poopdeck just forward of the mizzenmast, acts on the tiller by chain transmission.

157 top right The Christian Radich on the stocks, in 1937. Launching time is close because the anchor has been readied and festive flags are flying.

157 center right Such telegraphs mechanically relay orders from the deck to the engine room. A bell rings every time the watch officer or engineer move the dial arrows.

Christian Radich

The Christian Radich was built in 1937 at Sandefjord, in replacement of an earlier merchant navy schoolship, the brig Statsraad Erichsen. On her second voyage, in 1939, she was in New York for the World Fair, in company with the Danmark, when war broke out in Europe. The Danmark stayed in the United States but the Christian Radich sailed back to Norway where she was requisitioned by the Norwegian Navy and taken to the Horten Dockyard near Oslo. In April 1940 she was seized by the German Navy and put to use as a submarine depot ship. At the end of the war she was found in the German port of Flensburg, capsized and without her masts. She was towed back for repairs at the Sandefjord yard where she had been built and she resumed her normal duties in 1947.

In 1956 she took part in the first Tall Ships Race and then sailed on a six-month voyage (1956-67) to the West Indies and America for the filming of the internationally acclaimed wide-screen production Windjammer, a romanticized documentary. In the early seventies she also starred in the British TV serial The Onedin Line.

The Christian Radich is a frequent participant in the Tall Ships Races, often claiming honors and prizes. In 1976 she took part in the American Bicentennial transatlantic Tall Ships Race and went on to make a courtesy voyage to the Great Lakes, sailing all the way to Duluth on Lake Superior – 183 m above sea level. In 1978-1980 she sailed on a long voyage to the West Indies and to the US West and East Coasts. After her return to Norway she underwent a major and lengthy refit during which the cadets' hammocks were replaced by bunks. She was put back in service in 1983 and the following year took part in another transatlantic Tall Ships Race, to Quebec. In 1986 she sailed again to New York, for the centennial of the Statue of Liberty.

In those days the ship's normal program involved cruises for young men and women training for seafaring careers, from August through to June the following year, fitting in other activities such as Tall Ships Races, goodwill visits to foreign ports and occasional film work.

With the reduction of the Norwegian merchant

VESSEL	CHRISTIAN RADICH
LAUNCHED	1937
DESIGNER	Capt. Christian Blom
BUILDER	Framnæs Mek. Verksted A/S, Sandefjord, Norway
OWNER	Stiftelsen Skoleskipet Christian Radich, Oslo, Norway
FLAG	Norway
RIG	Full-rigged ship
TYPE	Schoolship
CONSTRUCTION	Steel
LENGTH EXTREME	73.50 m (241.1 ft.)
LENGTH HULL	62.50 m (205.1 ft.)
BEAM	9.76 m (32.0 ft.)
DRAFT	4.72 m (15.5 ft.)
TONNAGE	676 grt
DISPLACEMENT	1,100 td
SAIL AREA	1.360 mq (14,640 sq. ft.)
ENGINE	450 hp General Motors
USAGE	Sail training
COMPLEMENT	16 crew + 88 cadets

navy's intake of new officers and seamen, State funding of the Christian Radich had become erratic and, in an attempt to earn some of her keep, she operated a series of one-week passenger cruises in the Canaries during the winter of 1987-88. Likewise, during the winters of 1988-89 and 1989-90, she ran three-month school-at-sea cruises in the Mediterranean, with seventy Norwegian school students and their teachers.

In 1992 the ship took part in the Grand Regatta Columbus transatlantic Tall Ships Race Cadiz - Bermuda - USA - Liverpool.

Later in the 1990s she operated a pattern of winter cruises in the Caribbean, the Azores or the Mediterranean, with trainees aged 16-18 who were given general school education as well as instruction in seamanship and navigation. Since 1996 she runs summer excursion trips and sail training cruises open to anyone over the age of 12 (children aged 12-16 must be accompanied by a parent) – she no longer is a cadet schoolship and is basically competing in the same market as the other two Norwegian former schoolships, the Sørlandet and Statsraad Lehmkuhl.

In the summer of 2001, after taking part in the Cutty Sark Tall Ships Race in the North Sea, the Christian Radich sailed to New York in company with those other two square riggers and the Dutch barque Europa – all four ships under charter to the Sea Trek operation, an event organized by the Latter-day Saints (Mormons) to commemorate the 150th anniversary of their first wave of migration to the United States. From New York the Christian Radich sailed back to Oslo, via Brest, with "self-recruited" trainees.

158 top left The Christian Radich is a fast ship and is seen here as having left two competitors far astern.

158 center left This carved board displays the name of the Christian Radich.

158 center right Full-rigged ships seldom set a sail from the cro'jack, the lower yard on the aftermost mast. Here the Christian Radich is setting a triangular cro'jack sail.

158 bottom The time is struck every half hour during a watch, one clap for each elapsed half-hour. Claps are paired; thus 2 hours into a watch, "five bells" sounds as ding-ding, ding-ding, ding.

159 The Christian Radich at the start of a tall ships race. There is not much wind and the sails have not yet been trimmed to best effect.

160 With her black hull and lack of superstructures this full-rigged ship could be confused with a small merchantman of the 1860-1880s. However, the portholes along the center part of the hull betray her as a cadet ship.

161 top The launching of the Georg Stage on 22 September 1934. Sailing ships are very rarely launched with their masting in place; they are generally rigged and completed afloat.

161 center right The 1907 class of cadets and their officers and crew, on the first Georg Stage. The cadets were very young, between the ages of 14 and 17. They must also have been very crowded in the 'tween-deck, as the cadet complement was 80. It was also 80 on the present Georg Stage until 1980.

161 center left and bottom The sail plans of the old and current Georg Stage. The old ship, now named Joseph Conrad, has a rig that was old-fashioned when she was built, setting deep single topsails, rigged with short topsail and topgallant yards, and setting stunsails to extend the main and fore topsails and topgallants in light winds from abaft the beam. The sail plan of the current Georg Stage shows that this ship is bigger and has a more modern rig with double topsails, longer yards and no stunsails.

Georg Stage

"The littlelest of the biggest" used to say Captain B. Barner Jespersen of his Georg Stage when comparing that ship to the other steel-built square-rigged schoolships, but he was also well aware that she was among the most beautiful and elegant sailing ships of the 20th century. In fact very similar in size and appearance to many of the early iron or steel merchantmen built for the Atlantic trades.

And yet the Georg Stage, 41.60 m (136.5 ft.) hull length, is not the "littlelest," for her predecessor of the same name and rig was even smaller. That first Georg Stage, with a hull just 36.0 m (118.1 ft.) long, was built of iron in 1882 at the Copenhagen yard of Burmeister & Wain for the Stiftelsen Georg Stages

162 top The cro'jack (the lower yard on the mizzen mast) is a "dry" yard, without a sail bent to it, but here a flying cro'jack sail has been sent up from the deck, hauled out to the windward yardarm but not extending all the way to the lee yardarm (as the lee side would be blanketed by the spanker).

162 left A plunging view from the main royal. Going aloft to vertiginous heights is what separates square-rig sailors from cockpit yachtsmen, but

the latter have the worse time of it when they have to climb to their mastheads for some repair as their masts are not equipped for convenient climbing

163 The figurehead, representing Georg Stage, is gold-painted wood. The father of this man who died at 22 provided in his memory the funds to build the ship and endowed the foundation that operated her and her successor.

Minde (Georg Stage Memorial Foundation), financed by shipbuilder Frederik Stage and named after his son Georg who died at the age of 22. She was a schoolship used for training young Danes wishing to embrace seafaring careers. She operated annual six-month summer courses in the Baltic and North Sea with 80 cadets. In 1905 she was run down by a British steamer and sank with the loss of 22 cadet lives but she was raised, repaired and put back into service.

She was sold in 1934, to be replaced the following year by the present Georg Stage. Her new owner, the well-known Australian sailing-ship author Alan Villiers, renamed her Joseph Conrad, registered her as a yacht under the British flag and sailed her round the world on a "private" sail training voyage lasting more than two years, with a cadet crew comprising many different nationalities. At the end of that voyage, in 1936, he sold her to George Huntington Hartford, an American, who re-registered her under the Stars and Stripes and used for three years as a private yacht before presenting her to the U.S. Maritime Commission which used her from 1939 to 1945 as a training ship. In 1947 she became, by Act of Congress, the property of the Mystic Seaport Museum, in Connecticut, where she is preserved afloat to the present day, serving both as an exhibit and as a venue for the Museum's youth educational programs.

The second Georg Stage has been carrying on the work of her predecessor since 1935. At the end of each training year she is rigged down and laid up for winter in Copenhagen. At the start of the new season, March-April, she is rerigged and the sails are bent on.

The cadet contingent numbers 63 and is accommodated in the banjer, the orlop deck. The cadets still sleep in time-honored hammocks. Unlike the non-professional youth training vessels running cruises lasting only a couple of weeks or less, the training pace is more leisurely but, of course, far more in depth. Quayside training, drills and theoretical studies take up the first month and only then does she sets sail on day sails, anchoring at night.

Finally the Georg Stage sets sail on longer passages, in the Baltic and North Sea, sometimes beyond, notably on years when she takes part in the Cutty Sark Tall Ships Races in which she is a fairly regular participant. She sometimes sails further afield, for instance in 1992 when she sailed to America in the Columbus Grand Regatta and, also, in 1989 and 1995 when she visited her elder sister at Mystic Seaport. At the end of the season she returns to Copenhagen and is unrigged for the winter with the help of her cadets.

The Georg Stage is a repository of the skills and knowledge handed down, from master to master (often a former cadet), without a break from the days of merchant sail.

The courses nowadays are five months duration. Since 1981 there are also girl cadets, usually in the ratio 1:2, and some of the officers are also women. The cadets are aged between 17 and 21.

VESSEL	GEORG STAGE		
LAUNCHED	1934	CONSTRUCTION	Steel
DESIGNER	Å. LARSEN	LENGTH EXTREME	54 m (170.6 ft.)
BUILDER	Frederykshavn's Vaerft & Flydedok A/S, Frederiskhavn, Denmark OWNER Stiftelsen Georg Stages Minde, Copenhagen	LENGTH HULL	41.60 m (136.5 ft.)
		BEAM	8.50 m (27.9 ft.)
		DRAFT	4.2 m (13.8 ft.)
		TONNAGE	281 grt
		DISPLACEMENT	455 t (light); 506 t (load)
FLAG	Denmark	SAIL AREA	860 mq (9,257 sq. ft.)
RIG	Full-rigged ship	ENGINE	200 hp B&W Alpha diesel
TYPE	Schoolship inspired from merchant ships c. 1870	USAGE	Schoolship
		COMPLEMENT	10 crew, 63 cadets

During the 1920s Denmark had two large merchant navy cadets ships, the Viking and the København. Both were built specifically to combine cadet training with cargo-carrying.

The four-masted barque Viking had been in service since her commissioning in 1907. The magnificent Københaven, a five-masted barque, was one of the largest square-riggers ever built, grossing 3,9012 register tons and measuring 112.3 m (368.4 ft.) on the hull. She had been built in 1921 in Scotland for the Danish A/S "Det Ostasiatiske Kompagnie." This barque left Buenos Aires on 14 December 1928 and a week later she spoke by radio to a couple of steamers and that was the last that was ever heard from her and her company of 15 officers and men and 45 cadets… One of the big sailing disasters of the century. In the wake of this tragedy the Viking was sold in

Danmark

July 1929 to Gustav Erikson from the Åland Islands (Finland), the owner of the last big commercial fleet of Cape-Horners. (The Viking is still in existence today, preserved at Gothenburg, Sweden.)

So it happened that in 1930 Denmark no longer had a professional sail-training capacity. Despite the København's tragedy, such windjammers were considered to provide the best training possible for future officers and seamen, and the Danish State ordered the construction of a new ship to be named Danmark. That ship was launched on 19 November 1932 and commissioned the following June.

The Danmark had been running uneventful training cruises for six years when the outbreak of war found her in New York. Her management ordered her

not to return to Europe and she was laid up in Jacksonville, Florida. When the USA entered the war in late 1941, the Danes put her at the disposal of the United States Coast Guards who used her as an intensive schoolship until the end of the war, training 5,000 cadets on her. She was then returned to Denmark but the USCG had become totally converted to the value of such training and recommissioned, under the name of Eagle, the German barque Horst Wessel which had been seized as a war prize.

From 1946 until 1990 the Danmark operated two five-month training cruises every year like clockwork, one for future officers and one for future able-bodied seamen and bosuns. The first cruise started in January at La Spezia, Italy, and

164 top When launched in 1932 this ship was a Danish statement of continued faith in the training virtues of square- rig despite the traumatic loss in 1928 of the 4-masted bark schoolship København with all her crew and 45 cadets.

164 center Sailing close-hauled on the starboard tack, about to set the royals, or in the process of taken them in. In addition to the usual inshore sailing hazards from shoals and lee shores, tall ships have to cope with spectator boats and low flying aircraft at close quarters.

164 bottom Merchant ships and registered yachts must bear on their stern their name and that of their port of registry.

164-165 The Danmark was one of the most active schoolships, operating ten months a year until 1999. Today she only runs one training cruise yearly but is one of the last merchant navy schoolships to remain used for that purpose.

166 top right During the
Second World War the
Danmark was used as
training ship by the US Coast
Guards and sold them on the
merits of training under sail.
When they returned her to
her Danish owners after the

war they commissioned the
war-prize barque Eagle.

166 center left The
Danmark's figurehad is a
gilded King Neptune with a
crown of seaweeds
decorated with a starfish.

VESSEL	DANMARK
LAUNCHED	1932
DESIGNER	Åge Larsen, Denmark
BUILDER	Nakskov Skibs, Nakskov, Denmark
OWNER	Direktoratet for Söfartsuddannelser, Copenhagen (State owned)
FLAG	Denmark
RIG	Full-rigged ship
TYPE	Schoolship
CONSTRUCTION	Steel; teak deck
LENGTH	Extreme 77.00 m (252.6 ft.)
LENGTH	Hull 64.7 m (212.3 ft.)
BEAM	10.00 m (32.8 ft.)
DRAFT	4.47 m (14.7 ft.)
TONNAGE	790 grt
DISPLACEMENT	150 t deadweight
SAIL AREA	1,636 mq (17,610 sq.ft.)
ENGINES	486 hp Frichs
USAGE	schoolship
COMPLEMENT	19 crew + 80 cadets

would proceed to the Canaries, occasionally to the
West Indies, and on to the US East Coast. The voyage
would end in Copenhagen and the ship would
undergo refit for a couple months before starting on
her second annual voyage in August. That was to
various European destinations and the Canaries, and
ended just before Christmas at La Spezia. In those
days the ship had two masters and two permanent
crews, one for each voyage.

Her permanent crew numbers 19 and she carries
80 cadets. Since 1983 some of the cadets are girls.

Whenever possible the Danmark takes part in the
Tall Ships Races and various tall ship gatherings in
Europe and the USA.

In the early 1990s she underwent a major overhaul
spread over several years, running just one cruise a
year, for basic seamanship training. This remained the
pattern after the completion of the staged refit, owing
to the cancellation of the contract for the training of
future officers. Today the Danmark is one of the last
big square rigged merchant schoolships to remain
exclusively employed for that purpose. In early April
2000 she left Frederikshavn, her new homeport in
recent years, bound for the US Virgin Islands and then
on to the OpSail 2000 ports along the US East Coast;
she returned home on 16 August. In 2001 she sailed
from 7 August to 16 November, calling at various
Danish ports, the Canaries, Algesiras, the Azores and
Portsmouth.

166 bottom right The
Danmark's midship steering
wheel is double, allowing
2-4 cadets to take tricks at
the wheel at the same time.

166-167 bottom
The Danmark is of
riveted steel construction
with double bottom and
a watertight 'tween deck.
She has many watertight
bulkheads dividing the

hull into separate
compartments.

167 The Danmark is a
beautiful lady who had two
polygamous husbands:
during the long years when
she was sailing 10 months
a year she had two masters,
one for each semester
cruise, who used to say
they had two wives – a
shoreside one and the ship.

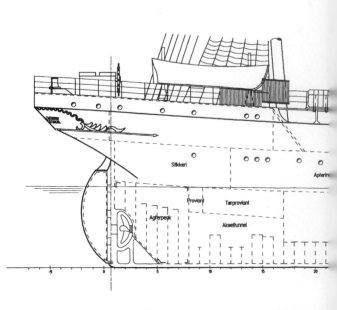

The Tovarishch was originally built as the German Navy schoolship Gorch Fock, the first of that name, in replacement of the barque Niobe that had capsized and sunk in a squall on 26 July 1932, with the loss of 69 lives. This vessel is the first of a series of six schoolships designed and built by Blohm & Voss of Hamburg between 1933 and 1958. Built to Lloyd's top specifications, she was launched on 3 May 1933 and commissioned on 27 June. Originally she carried a single spanker, later replaced by the double spanker she bears to the present day.

Each year until the outbreak of war the Gorch Fock (I) made several short cruises in the North Sea and Baltic and one long cruise, usually transatlantic. During the war she carried on training naval cadets in German home waters, and was given a more powerful auxiliary engine in 1942, a 220 hp MAN, to increase manoeuvrability in mined waters. On 1 May 1945 her

Tovarishch

168 center The ship is underway under bare poles and cadets are sent up the foremast to cast off the sails' gaskets so that sail may be set. The first up go the furthest aloft and the furthest out along the yardarms.

*168 bottom
The area behind and around the Tovarishch's double wheel, enclosed by a wooden safety railing, was known on the wooden fighting ships of old as the "cockpit" – the origin of the yachting expression.*

168 top The white main upper and lower-topsail yards are clearly seen, with their sails furled. When alongside a quay or other ships, or when transiting through a lock, the yards are usually braced hard to one side to avoid snagging shoreside structures such as lamp posts, cranes or sheds, or the rigging of the other ships.

168-169 The Tovarishch under full sail on the starboard tack in a very light breeze that barely fills the sails and hardly ripples the sea.

crew scuttled at Stralsund to prevent her capture by the Russians.

She was however refloated in 1948 by the Russians who repaired her at Wismar and Rostock, in East Germany, and renamed her Tovarishch ("Comrade"). The repairs were completed in 1951 and the barque was allocated to the Kherson Nautical Preparatory College "Lieutenant Schmid" in the Ukraine, to train cadets for the Soviet merchant military navies.

Until 1957 she conducted all her cruises in the Black Sea. In 1957-58 she sailed on a long voyage to the Indian Ocean and Atlantic. Her 1942 engine was replaced by her current 550 hp _koda and her sail area was increased by 6% during a refit in 1967-68.

In 1974 she and the Kruzenshtern were the first Soviet vessels to take part in a Tall Ships Race. Both barques also took part in the 1976 transatlantic race, after which the Tovarishch was restricted to the Black Sea, because she was no longer considered seaworthy enough for extended voyaging.

After a refit in 1989, she reappeared in the West from 1990 onwards in various tall ship events. With the combination of perestroika and the economic implosion of the USSR, the Kherson Nautical College made berths available to Western trainees, mostly from Germany, to raise hard currency. When the Ukraine parted company with the former Soviet Union in 1992, the Tovarishch became Ukrainian-flagged, carrying on much as before.

In 1992 she took part in the Columbus Regatta to America. The following year a youth organization from Newcastle, England, sent some teenagers to sail on her, following which positive experience the organization decided to support the overhaul necessary to enable the ship to carry on sailing. Thus

VESSEL	TOVARISHCH
Launched	1933
Designer	Blohm & Voss, Hamburg
Builder	Blohm & Voss, Hamburg
Owner	Kherson Nautical College
Flag	Ukraine
Rig	Barque
Type	Schoolship
Construction	Steel
Length Extreme	82.10 m (269.4 ft.)
Length Hull	73.64 m (241.6 ft.)
Beam	12.02 m (39.4 ft.)
Draft	5.23 m (17.2 ft.)
Tonnage	1,392 grt, 230 nrt
Displacement	1,350 t standard, 1,760 t load
Sail Area	1,857 mq (19,989 sq. ft.)
Engine	550 hp Skoda
Usage	Merchant Navy Schoolship and adventure sail training vessel
Complement	225: 45 crew + 180 cadets and trainees/passengers

170 top The Tovarishch on the port tack and in the process of setting the main royal, near the starting line of a Tall Ships Race. The full-rigger in the background appears to the Christian Radich. A three-masted schooner can just be made out behind the Tovarishch's spanker boom.

in May 1995, the Tovarishch arrived at Newcastle for maintenance in dry dock.

The docking revealed a horror story and the necessity of repairs estimated at £2 million (approx. $3 million), far more than could be afforded by the Ukrainian owners or the ship's Western supporters. The barque was prevented from leaving by the British maritime authorities on grounds of unseaworthiness. Subsequently she was towed to nearby North Shields to await further developments. She languished there until May 1997, when she was towed to Middlesborough for possible repairs at a proposed National Tall Ships Center. Nothing came out of that and the vessel was threatened with seizure for unpaid debts.

The German association Tall-Ship Friends came up with rescue deal whereby she would be towed to a free berth in Wilhelmshaven and be repaired in Germany as funds were being raised. The ship was towed to Wilhelmshaven in September 1999. Repairs and modernization being carried out include rebuilding the accommodation and the engine so that the Tovarishch can be, once again, a Ukrainian schoolship and a sail training ship with trainees from all over the world.

170 bottom The Tovarishch running free in the van of a gaggle of tall ships. The radar on the foremast, above the foreyard, has a "cage" of hoops to prevent rigging lines from getting caught by the rotating aerial. This is the main radar.

171 The wooden battens across the shrouds, known as "Lord Nelsons," are more comfortable, when climbing aloft than rope ratlines, but they create more windage. The Tovarishch did not always have them, as can be seen on the other pictures.

T he Eagle, the schoolship of the US Coast Guard, was launched on 30 June 1936 for the German Reichsmarine (Navy) under the name of Horst Wessel. She is one of six nearly identical ships designed and built by the Blohm & Voss shipyard in Hamburg between 1933 and 1958.

The first of the series was the Gorch Fock, still in existence under the name of Tovarishch. The Horst Wessel, named after a Nazi party hero, was built to basically the same plans, with the same beam, but lengthened by a little over 7 meters. The third, the Albert Leo Schlageter, launched in 1937, is another "big class," a sistership of the Horst Wessel; she is now the Sagres II. Those three ships were all built for the German Navy.

Eagle

The Mircea was the fourth, a "small class," sistership of the Gorch Fock, built in 1938-39 for the Romanian Navy. The fifth, named Herbet Norkus, another "big class," was being built in 1939 for the Reichsmarine when Second World War interrupted further work on her. In 1947 the Allied forces of occupation loaded that hull with surplus war explosives and towed it out to sea where it was blown up.

The three prewar German Navy schoolships were distributed among the victors as war prizes. In 1958 the new German Federal Navy had a new Gorch Fock built to the "big class" plans.

Early in the war the Horst Wessel was converted to a cargo ship, transporting men and supplies throughout the Baltic Sea. She was fitted with a light

armament and is reputed to have downed three Soviet aircraft.

At the end of the war the USCG obtained the Horst Wessel in replacement of the Danmark and renamed her Eagle. A Coast Guard crew, helped by the German crew still on board, sailed the barque in 1946 from Bremerhaven to her new homeport in New London, Connecticut.

The Eagle's original figurehead was a Third-Reich-style eagle; it was replaced by a sculpture of a bald eagle, the eagle on the US coat of arms. The original double spanker was replaced by a single spanker, but since 1990 the barque is once more rigged with a double spanker.

The Eagle trains both cadets from the Coast

172 top In this unusual viewing angle of the Eagle, the sails are clewed up, hanging in their gear of buntlines and clewlines, ready to be furled or set, as the case may be.

172 bottom This stern wheel is the typical steering found on

medium sized iron and steel merchantmen. Two men at most are needed to work such a wheel. The steering mechanism is inside the long box. The wheel's shaft becomes a double-threaded screw gear moving coupling rods acting on the rudder stock.

172-173 When the wind is forward of the beam, the angle at which the yards are braced decreases from the lower yards to the royal yards, a pattern known as feathering. Thus the higher sails are the first to luff when the ship is steered too close to the wind, warning the helmsman before the lower, major sails are taken aback.

173 bottom left A stopper block with the rope ends prevented from flying away by crown splices wider than the holes.

173 bottom right Bracing the foreyard and fore topsail yards to starboard. This is teamwork. The gang to port (left) only has to feed out the port braces as the port yardarms swing forward.

USCGC EAGLE
WIX 327

VESSEL	EAGLE
LAUNCHED	1936
DESIGNER	Blohm & Voss, Hamburg, Germany
BUILDER	Blohm & Voss, Hamburg, Germany
OWNER	United States Coast Guard
FLAG	USA
RIG	Barque
TYPE	Schoolship
CONSTRUCTION	Steel
LENGTH EXTREME	89.73 m (294.4 ft.)
LENGTH HULL	80.70 m (264.8 ft.)
BEAM	11.92 m (39.1 ft.)
DRAFT	5.18 m (17.0 ft.)
TONNAGE	1,500 grt
DISPLACEMENT	1,634 t standard; 1,816 t load
SAIL AREA	1,983 mq (21,345 sq. ft.)
ENGINE	1,000 hp Caterpillar
USAGE	Coast Guard and Officer Candidate schoolship
COMPLEMENT	215-225: 75 professionals + 140-150 cadets

174 bottom This picture of the Eagle motorsailing shows the fore-and-aft sails of a barque. Square-rigged ships are unable to sail with only those sails set. This photo was taken before 1990 when the spanker seen here was replaced by the double spanker than can be seen on the previous page picture.

174-175 The figurehead of the Eagle is, naturally enough, an eagle – the bald eagle that is part of the coat of arms of the USA. This gilded eagle replaces an earlier eagle which the barque had when she was named Horst Wessel.

175 top right Traditional brass compass binnacles such as this one keep the trainees busy polishing them. The two iron balls greatly reduce the effect of the steel hull on the magnetic compass.

175 bottom left The mechanical wheel is sufficient to steer the Eagle. The treble wheel between the mizzen mast and charthouse, with hydraulic transmission, is very much a schoolship feature; it allows up to six cadets to steer the ship at the same time.

175 bottom right The brass heel indicator fixed behind the charthouse, in front of the binnacle. The vertical arrow is hinged at its top and remains vertical when the ship heels. The angle of heel can be read off the graduated arc segment.

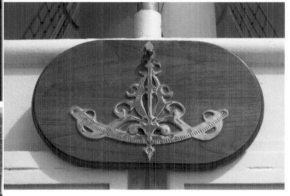

Guard Academy and officer candidates from the services' Officer Candidate School program.

Academy cadets sail two or three times during their four-year curriculum. Most officer candidates sail for two weeks during their 17-week course. The typical manning of the barque consists of 75 professionals and 140-150 cadets or officer candidates. The professional crew consists of a permanent core of six officers and 29 enlisted seamen augmented by reservists. Since the 1980s girl cadets have been admitted and usually number about 20.

The ship normally sails 15 to 17 weeks a year, in summer, operating two "long" cruises followed by a two-week one. She usually operates along the US East Coast but frequently sails further abroad, notably to Europe and sometimes taking part in Tall Ships Races. She took part in the 1988 Australian Bicentennial Tall Ships Race and in 1989 she paid her first visit to the Soviet Union, calling at Leningrad. She always is the flagship of the US East Coast OpSails. She visited Hamburg and the yard of Blohm & Voss on her sixtieth birthday in 1996.

One of the duties of the USCG is the enforcement of US safety and other rules pertaining to shipping. Yet for many years the Eagle was sailing under many exemptions from those rules.

That embarrassment was remedied during a major refit in 1981-82 when she was modernized and fitted with additional watertight bulkheads. At the same time a new engine was installed and the former open cadet berth deck with hammocks was divided into smaller dormitories with bunks. The Eagle is very well maintained and is expected to sail into the 21st century for many decades to come.

Sagres II

The Sagres is the third of the six Gorch Fock Class barques, one the "big class" sisterships like her immediate predecessor Eagle ex-Horst Wessel.

Like that preceding vessel, the Sagres was built for the German Reichsmarine and originally bore the name of a Nazi party hero, in her case that of Albert Leo Schlageter. Her keel was laid down in June 1937 in the same Blohm & Voss Hamburg yard were all those sisterships were built; she was launched on 30 October and commissioned on 1 February 1938.

The Albert Leo Schlageter carried a complement of 298 crew and cadets and made one long and one short voyage to South America before the outbreak of war. At the beginning of the hostilities she was turned into stationary headquarters for naval NCO Training. She

returned to sailing duties in 1944, and on 14 November that year, while transporting troops, she hit a Russian mine off Sassnitz and suffered extensive damage to the engine room. She was towed to Flensburg and then to Kiel where she was seized by the Americans in 1945.

Having picked the Horst Wessel for her Coast Guard, America had no use for a second schoolship and, in 1948, passed on the surplus barque to the Brazilian Navy which renamed her Guanabara, after the bay of Rio de Janeiro. The Brazilians operated the Guanabara along with another schoolship they already had since 1934, the four-masted schooner-barquentine Almirante Saldanha. Meanwhile the Portuguese Navy was running, since 1924, a school

barque, named Sagres after the port in southern Portugal where Prince Henry the Navigator (1394-1460) had founded Europe's first navigation school. That Sagres was the former German Cape-Horner Rickmer Rickmers, built in Bremerhaven in 1896, and she was aging. It so came to pass that the Portuguese bought the Guanabara from their erstwhile colony in October 1961, and they transferred the name of Sagres to their new acquisition.

The Almirante Saldanha kept sailing until 1964, after which she was converted to a motor vessel used for oceanographic research. In 2000 the Brazilian Navy commissioned the brand new schoolship Cisne Branco, a sistership of the Stad Amsterdam.

To avoid confusion, the old and the new Sagres are often called Sagres (I) and (II); however there was an

176 top The Sagres, like most schoolships, carries three different types of boats. The two big motorized launches on sleds amidships are for ferrying crew and guests between shore and ship at anchor; the smaller tenders on davits aft are for practicing pulling with oars and for painting the outside of the hull; the self releasing liferafts in canisters will hopefully never be needed.

176 bottom The motto on the stern wheel, in ancient Portuguese, means "Honor the Fatherland that is looking upon you."

176-177 This picture conveys the size and power of the big square-riggers. The red Lusitanian crosses are the hallmark of the Sagres and are the same as those that adorned the sails of the Portuguese cogs, caravels and carracks of the Age of Discovery.

177 bottom left The "labor-creating" big treble wheel is the same as on the US Coast Guard's Eagle, Sagres' sistership. The white object on a brass stand to the left of the magnetic compass binnacle is a gyrocompass repeater. The pedestal to the right of the binnacle is the engine room telegraph for sending speed instructions to the engineer.

177 bottom right In this wide-angle shot of the Sagres proceeding under reduced canvas, the anchor is just below water, indicating that the ship is about to drop it or that she is just getting underway under sail.

178 top
The gilded ornamental scroll work on the Sagre's trailboards includes the coat of arms of the town of Sagres. These trailboards, still common on today's tall ships, are the distant echo of sweeping timbers that formed the beakhead on the old galleons.

178 bottom left
A flying-fish view of the Sagres sailing on a broad reach on the port tack. From inboard outwards, the headsails are named fore-topmast-staysail, inner jib, outer jib and flying jib.

178 bottom right
The Sagres under full sail reach the best point of sailing for square-riggers. The square sails on the foremast, are named, from the deck upwards, fore-course, fore-lower-topsail, fore-upper-topsail, fore topgallant and fore-royal.

179 A lookout is always kept in the bows. The bow bell is used to alert the officer of the watch, by the wheel, to the sighting of shipping or danger ahead. The lookout also repeats on that bell the half-hourly strikes struck on the main bell aft.

earlier Sagres which had been built in England in 1858 and used as a Portuguese Navy schoolship from 1882 to 1898. Both 20th century Sagres are easy to distinguish from other ships by the red Lusitanian crosses on their sails, the same that adorned the sails of the Portuguese caravels and carracks of the Age of Discovery. Those two Sagres can be told apart from one another on photographs by the single spanker of the earlier one and the double spanker of the present one.

The old Sagres was renamed Santo André and

VESSEL	SAGRES		
LAUNCHED	1937	DRAFT	5.30 m (17.4 ft)
DESIGNER	Blohm & Voss, Hamburg	TONNAGE	-
BUILDER	Blohm & Voss, Hamburg	DISPLACEMENT	1,725 t standard, 1,869 load
OWNER	Portuguese Navy	SAIL AREA	1,935 mq (20,828 sq. ft.)
FLAG	Portugal	ENGINE	1,000 hp
RIG	Barque	USAGE	Naval schoolship
TYPE	Schoolship	COMPLEMENT	203: 10 COs, 17
CONSTRUCTION	Steel		NCOs, 113 men,
LENGTH EXTREME	89.48 m (293.6 ft.)		63 cadets
LENGTH HULL	81.28 m (266.7 ft.)		(incl. 12 girls)
BEAM	12.02 m (39.4 ft.)		

181 bottom left The Sagres' main bell, by the treble steering wheel, is engraved with the year when the ship was first commissioned in the Portuguese Navy. It is struck every half hour, once 30 minutes after the start of a watch, twice for the first hour, etc., until "eight bells" mark the end of a four-hour watch.

181 right On this head-on view the yards appear foreshortened because they are braced to port. Even if set square they would not be as long as those of deep-sea merchantmar of similar size. Most schoolships have slightly shortened yards for easier sail handling by raw trainees.

180-181 The sails on the mizzenmast are named, from top downwards, mizzen topsail, upper spanker and lower spanker; they are taken in in that order when the wind freshens. The double spanker is easier to handle than the single spanker found on many other barques and ships.

180 bottom left The officers' mess room, in the poop accommodation, laid out for a formal occasion.

180 bottom right The Captain's day room is where he does his paperwork and receives private guests when in port. Guests received in that room are often treated to the Captain's own reserve of port wine which surpasses even the extremely good port served to VIPs in the main saloon.

181 top left The figurehead represents Prince Henry the Navigator (1394-1460) whose geographical curiosity, crusading spirit and desire of extending trade to regions unknown made him a patron of maritime exploration. He attracted Christian, Jewish and Muslim geographers and cartographers to his court at Sagres and sponsored the first Portuguese voyages of discovery.

laid up as a supply and depot ship at the Alfeite dockyard near Lisbon. In 1983 she was sold to a German association which is preserving her as a museum ship in Hamburg after restoration to her original Cape-Horn appearance and to her original name of Rickmer Rickmers.

The present Sagres is a very well-maintained and well-sailed ship. She is a frequent participant in the Tall Ships Races and other windjammer events. In her career to date she has called at more than 113 ports in more than 45 countries. The North and South Atlantic are her home waters but she has made (at least) two circumnavigations, in 1978-79 and 1983-84, the latter including the Osaka World Sail Festival. In 2000 she took part in the 500th anniversary celebrations of the discovery of Brazil by the Portuguese navigator Pedro Alvarez Cabral (1460? - 1526?), sailing to Brazil in company with the Cisne Branco, which was on her maiden voyage from Amsterdam, and of the Uruguayan three-masted schooner Capitán Miranda. The three schoolships then sailed to the USA to take part in OpSail 2000.

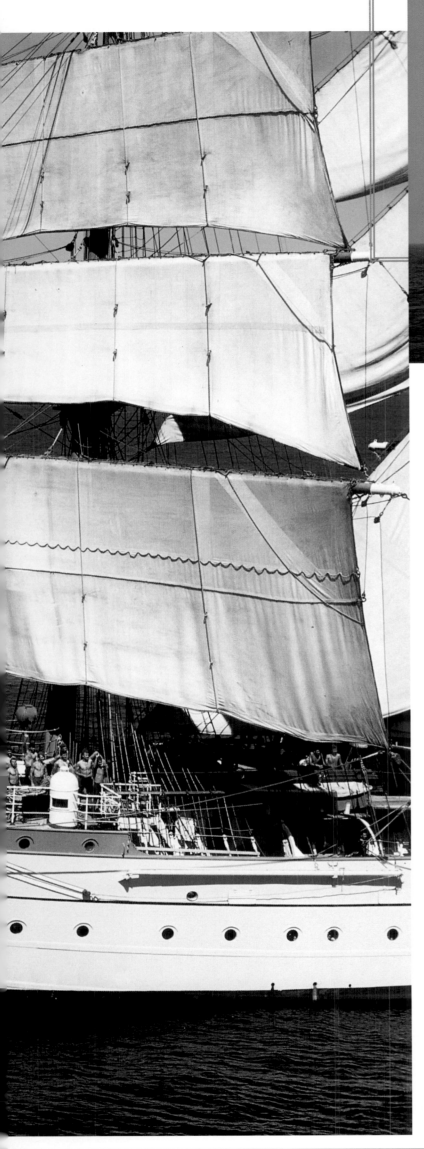

The Mircea (pronounced "Mircha") is the fourth of the six Gorch Fock Class barques and the exact sistership of the original Gorch Fock (now the Tovarishch). The other barks have hulls approximately 7.40 m (24 ft.) longer. Of all the family, Mircea was the only one not built for the German Navy: she was ordered by, and built for, the Romanian State, as a training ship for the Naval School at Constanza the country's major seaport.

This Mircea is the second Romanian schoolship bearing that name. The first, a brig built to order at Blackwall near London, was launched in 1882, the year after the proclamation of the Kingdom of Romania which itself followed closely the war of 1877-78 in which the Ottoman Turks were finally completely ousted from the country they had occupied or held in vassalage since the late Middle Ages. Their last foothold in Romania had been Dobrogea, the coastal province with Constantza.

The brig was named Mircea after Prince Mircea Staria

Mircea

(1333-1418) of Muntenia (Eastern Wallachia) who had retaken Dobrogea from the Turks and under whom Romania had become a sea trading country for a while.

The brig performed her training duties until retired by age. The present Mircea is her replacement. The keel of the new ship was laid on 15 April 1938, the hull launched 22 September and the completed ship delivered to her owners on 16 January 1939. The new barque took on the name of her predecessor and was given a splendid figurehead representing prince Mircea; the reference used by the sculptor was a mural painting in the mediaeval monastery of Kosia.

The barque was commissioned at Constantza in April 1939. Since the previous year, the Naval School included a Merchant Marine Department for the education of aspiring merchant navy deck officers, engineers, radio operators and pursers. Thus the Mircea was to provide training for both

182-183 Very unusually for large square-riggers with double topsails, the Mircea's courses (lower square sails) and upper topsails have a reef band each, seen here as horizontal festooned lines. Taking a reef in a square sail is one of the more demanding jobs aloft but is not necessary on that type of rig.

183 The Mircea and Tovarishch are the "small sisters" of the Gorch Fock class, with hulls 9% shorter than those of the "big sisters." Their rigs are however less than 3% shorter and their yards the same length, so those smaller barques appear more canvassed, loftier and even more graceful.

The Mircea took part in tall ship gatherings in London and Amsterdam in 1975 and took part in the 1976 US bicentennial transatlantic Tall Ships Race.

In 1990, following the December 1989 revolution, the Naval Officer School "Mircea Cel Batran" was re-organized under the name Naval Academy "Mircea Cel Batran". The Mircea carried on sailing a while but was in need of a $5 million refit to be carried out in stages and partly financed by making berths available to foreign "holiday trainees," following the example set by other former Eastern Block schoolships. She was expected at Rouen 1999 but cancelled, perhaps concerned the same thing might happen to her as had happened to the Tovarishch in Newcastle in 1995. No news has been heard from her since then, the suspicion being that she is laid up waiting for money for repairs.

184 top The white domed cylinder at the after corner of the fo'c'sle deck is a lamp tower of very traditional design. Those towers hold the port and and starboard side-lights that originally were oil lamps requiring such elaborate sheltering against storm winds and breaking seas.

184 bottom This small hydraulic steering wheel with an oversize rudder angle indicator lacks the beauty of its counterparts on the Eagle and Sagres. The modernistic 1930s-style painted binnacle is on a par with the wheel; those fittings look like, and probably are, postwar Soviet designs.

naval and merchant navy cadets, but she only did so for one regular training cruise in the Mediterranean before war engulfed Europe. During the war years, only naval cadets were trained, on short cruises in home waters.

At first neutral, Romania eventually entered the war on the Axis side and was subsequently occupied by the Soviet Army which hoisted the Red Flag on the Mircea. The barque would undoubtedly have become a war prize like her German sisters had not Romanian communists seized power soon after the war; the Mircea was returned to a government friendly to Moscow.

Training cruises resumed in 1946, still only for naval cadets until 1959 when the Naval School re-established its Merchant Marine Department. During those years, and until 1965, the ship sailed in the Black Sea and Eastern Mediterranean.

The Mircea was back at the Blohm and Voss yard from January to February 1966 for a major refit where the masting and rigging were overhauled, additional watertight bulkheads were built, the original engine replaced by a 1,100 hp MAK, electrical systems renewed and modernized, and a new suite of sails was made.

After that refit the barque resumed her training cruises, no longer exclusively in the Black Sea and Eastern Mediterranean. She visited other parts of Europe, Africa and North America. In 1969 the Naval School ship was renamed Naval Officer School "Mircea Cel Batran."

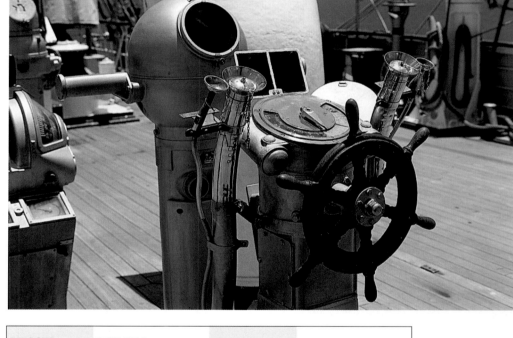

VESSEL	MIRCEA		
LAUNCHED	1938	LENGTH HULL	73.70 m (241.8 ft.)
DESIGNER	Blohm & Voss,	BEAM	12.00 m (39.4 ft.)
	Hamburg, Germany	DRAFT	5.20 m (17.1 ft.)
BUILDER	Blohm & Voss,	TONNAGE	1,312 grt
	Hamburg	DISPLACEMENT	1,630 t standard,
OWNER	Naval Academy		1,760 load
	"Mircea Cel Batran,"	SAIL AREA	1,748 mq
	Constantza		(18,815 sq. ft.)
FLAG	Romania	ENGINES	1,100 hp MAK
RIG	Barque	USAGE	Naval and mercantile
TYPE	Schoolship		schoolship
CONSTRUCTION	Steel	COMPLEMENT	185: 65 officers and
LENGTH EXTREME	82.28 m (269.9 ft.)		crew, 120 cadets

185 The clunkiness of the steering station above is more than made up by the delightful figurehead representing Mircea Staria (1383-1418), the Romanian prince who retook Romania's coastal province from the occupying Turks. The model for that sculpture is a mural painting in a Mediaeval monastery.

Gorch Fock II

In 1945, for the second time in less than 30 years, Germany had lost her sailing schoolships as a result of loosing a war. In particular, the German Navy had lost all three of the barques it was operating just before the war: the 1933 Gorch Fock (now the Tovarishch) and her slightly larger sisters Horst Wessel (now the Eagle) and Albert Leo Schlageter (now the Sagres), as well as the unfinished Herbert Norkus (blown up). When the German Navy reappeared, under new management and under a new name (Bundesmarine), one of the very first new ships it decided to have built was a sailing schoolship.

The prewar Gorch Fock class had proved to be ideally

suited for the job and the Hamburg yard of Blohm & Voss was once more contracted to build a barque, to the same design as the "big sisters." The new barque was to be named Gorch Fock, like the first of the series – both named after the pen name of Johann Kinau (1880-1916), a German sea-novelist and poet.

The general class design already had improved safety features introduced in the wake of the capsizing in 1932 of the barque Niobe. In 1957, the year before the building of the new Gorch Fock, there had been another disaster, the foundering in a hurricane of the German four-masted barque Pamir, and that prompted the introduction of watertight superstructures,

additional watertight bulkheads and the capability of recovering from a 90° knockdown.

The keel was laid down in early 1958; the new barque was launched on 25 August and commissioned on 17 December the same year.

The Gorch Fock trains CO and NCO candidates. Female cadets will also be embarked as of May 2002, although women in other ranks have been sailing on that barque since 1989. The Gorch Fock sails long seasons and winters in her base port of Kiel. Most years she runs three cruises of different lengths, one at least including destinations beyond Europe and the Canaries.

186 top This stern view with the yards set square and the sails set shows the typical "pyramid" proportions of a square-rig sail plan but does not show the ship under sail with a wind from dead astern: the Gorch Fock is motoring with her square sails aback.

186 bottom This name board is unusually located aft, abreast of the charthouse, as can be seen on the main picture. It is more customary on sailing ships to put the name boards near the bows. Ships also carry their name on the stern.

186-187 The Gorch Fock is seen here motoring, with the apparent wind setting her square sails aback. This is a typical "parade of 'sail'" situation where ships have to follow headings without regard to the wind but still set some sails for the benefit of shoreside onlookers.

187 bottom right The Gorch Fock is dressed overall, with flags, for a festive occasion. Those signal flags are not hoisted in random order but in a set order arranged for color balance and to avoid spelling any meaning.

VESSEL	GORCH FOCK		
LAUNCHED	1958	LENGTH HULL	81.26 m (266,6 ft.)
DESIGNER	Blohm & Voss,	BEAM	12.00 m (39.4 ft.)
	Hamburg	DRAFT	5.00 m (16.4 ft.)
BUILDER	Blohm & Voss,	TONNAGE	1,499 grt; 882 nrt
	Hamburg	DISPLACEMENT	1,760 t standard;
OWNER	German Federal Navy		1,870 t load
FLAG	Germany	SAIL AREA	1,952 mq
RIG	Barque		(21.011 sq. ft.)
TYPE	Schoolship	ENGINE	1,600 hp Deutz MWM
CONSTRUCTION	Steel	USAGE	Naval schoolship
LENGTH EXTREME	89.32 m (293.0 ft.)	COMPLEMENT	80 crew + 160 cadets

The maiden voyage, starting in 1958, was to Tenerife. In 1959, a year with no Tall Ships Race, she cruised in the North Sea. 1960 was her first occasion of joining a Tall Ships Race, the third such event, from Cannes to Naples, which she won. The Gorch Fock is a very regular participant in those international sail training races, often winning first place and consistently in the top league. She has taken part in all five transatlantic Tall Ships Races held to date, in 1964, 1976, 1980, 1992 and 2000.

She underwent modernization in 1985, including the installation of a cafeteria and of a watermaker. The cadet berth-deck still retained its hammocks, however. She made her first round-the-world voyage in 1987-1988, attending the Australian Bicentennial celebrations in Sydney.

Another major refit was conducted in 1990-91, during which a new 1,600 hp engine was fitted, twice the power of the original one. Ducted air conditioning and heating were also installed.

In 1996-97 the Gorch Fock made her longest voyage to date (343 days), sailing to 18 ports in 16 countries – Mediterranean, Suez Canal, Red Sea, South China Sea, Mauritius, Cape Town, Brazil, West Indies and Azores.

188 top The cadet steering station with the same treble wheel as on the Eagle and Sagres. The compass in front of the wheels is the steering compass; the one at the front of the picture is used for taking bearings. A white gyrocompass repeater can be seen to the right.

188 center A gyroscopic bearing compass for taking the bearings of landmarks and the angles between them to determine the ship's position. Gyrocompasses are more accurate and steadier than magnetic compasses. They are driven by a gyroscope inside the bowels of the ship.

188 bottom The Gorch Fock's figurehead is an unusually stylized eagle that cannot quite make up its mind if it is, perhaps, an albatross or possibly it is the other way around.

189 Square-riggers at sea under a full press of sail are a timeless sight of timeless grace. Fortunate are those who sail on them. The Gorch Fock regularly undertakes long ocean passages.

In early December 2000 the barque began a nine-month refit program, her most expensive to date, costing over 1,000,000. More powerful new generators are being fitted to cope with all the new mod-cons and electronics. The hull is being extensively replated, with welded seams. The original plates were riveted; fake rivet heads are being stuck on the new plates to preserve the original appearance. The accommodation is being completely redesigned and has cabins for the female cadets embarked in May 2002.

The Amerigo Vespucci, one of the largest sailing ships in service today, is the schoolship for the cadet officers of the Leghorn Naval Academy of the Italian Navy. She is named after the Florentine cartographer (1454-1512) who drew the first maps of the new continent discovered by the Genoese navigator Christopher Columbus and who signed them with his name which later became attached to the new world itself – America.

This ship was actually the second of two sisterships, the first one of which had been launched in 1928 under the name of Cristoforo Colombo. That other ship was seized by the Soviet Union in 1949 for war damages, renamed Dunay and used in the Black

190 top left Schoolships nearly always have crests or medallions, replicas of which, usually in smaller size, are given as souvenirs to visiting VIPs. This is a bronze medallion of the Amerigo Vespucci.

190 top right and 190-191 The Amerigo Vespucci is big for a three-masted vessel and has a great beam for her length; she also is a three-decker. With those characteristics and

her long bowsprit with separate jibboom, she is reminiscent of the last sailing ships-of-the-line that were iron-clad and had auxiliary steam propulsion.

190 bottom
Tall ships never fail to be
the center of attraction
wherever they go.
Sometimes the attraction is
too strong; collisions
between spectator boats

and between spectator
boats and tall ships are not
unheard of, despite
warnings and, in tall ships
festivals, parade lanes
being made off-limits to
spectator craft.

Amerigo Vespucci

Sea by the Soviet Navy until laid up in 1963; she was broken up in Odessa in 1971.

The Amerigo Vespucci has three decks and is reminiscent of the sail-and-steam ships of the line of the 1850s and 1860s, including her long bowsprit and jibboom, her stern walk, gilded figurehead, trailboards and much brightwork about the weather deck. However she has portholes instead of gun ports, and the immaculate weather deck is "luxury yacht" teak. There is a recent futuristic wheelhouse amidships, with a glass top that looks like a starship set for a SF movie. The wheel there, of moderate size, is still of traditional appearance but the steering is electric-hydraulic. When under sail, however, the ship is normally steered from the a massive quadruple wheel near the stern, which has manual transmission and which is manned by up to eight men.

For auxiliary propulsion the Amerigo Vespucci has twin 1,500 hp electro-diesel engines – an unusual system for a tall ship, with the engines driving two alternators that provide the power to an electric motor coupled to a single four-bladed propeller.

The Amerigo Vespucci is a sea-going classroom,

193 The figurehead represents Amerigo Vespucci, the Florentine navigator who made, for Spain and Portugal, two to four voyages to the lands across the Atlantic and whose maps were the first to show those lands as a new world.

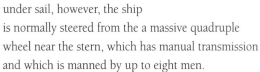

192 top left The Amerigo Vespucci carries a large number of boats. These are used for boatmanship exercises and to ferry the large ship's company (in excess of 370 men) between ship and shore.

192 top right The stern galley, or "captain's walk," reserved to the captain and his guests, is a 19th century feature, one that in fact goes back to the age of the carracks, before even the galleons. The blue-and-red striped tent on the poop deck is erected in harbor for receptions.

192 center and bottom The two most immediate differences between the Amerigo Vespucci and the last three-decker ships-of-the-line of the 1850s are the rows of portholes instead of gunports and the double topsails. Although the more handy double topsails appeared during the 1850s on merchantmen, men-o'war remained faithful to the last to the deep single topsails with many reef bands. The bridge abaft the foremast is an "anachronism."

VESSEL	AMERIGO VESPUCCI
LAUNCHED	1931
DESIGNER	Lt. Col. Francesco Rotundi
BUILDER	Castellamare di Stabia shipyard, Naples, Italy
OWNER	Italian Navy (Leghorn Naval Academy)
FLAG	Italy
RIG	Full-rigged ship
TYPE	Schoolship
CONSTRUCTION	Steel
LENGTH	
EXTREME	100,60 m (330.1 ft.)
LENGTH HULL	82.30 m (270.0 ft.)
BEAM	15.50 m (50.9 ft.)
DRAFT	7.20 m (23.6 ft.)
TONNAGE	2,686 t Thames Measurement
DISPLACEMENT	3,543 T (standard) 4,146 T (load)
SAIL AREA	2,580 mq (27,771 sq. ft.)
ENGINES	2 x 1,500 hp Fiat-Marelli electro-diesels (1 propeller)
USAGE	Naval training ship
COMPLEMENT	267 crew, 105 cadets

a drill ship and a seamanship school, and she also serves admirably her ambassadorial functions when in foreign ports. Her rig is perfectly traditional and to scale and offers all the sail handling training that can be desired. She is immaculately kept, with brasswork gleaming and the halyard falls neatly coiled in tubs. In harbor the cadets, in smartly tailored and well-pressed uniforms, wearing white gloves and caps, make a big show of racing up the masts and manning the yards Before embarking they have already practiced on a couple of full-scale fully-rigged masts erected in the grounds of the Academy. There are safety nets around the feet of those masts, but not on the ship.

The Amerigo Vespucci is based at La Spezia and most years commissions in June for a short Mediterranean cruise with the crew only, for their own training and work-up – the deckhands are generally

194 Motoring under "bare poles." Note the old-fashioned catheads, those two stout beams protruding from the foredeck on either side of

the bows. They are used to bring the stock anchors up to deck level. A fluke is then fished with a loop to bring it inboard, just over the side.

195 top left All ropes serving a purpose on a square-rigger have their own name that seldom includes the word rope. The bell rope is one of the few ropes found aboard a tall ship and is traditionally decoratively knotted. In addition, this one has been painted in the colors of the Italian flag.

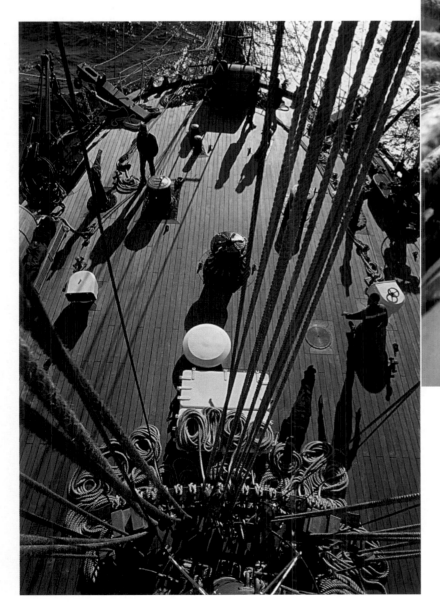

195 top right The highly-polished capstan crown cap reflects the masting. The capstan not being used at this time, its bars are stowed out of the way in racks.

195 bottom left The falls of the lifts that control the horizontal angle of the yards, and of the sheets that control the lower corners of the lower topsail, topgallant and royal, all lead to pin rails in front of the masts. Their tails (excess lengths) are here coiled on deck.

195 bottom right Looking up along the foremast. The lower yard is held away from the mast by a crane so that the yard is in the same plane as the ones above it. The hoop circling the mast is to prevent lines and tackles from fouling one another.

new enlisted recruits. Then, in July, after the end of the academic year, the first year officer cadets go on a three-month voyage, July to September, to the Atlantic, the North Sea and sometimes the Baltic.

With the windage of her high sides and her heavy displacement, the Amerigo Vespucci is not a fast sailer, particularly to windward, a reason why she seldom actually races in the Tall Ships Races, although she often turns up at the port gatherings of those events, adding a valuable contribution to the forest of lofty masts and yards . She did take part in the Tall Ships 2000 series, in the Genoa-Cadiz, Cadiz-Bermuda and Boston-Halifax races. She achieved Second in Class and Third Overall places on corrected time (on handicap) for the transatlantic leg.

The ship often sails on extended cruises, for instance to take part in the American OpSail parades held on special commemorative occasions such as the 1976 American Declaration of Independence bicentennial, the Columbus quincentenary OpSail in 1992 and OpSail 2000. She has sailed many time across the Atlantic and has visited South America. She is also a frequent participant in European tall ship festivals.

196 top The fo'c'sle head deck is flush with the midships spardeck (but there is a raised poop deck right aft). The raised wheelhouse between the fore and main-masts has a transparent top which is protected by a netting from falling blocks and other objects.

196 center left Heavy hauling – be it halyards, braces, sheets, course tacks or boat falls – is a feature of work on windjammers. It requires coordination but also alertness from the leader in case something has jammed aloft.

196 bottom Morning muster of the crew. The names are called to make sure no one is skulking below deck or has gone overboard unnoticed; the captain has completed his inspection of the ship and on the stroke of 8 a.m. orders "eight bells" to be struck.

196 center right The poop deck. The cage-like cylinders stacked on deck are tubs in which the falls of the lines from aloft can be kept safely coiled. They are not in use here; the men working at the mizzen pinrail are surrounded by quite a jumble of falls on deck.

197 The Amerigo Vespucci carries eleven boats, four of which, the palischerni, have both oars and sail. They are sometimes used in flat calms to make the cadets tow the ship as was sometimes done in the days before auxiliary propulsion. They are also used for crew regattas.

198 top In harbor, when there are visitors, the lines surrounding the masts are made neater with this decorated "cummerbund," and the tails of the falls are neatly coiled in tubs.

198 center A cheekless metal block used for the hoist of a crane or boat boom.

198 bottom A triple tackle with wooden-cheeked blocks. Older style blocks have an external rope strapping; these have internal metal strapping. The Amerigo Vespucci still makes much use of natural manilla fiber.

198-199 In the maze of standing rigging and running rigging, every line and stay has its own name. The maze is only apparent; there is a logic to this architecture of rope and canvas that is the end product of centuries of square-rig evolution.

199 bottom left Deadeyes and lanyards are the traditional wooden-ship era method of making stays and shrouds taught and securing them to the hull. they are an unexpected feature of the steel-built Americo Vespucci, steel ships normally having threaded bottlescrews for the purpose.

199 bottom right These cylindrical-topped boxes found around the weather deck protect and hide liferafts. The tails of the clewlines and buntlines are coiled on deck; on northern ships those coils would be hung from their pins to prevent them from being washed by seas into the scuppers.

200 bottom The great cabin in the stern serves as the captain's dining room and for official receptions. It is decorated with many mementoes of the ship's life, cruises and ports of call

201 top left This highly ornamental ship's lantern of 17th century design is taken down when the ship is at sea.

201 top right The Captain's private day room is decorated and furnished in late 19th century nautical style with a touch of the 1930s.

201 bottom This far more more modest but just as effective wheel is normally used when the ship is motoring. It is located in the forward wheelhouse. Its transmission is electro-hydraulic. Under the brass binnacle is a conventional magnetic steering compass; there is also a gyrocompass repeater.

200-201 Three of the four wheels in the poop deck wheelhouse. They are the ones normally used when the Amerigo Vespucci is under sail. They are manned by eight cadets at a time.

The Juan Sebastian de Elcano, the schoolship of the Spanish Navy, is used for the training of the midshipmen from the Naval Academy of Marín and as in itinerant goodwill ambassador for her country. She is the oldest schoolship currently in service but is maintained in top condition and was given major refits in 1956 and 1978. With her near-sistership Esmeralda she is the largest schooner in existence, and has a greater length and tonnage than most of the square-riggers currently in service.

Her hull plans were drawn by Echevarrieta y Larrinaga, the Cadiz shipyard where she was built; her rig was designed by Charles Ernest Nicholson of Camper & Nicholson's, the reputed English yacht designers and builders. Her keel was laid on 24 November 1925; she was launched on 5 March 1927. The Navy took delivery on 28 February 1928 and

commissioned her on 17 August of that year.

The masts are named fore, main, mizzen and spanker masts in English; the Spanish names translate as fore, fore-main, aft-main and mizzen masts – but on the Juan Sebastian de Elcano they are called Blanca, Almansa, Asturias and Nautilus, from the names of four earlier Spanish naval schoolships. They are all the of same height, 48.7 m (159.8 ft.). Almansa and Asturias carry identical sails; the Nautilus boom is longer than the identical booms of the three other masts. Blanca carries a double topsail and a topgallant above, meaning that the correct name for the rig is "four-masted topgallant schooner," although the

202 top The Juan Sebastian de Elcano's ensign is the flag of Spain displaying the kingdom's coat of arms with a crown and, quarterly, the arms of Castile, Leon, Aragon and Navarra with France en surtout, flanked by the Pillars of Hercules and carrying the motto Plus Ultra.

202 bottom Cadets furling the square foresail. The latter's running rigging is no different from that a square-rigger's course but its yard is placed much higher.

202-203 This picture shows well the two-island superstructure of the hull, with its two "Liverpool houses" dividing the main deck between fo'c'sle and poop into three well-decks. The square sails are here furled and the upper topsail and topgallant yards are in their lowered position.

203 top The Juan Sebastian de Elcano's figurehead is a gilded classical crowned female figure and includes an escutcheon bearing the rampant lion of Leon – not the coat of arms of Juan Sebastian de Elcano which includes a globe and the motto Primus circumdistime (First around the Globe).

Juan Sebastian de Elcano

schooner is often called a "topsail schooner," a generic term designating all schooners setting one or more square sails above the gaff foresail.

The hull has a long poop deck extending almost to Asturias, and a short fo'c'sle. The long main deck between poop and fo'c'sle is divided into three "well decks" by two Liverpool houses, deckhouses occupying the full width of the hull and so called because they were first seen on some late 19th century ships from Liverpool. Catwalks linking the Liverpool

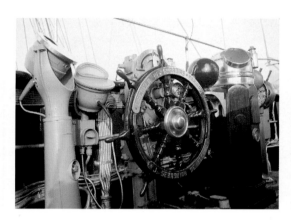

houses allow to walk at a level from the poop deck to the fo'c'sle deck without having to go down to the well decks or to walk through the deckhouses.

The 226 complement indicated in the data panel is a nominal figure published by the Navy; in practice the complement usually numbers between 250 and 300.

The schooner is named after Juan Sebastian de Elcano (1476-1526), the first navigator to sail round the world. He was one of the officers in Ferdinand Magellan's fleet of five ships that left Spain in 1519 to seek a westward route to the Spice Islands.

VESSEL	JUAN SEBASTIAN DE ELCANO		
LAUNCHED	1927	**LENGTH EXTREME**	112.80 m (370.1 ft.)
DESIGNERS	Echevarrieta y Larrinaga	**LENGTH HULL**	94.11 m (308.8 ft.)
	(hull); Camper &	**BEAM**	13.15 m (43.1 ft.)
	Nicholson's (rig)	**DRAFT**	7.46 m (24.5 ft.)
BUILDER	Echevarrieta y Larrinaga	**TONNAGE**	2,478 grt
	yard, Cadiz, Spain	**DISPLACEMENT**	3,671 t
OWNER	Spanish Navy	**SAIL AREA**	2,467 mq (26,555 sq. ft.)
FLAG	Spain		– 3,153 mq
RIG	Four-masted topgallant		(33,939 sq.ft.) all on.
	schooner	**ENGINE**	1,500 hp Sulzer-Bazan
TYPE	Schoolship	**USAGE**	Naval schoolship
CONSTRUCTION	Steel	**COMPLEMENT**	226 including
			80-90 cadets

204 top The flying-bridge wheel, surrounded by a battery of compasses and engine room repeaters. The brass inscription on the rim reads Escuela de Guardias Marinas – "Naval Officers' School."

204 bottom. On this picture the gaff fore-topsail partially blankets (takes the wind out of) the square topsails and topgallant, and the square sails in turn are blanketing the headsails.

204-205 The Juan Sebastian de Elcano is among the biggest sailing vessels of her time and the biggest schooner in existence. However she would be dwarfed by the 1902 Thomas W. Lawson, an American 7-masted schooner that measured 112.62 m between perpendiculars (Elcano is only 79.10 m).

205 bottom left The foredeck with the tack of the fore-staysail and the plates covering the tops of the hawse pipes (slid forward when the anchor chains are hauled in or let out). The white vertical object is a mushroom ventilator allowing fresh air to reach the chain locker below.

205 bottom right The stern wheel bears the same inscription as the flying bridge one. There is plenty of brasswork around the Juan Sebastian de Elcano's decks, and it is polished daily by the cadets.

The expedition suffered heavy casualties caused by scurvy, fighting and shipwreck. Magellan himself was killed in an affray with natives in the Philippines and de Elcano, the senior officer left, took command of what remained of the expedition. He sailed on, still west-about, and reached home in 1522 in the Victoria, the sole remaining ship.

The schooner Juan Sebastian de Elcano is worthy of her name, having herself sailed round the world ten times, ten voyages among the 71 training cruises made before 2001. Those cruises have taken her to 60 countries and to more than 130 ports. The schooner is a familiar sight in the Tall Ships

Races and tall ship harbor festivals. Among other races and events, she took part in the 1976 American Bicentennial Tall Ships Race, the 1988 Australian Bicentennial, and the 1992 Columbus Grand Regatta in which she was the flagship because of the Spanish connection and because the transatlantic part of the race departed from her homeport of Cadiz. The Juan Sebastian de Elcano also was at Sail Osaka 97 and took part in the Tall Ships 2000 race from Cadiz to Bermuda, after which she took part in OpSail 2000 events in various US ports such as Norfolk, VA, and New York.

207 bottom
These fancy brass treads of this ladder are indicative of the attention to finish given to pre-war schoolships. Modern units tend to be much more utilitarian in finish, something that might be preferred by the cadets whose job it is to keep the brass shining!

206-207 Note the arrangement of the stays between the topmasts, the tall deck-mounted radar before the foremast, the radio satellite dome and three tall whip antennas before the mainmast, and the ensign surprisingly flown from a staff when one would expect it to be flown at sea from the jigger gaff.

207 top and center Two views of the Juan Sebastian de Elcano's great cabin under the poop. With stained glass windows, glass-fronted cabinets and the opulent woodwork, one could be forgiven for forgetting one is aboard a sailing ship, not a palace on land. However, all the displayed cruise mementoes, trophies and souvenirs, must surely either be screwed down or safely stowed away when at sea.

In 1942 the Spanish Navy ordered a sistership of the Juan Sebastian de Elcano to be built by the Cadiz yard of Empresa de Construcciones Navales Militares Bazán S.A. This new schooner was to be named Juan de Austria. Her keel was laid down that year but, mainly for financial reasons, building progress was extremely slow. The hull was still unfinished when an ammunition factory blew up in August 1946, causing such massive damage to the shipyard that further work had to be halted and the yard became insolvent. It was saved by being nationalized under the name of Empresa Nacional de Construcciones Navales Militares Bazán S.A. Despite this, work did not resume on the Juan de Austria.

Spain's economy was still suffering from the aftermath of the Civil War. A large debt to Chile had been incurred and the Spanish State was unable to keep up with repayments. Spain offered repayment in kind, in manufactured goods, notably in the field of naval construction. The Chileans were interested in the languishing Juan de Austria and thus took possession of that ship on 23 October 1952, for a valuation of US $2,980,000.

Construction resumed and the hull was launched

208 top The square sails of the Esmeralda are "schooner-fashion," but the gaff foresail and gaff fore-topsail are here replaced by staysails, "barquentine fashion."

208 bottom This oil painting depicts the original Esmeralda, a Spanish 44-gun frigate captured at Callao (Peru) in 1820 by the Chileans fighting for independence in a daring cutting-out raid led by Scottish-born Lord Thomas Cochrane, a former officer in Nelson's navy.

Esmeralda

208-209 Whereas the Juan Sebastian de Elcano has a short fo'c'sle and two Liverpool houses on the main deck, the Esmeralda has a very long fo'c'sle and no liverpool house, albeit quite a large deckhouse on the main deck, with a top extending to the sides with awning decks.

209 bottom right The ship's builder's plaque. The date, April 1954, was the month when work was completed. The building had begun in 1942 for the Spanish Navy but was halted by an ammunition explosion destroying much of the shipyard, and by lack of money. The ship was completed for the Chilean Navy.

VESSEL	ESMERALDA
LAUNCHED	1953
DESIGNER	Echevarrieta y Larrinaga (hull); Camper & Nicholson's (rig)
BUILDER	Empresa Nacional de Construcciones Navales Militares Bazán S.A., Cadiz
OWNER	Chilean Navy
FLAG	Chile
RIG	Four-masted schooner-barquentine
TYPE	Schoolship
CONSTRUCTION	Steel
LENGTH EXTREME	113.00 m (370.7 ft.)
LENGTH HULL	94.00 m (308.4 ft.)
BEAM	13.11 m (43.0 ft.)
DRAFT	6.00 m (19.7 ft.)
TONNAGE	2,276 t TM
DISPLACEMENT	3,222 t standard; 3,673 t load
SAIL AREA	2,852 mq (30,699 sq. ft.)
ENGINES	1,400 hp Fiat
USAGE	Naval schoolship
COMPLEMENT	237 officers and crew; 100 cadets

on 12 May 1953 under the name of Esmeralda. She is the sixth Chilean Naval vessel to bear that name, the first having been a Spanish frigate captured by the Chileans in 1820, during the War of Independence – that signal action was led by Lord Thomas Cochrane (1775-1860), founder of the Chilean Navy and former officer in Nelson's Navy.

Some modifications were made to the original Echevarrieta y Larrinaga hull plans. The two Liverpool houses were dispensed with (replaced by a conventional deckhouse with bridge above), and the fo'c'sle was extended almost to the main mast. Thus the Esmeralda can easily be distinguished from the Juan Sebastian de Elcano in profile view, although an even more conspicuous change was introduced to Charles Nicholson's sail plan: the gaff foresail was replaced by two main-mast staysails, effectively transforming the topgallant schooner rig into that of a quasi-barquentine. However the foremast's disposition was not altered, retaining the tall lower-mast typical of

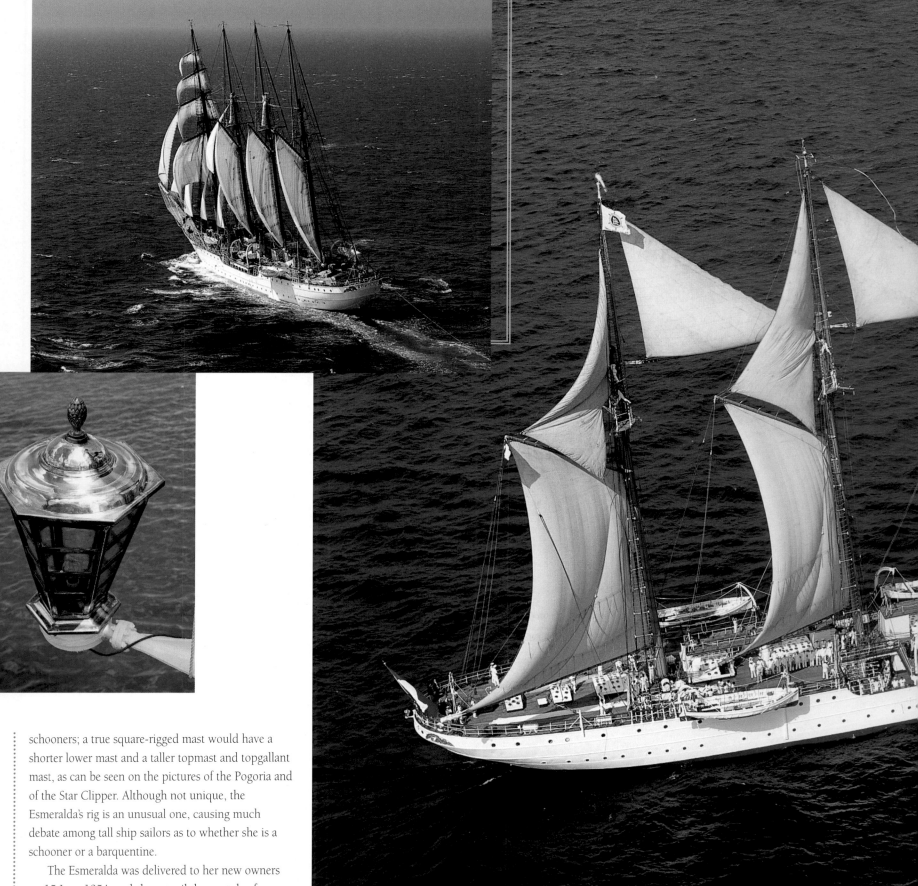

schooners; a true square-rigged mast would have a shorter lower mast and a taller topmast and topgallant mast, as can be seen on the pictures of the Pogoria and of the Star Clipper. Although not unique, the Esmeralda's rig is an unusual one, causing much debate among tall ship sailors as to whether she is a schooner or a barquentine.

The Esmeralda was delivered to her new owners on 15 June 1954, and she set sail the next day for Valparaiso, her intended base port, by way of Las Palmas, New Orleans (where a desalination plant was installed) and Panama.

She has since then been very actively used for the training of midshipmen and young recruits. She also performs as a goodwill ambassador, entertaining heads of State and of government and other dignitaries, and being open to the public for visiting. The Esmeralda has visited more than 300 ports in all parts of the world and is one of the schoolships that sail the greatest number of miles per year. She has made several circumnavigations and is a frequent visitor to North America, Europe and the Far East. She holds the daily run record for ships of her type, having

achieved an average of 16 knots for twenty-four hours.

The Esmeralda entered Tall Ships Races in 1964, 1976, 1982, 1988 (Australia), 1990, 1992 and 2000, and was awarded the Cutty Sark Trophy for international friendship in the 1982 and 1990 races. She took part in the 1964, 1976, 1986, 1989 and 2000 American OpSails and has been present at other tall ships gatherings, such as Osaka's World Sail 83, Rouen's Armada de la Liberté in 1994, Hamburg's Harbor Birthday 1997 and Sail Bremerhaven 2000.

212 top The Esmeralda has fine lines and a powerful rig; she is capable of a fair turn of speed, as can be judged from the wake on this photograph.

*212 center
An old fashioned lantern near the stern, lighted after dark when the ship is at anchor.*

212-213 The crew is here assembled on deck by divisions, by their working stations. One division per mast plus one for the headsails. Gaff sails may have a better windward performance than square sails but on large ships they become immense, very heavy to hoist and difficult to control.

213 bottom left
The motto on this
wheelhouse literally means
"To vanquish or to die"
but is better translated as
"Victory or Death."
The crest above the motto
is the coat of arms of
Chile which features
allama and a condor, two
symbols of the Andes.

213 bottom right
The Esmeralda's
figurehead is a condor, the
"king of the Andes" which
is part of the coat of arms
of several South American
republics.

VENCER O MORIR

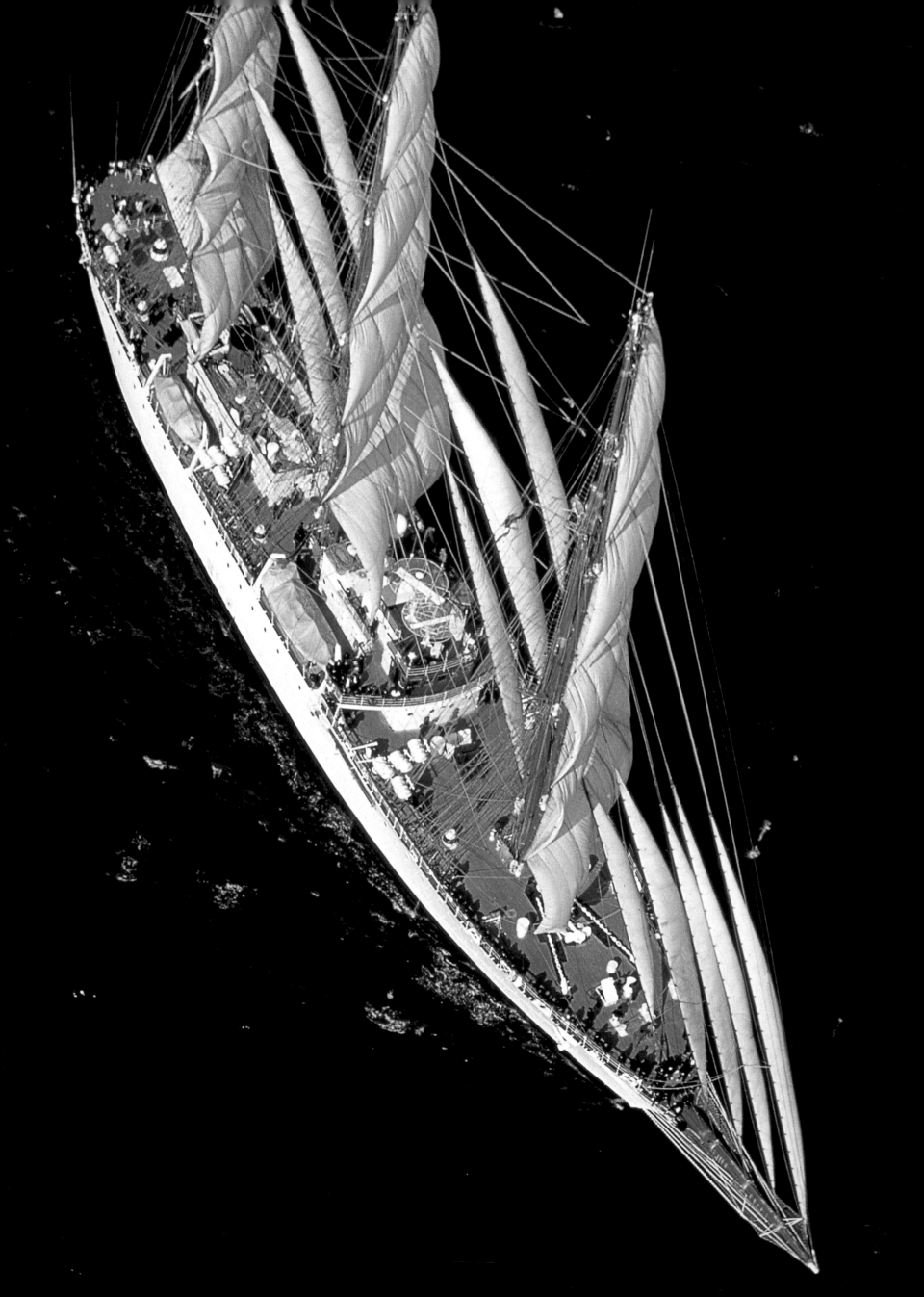

Libertad

The Argentinean Navy has a schoolship tradition going back to 1872, when the auxiliary steamship General Brown was affected to the newly founded Naval School. That ship was replaced in 1974 by the Uruguay, a steam gunboat rigged as a barque which served as a schoolship until 1883 (The Uruguay is still in existence as a museum ship at Buenos Aires or Tigre). The ship-rigged steam corvette La Argentina served as the Navy's schoolship from 1883 until 1891 and was succeeded in 1898 by another ship-rigged steam corvette, the Presidente Sarmiento.

The Presidente Sarmiento operated 37 annual training cruises, including 6 circumnavigations, logging 1,100,000 miles before being converted to a stationary schoolship in 1938. She served in that capacity until 1961 and is now preserved as a

214 The Libertad has a flush upper deck linking the fo'c'sle to the poop deck; this is known as a spardeck. The main deck is below, entirely covered.

215 left Leaving a sheltered bay under power. Once clear of the shore the sails will be sheeted-in and trimmed to the wind.

215 top right A harbor "display style" favored by the Libertdad, with yards placed at equal spacings and the sails hanging in their gear.

215 center right The bridge is located above the midship deckhouse (between foremast and mainmast), and has an open-railed flying bridge above.

215 bottom right The pinrails around the foot of a square-rigged mast are where the lower topsail, topgallant and royal sheets lead to, and also the yards' lifts.

VESSEL	LIBERTAD		
LAUNCHED	1956 (commissioned 1963)	LENGTH EXTREME	103.7 m (340.2 ft.)
DESIGNER	Argentinean Navy Design	LENGTH HULL	91.78 m (301.1 ft.)
OFFICE BUILDER	A.F.N.E. (Naval dockyard),	BEAM	14.31 m (46.9 ft.)
	Rio Santiago, Argentina	DRAFT	6.64 m (21.8 ft.)
OWNER	Argentinean Navy	TONNAGE	2,587 t TM
FLAG	Argentina	DISPLACEMENT	3,027 T standard; 3,765 T load
RIG	Full-rigged ship	SAIL AREA	2,652 mq (28,546 sq. ft.)
TYPE	Schoolship	ENGINES	2 x 1,200 hp Sulzer (1 propeller)
CONSTRUCTION	Steel	USAGE	Naval schoolship
		COMPLEMENT	263 crew + 88-150 cadets

bulk cargo, it caused a rethink about the Libertad's intended rig which was redesigned as that of a three-masted full-rigged ship. The Libertad was the world's longest full rigged ship in service until 1982, when the Dar Mlodziezy, a hair longer, claimed the title.

The Libertad was commissioned on 28 May 1963 and sailed on her maiden voyage on 19 June that same year.

She has won six times the Boston Teapot Trophy which is awarded annually by the International Sail Training Association to the sail training vessel having covered the greatest distance under sail over a period

217 top left An exquisite perspective of clipper bows and gracious figureheads. In the foreground, the Juan Sebastian de Elcano; outboard of her, the Libertad.

217 center right Under full sail. Note the white liferaft canisters carried on the shrouds and the satellite aerial dome in front of the main course.

museum ship at Buenos Aires.

The Libertad is Argentina's fifth schoolship. She was designed and built by the Navy; her keel was laid down on 11 December 1953 at the Naval Dockyard at Rio Santiago, near Buenos Aires, and she was launched on 30 May 1956. She has a spardeck. the flush upper deck from fo'c'sle to poop, a feature not found on the earlier-built schoolships but which now also exists on the Dar Mlodziezy and her sisterships. It was originally intended to rig the Libertad as a four-masted barque.

On 10 August 1957 the German cargo-and-cadet four-masted barque Pamir sailed from Buenos Aires with a cargo of 3,780 tons of grain in bulk. On 21 September she was hit by hurricane Carrie off the Azores and foundered with the loss of 80 out of 86 souls on board. Even though the disaster was not caused by her rig but by the shifting in the hold of her

216-217 The Libertad was the largest full-rigged ship in service until 1982 when she was "overtaken" by the Dar Mlodziezy.

216 bottom A souvenir medal from the Libertad. Such gifts, also including china plates with a picture of ship, are given to honored guests.

217 bottom Ghosting along in light airs. The possibility to keep predictable schedules is the main reason why all the big sailing ships today have auxiliary engines.

of 124 hours. In 1966 she crossed the North Atlantic under sail alone, from Cape Race (Canada) to an imaginary line joining Dublin to Liverpool, covering 2,059 miles in 8 days and 12 hours, a record for that passage by a tall ship.

The Libertad does one training cruise a year, of about six months duration, with midshipmen from the Naval School at Rio Santiago. The itineraries vary and average 22,000 miles. By the end of 2000 she had sailed more than 740,000 miles, had totalled 17 years away from home, had called at 470 ports in 60 countries, and had trained more than 10,000 officers and sailors.

She regularly takes part in the Tall Ships Races and international tall ship gatherings. She took part in the first transatlantic Tall Ships Race in 1964 and the OpSail that followed, and in 1970 she called at Sydney for the bicentennial of the discovery of New South Wales. She took part in the 1976 American Bicentennial Tall Ships Race and OpSail, in the 1984 Tall Ships Race and Quebec 450; she was in the 1986 New York OpSail and less than a month later was in Bremerhaven, Germany, to join a Cutty Sark Tall Ships Race. She took part in the Hong Kong to Osaka race in 1987 and in the Columbus Regatta in 1992. She was at the Rouen festivals of 1989, 1994 and 1999. In 2000 she took part in the Tall Ships 2000 race, OpSail 2000, Sail 2000 Amsterdam and Bremerhaven 2000.

218 top The figurehead is an effigy of Liberty, wearing a Phrygian hat. The Libertad is the last tall ship to have been built with riveted hull plates.

218 bottom left The Libertad is unusual among the tall ships for having a cruiser stern. The emblem, with a Phrygian hat, is the arms of the Republic of Argentina.

218 bottom center The Libertad's crest. A.R.A. stands from Armada de la Republica Argentina, serving the same purpose as H.M.S. in front of British war ship names.

218 bottom right The Libertad motoring in a parade, dressed over all with flags and setting her staysails for "show;" this is not a sailing configuration.

219 Sailing with a following wind, under courses and lower topsails. The Libertad has a narrow entrance and a very good turn of speed.

220-221 The Gloria is the first of four barques built in Spain for Latin American navies. She is also the first square-rigged schoolship of welded construction as opposed to riveted.

220 bottom left The bronze crest of the Colombian Navy schoolship Gloria.

221 top The Gloria's style of parade display is to have all the square sails unfurled and hanging in their gear, with the hoisting yards in their up position.

221 bottom On formal parades and in naval reviews the ship is dressed overall with her signal flags and the cadets man the yards.

The age of deepwater merchant sail came to a final end with the Second World War. After then, the only tall ships still to grace the oceans were schoolships, and their future was also in doubt. The first Tall Ships Race, in 1956, was largely conceived as an exercise in nostalgia, as a one-off event that was likely to be last gathering of a tall ship fleet. Between 1939 and 1967 only four new such vessels were commissioned: Indonesia's barquentine Dewaruci (in 1953), Chile's four-masted barquentine Esmeralda (in 1954), West Germany's

Gorch Fock II (in 1958) and Argentina's full-rigged ship Libertad (in 1960).

Those four vessels are still in the pre-war style and tradition, the last of the "classic" schoolships. But then came the Gloria, the Colombian Navy's schoolship, commissioned in 1968 at the time of the very trough of square-rigged shipbuilding, and she proved to be the first of a new generation although there were to be a further nine years before the next big square rigger was to be commissioned.

The design of the Gloria, made by Senermar of

Madrid, was done with the help of tank testing of hull models and wind-tunnel testing of rig models, and the building, at the ASTACE yard of Bilbao, also in Spain, was done using modern methods of construction. However there is nothing really revolutionary in the Gloria's design and rig and, if anything, the break with traditional concepts and craftsmanship produced some regressive aspects: the lofty bridge amidships causes much windage and the mainsail often cannot be set because it completely blocks the forward vision of the helmsman, and a slight lack of symmetry in the construction of the two sides of the hull necessitates to keep the rudder at a small angle to steer a straight course. The Gloria, launched in the last quarter of 1967, was named after the wife of the late Colombian Defence Minister General Gabriel Rebeiz Pizarro.

The ship was delivered to her owners in Bilbao in September 1968 and was

Gloria

commissioned in November that year, after her arrival in Colombia. She trains midhsipmen in their third year at the Naval Academy, to practice their academic knowledge in the fields of navigation, seamanship and leadership; she also provides seamanship training to enlisted seamen and warrant officers, and is a goodwill ambassador of the Republic of Colombia. During her first 33 years of extremely active service she has trained more than 700 officers and 4,500 enlisted men and women. Her usual complement consists of 10 commissioned officers, 30 warrant officers, 20 crewmen, 5 instructors and 80 cadets. The average age of the latter is nineteen.

The Gloria sails far and wide and takes part in most Tall Ships Races and big international tall ship events in the Americas, Europe and the Far East. Just to mention a few highlights, she sailed round the world in 1970; took part in the American Bicentennial 1976 Tall Ships Race from Bermuda to Newport, New York and Boston and then sailed on to Europe; she took part in the 1980 Tall Ships Race in Europe, in the 1982 Philadelphia Tercentennial, in the 1984 Tall Ships Race from Puerto Rico to Bermuda and Halifax and the Quebec gathering, in the 1986 New York OpSail, the 1988 Australian Bicentennial Tall Ships Race, the 1989 French

Revolution bicentennial gathering in Rouen, Sail Amsterdam 1990, the 1992 Columbus Regatta, the 1997 Tall Ships Race to Osaka, Japan. In 1999 she took part in the San Francisco Gold Rush Race and visited British Columbia. In Year 2000 she participated in OpSail 2000, in the Halifax-Asmsterdam Tall Ships and then called at Brest, France.

She is the first of four barques designed by Senermar and built by ASTACE, the others being Ecuador's Guayas (1976), Venezuela's Simon Bolivar (1979) and Mexico's Cuauhtémoc (1982), each a little bigger than the predecessor.

222 top
The figurehead of the
Gloria is a Winged Glory.

222 bottom
The painted crest of the
Colombian Navy
schoolship Gloria, below
the bridge windows.

222-223 In this particular
parade the wind and
course directions allowed
the sails to be set. The crew
man the rails insted of the
yards.

223 bottom The ensign of
the Gloria is the flag of
Colombia bearing the
country's arms with
Phrygian cap (a symbol of
liberty) and a condor.

VESSEL	GLORIA		
LAUNCHED	1967	LENGTH HULL	64.60 m (211.9 ft.)
DESIGNER	Senermar (Sener	BEAM	10.60 m (34.8 ft.)
	Sistemas Marinos S.A.),	DRAFT	5.00 m (16.4 ft.)
	Madrid, Spain	TONNAGE	997 grt
BUILDER	Astilleros y Talleres	DISPLACEMENT	1,150 t standard;
	Celaya (ASTACE),		1,380 t load
	Bilbao, Spain	SAIL AREA	1,400 mq
OWNER	Colombian Navy		(15,070 sq. ft.)
FLAG	Colombia	ENGINE	530 hp Naval Stork
RIG	Barque		RHO 216 (1968)
TYPE	Schoolship	USAGE	Naval schoolship
CONSTRUCTION	Steel	COMPLEMENT	50-60 crew + 80 cadets
LENGTH EXTREME	76.00 m (249.3 ft.)		

Guayas

to the Ecuadorian Navy on 23 July 1977.

The Guayas is named after Ecuador's largest river, itself named after a cacique (native chieftain) of the Huancavilca tribe which used to live in the Guayaquil region.

The cadets are guardiamarinas (midshipmen) from the Naval Academy at Guayaquil. Although the ship could carry more than 80 cadets, the cadets usually number between 42 and 48, outnumbered by the 72-89 ratings and petty officers most of whom are also undergoing training. The commissioned officers number 14 or 15. The Guayas does not have a permanent captain; she changes commanding officer almost every year. The first training cruise took place in 1978 and was a counter-clockwise circumnavigation of South America, calling at ten foreign ports. The ship normally operates

The next schoolship to be built after the launch of the Gloria in 1967 was Ecuador's Guayas, launched nine years later. The Guayas is a sistership of the Gloria, with minor modifications above the waterline and to the general arrangement. A happy modification, which improves looks and reduces windage, concerns the bridge reduced to a flying bridge no longer enclosed – but nonetheless still in the same high position, with forward vision blanketed by the main sail.

The Guayas is 2.40 m (7.9 ft.) longer in sparred length and 2.80 m (9.2 ft.) longer on the hull than her older sister. Her auxiliary propulsion engine is of a different make and slightly more powerful.

Ecuador's decision to have a naval schoolship built was taken in 1974; the contract with the Spanish yard was signed on 22 May 1975 and the keel was laid down on 1 June 1976. The hull was launched less than five months later, on 22 October. Completed and fitted out afloat, the barque was formally handed over

VESSEL	GUAYAS		
LAUNCHED	1976	LENGTH HULL	67.40 m (221.1 ft.)
DESIGNER	Senermar (Sener Sistemas	BEAM	10.60 m (34.8 ft.)
	Marinos S.A.), Madrid,	DRAFT	4.70 m (15.4 ft.)
	Spain	TONNAGE	934 grt
BUILDER	Astilleros y Talleres	DISPLACEMENT	1,153 t standard;
	Celaya (ASTACE)		1,300 t load
	Bilbao, Spain	SAIL AREA	1,410 mq (15,177 sq. ft.)
OWNER	Ecuadorian Navy	ENGINES	700 hp General Motors
FLAG	Ecuador	USAGE	Naval cadet ship
RIG	Barque	COMPLEMENT	172 berths – usually
TYPE	Schoolship		sails with 14-15
CONSTRUCTION	Steel		officers, 72-89 men
LENGTH EXTREME	78.40 m (257.2 ft.)		and 42-48 cadets.

one training cruise a year, of variable but substantial duration, although she did not sail in 1979, 1990, 1993, and 1997. The destinations are variable and have included the Caribbean, both coasts of the Americas, the Atlantic, North Sea and Baltic, Polynesia and Australia.

Guaya's first appearance in international tall ship events was in 1980 when she took part in a Tall Ships Race from Cartagena (Colombia), to Norfolk VA, in which she came second, and from Boston to Kristiansand (Norway), in which she came third; she then joined the Cutty Sark Tall Ships Race from Kiel (Germany) to Amsterdam, via Karlskrona (Sweden) and Frederikshavn (Denmark).

In 1981 she sailed to Hawaii and Acapulco; in 1982, to the Marquesas Islands and Punta Arenas in southernmost Chile. Another circumnavigation of South America was made in 1983; 1984 saw her in Hawaii, California and along the Mexican West Coast. In 1985 she sailed to Easter Island and to Juan Fernandez, the island off Chile where Alexander Selkirk (1617-1721) had been marooned for more

than four solitary years in 1704-08, an adventure for which he became immortalized by Daniel Defoe under the name of Robinson Crusoe.

In 1986 the Guayas took part in the big tall ship parade celebrating the centennial of the Statue of Liberty in New York. The 1987 and 1988 cruises were combined into a single extra-long voyage calling at Tahiti and Fiji, Brisbane, Hobart, and Sydney for the Australian Bicentennial. The barque then sailed home via New Zealand, Peru and Chile.

The next two voyages were to the Caribbean, and then, in 1992, the Guayas sailed to Lisbon to take part in the Columbus Regatta race to Cadiz, Tenerife and Puerto Rico. The following three voyages took place in Caribbean waters and the Gulf of Mexico, and in 1998 the Guayas called, not for the first time, at Havana, and also at several US Gulf and Atlantic ports. In 1999 she sailed to San Francisco with calls at Acapulco, San Diego and Monterrey. In 2000 the Guayas took part in OpSail 2000, San Juan - Miami - Norfolk - Baltimore - New York - New London.

226 top The Guayas sailing under a quasi staysail-barquentine sail arrangement, the mainmast square sails not being set.

226 center The condor is a frequent figurehead subject for tall ships from the Andean republics.

226-227 Falls from aloft are extremely rare. When they do happen, it is usually experienced sailors who are the victims – they can become overconfident.

228-229 The horizontal lines called "brails" that are used to gather the spanker against the mizzen mast (the gaff being left up).

228 bottom left A heel indicator with compass rose decoration and a dial needle in the shape of a dirk.

Simon Bolivar

The barque Simon Bolivar is the third ship from the Senermar - ASTACE "stable." Her keel was laid down on 6 June 1979 at the ASTACE yard in Bilbao, Spain; the hull was launched on 21 November the same year and the owner, the Venezuelan Navy, took delivery on 12 August 1980.

Whilst retaining the same 10.60 m (34.8 ft.) beam, the Simon Bolivar is 2.40 m (7.9 ft.) longer on the waterline than her younger sisters, the Gloria and the Guayas, and is 4 m longer, with bowsprit, than Guayas. She appears much bigger because her superstructures have been reduced – the tall bridge just abaft the main mast, found on her younger sisters, has been dispensed with, replaced by a lower and more conventionally placed chartroom on the poop deck abaft the mizzen mast. To the casual observer, the Simon Bolivar is easy to differentiate from her sisters, including her younger sister, the Cuauhtémoc, by the distinctive livery of her hull, white but with a broad black band at main deck level and with painted gun ports beneath it. This pattern is also instrumental in elongating her profile. Actually, this color scheme of painted gunports on a white hull, as opposed to painted on a white band on an otherwise black hull,

228 bottom right The compact wheel box indicates the transmission is hydraulic. Note another heel indicator fixed to the mast.

229 bottom The Simon Bolivar's figurehead is an effigy of Liberty draped in the flag of Venezuela.

VESSEL	SIMON BOLIVAR
LAUNCHED	1979
DESIGNER	Senermar (Sener Sistemas Marinos S.A.), Madrid, Spain
BUILDER	Astilleros y Talleres Celaya (ASTACE), Bilbao, Spain
OWNER	Venezuelan Navy
FLAG	Venezuela
RIG	Barque
TYPE	Schoolship
CONSTRUCTION	Steel
LENGTH EXTREME	82.40 m (270.3 ft.)
LENGTH HULL	70.00 m (229.7 ft.)
BEAM	10.60 m (34.8 ft.)
DRAFT	4.35 m (14.3 ft.)
TONNAGE	934 grt
DISPLACEMENT	1260 T standard
SAIL AREA	1,650 mq (17.760 sq. ft.)
ENGINE	750 hp General Motors
USAGE	Naval schoolship
COMPLEMENT	16 officers, 76 crew and 102 cadets

230 top The Simon Bolivar under full sail. The sailor standing on the fore-royal yard gives an idea of the scale.

230 center The Simon Bolivar's great cabin is decorated and fitted out in traditional style.

230 bottom A bronze bust, in the great cabin, of Simon Bolivar (1783-1830), the Venezuelan-born liberator of Venezuela, Colombia, Ecuador, Bolivia (named after him) and Peru.

231 The Simon Bolivar has a classical deck layout, with raised foredeck (fo'c'sle) and poopdeck, with the maindeck one level down in between.

distinguishes her from all other three-masted square riggers. Although still carrying the same sail plan of twenty-three sails, including ten square sails, she sets 250 and 240 m (2,690 - 2,580 sq. ft.) more than the Gloria and Guayas respectively.

The Simon Bolivar is named after Venezuela's national hero (1783-1830) who wrested independence from Spain for his country and many other South American countries. The barque's figurehead is an effigy of Liberty, wearing a Phrygian cap and breaking the chains of servitude. No bad feelings, though: after leaving Bilbao she paid, on her maiden voyage, courtesy visits to the Spanish ports of El Ferrol, Cadiz, Barcelona and Palma de Mallorca, before setting sail for her homeport of La Guaira for the first time.

Her complement is typically 16 officers, 76 crew and 102 cadets, including up to 18 young women – the latter being admitted aboard since the early days

when the practice was still highly unusual in naval schoolships.

The Simon Bolivar undertakes one long training voyage a year. Her first regular one, La Guaira to La Guaira, was in 1981 and took her to the East coast of the USA and then across to Western Europe and back home via the Canaries. The next year she followed a similar route, attending Philadelphia's 300th anniversary tall ship celebrations and taking part in the transatlantic Tall Ships Race to Lisbon. The bark is a regular participant in the Tall Ships Races and other tall ship events. In 1984 she raced from Puerto Rico, Bermuda and Halifax and sailed on with the fleet up the St. Lawrence river to take part in the town of Quebec celebrations marking the 450th discovery of Canada by the French navigator Jacques Cartier (1491-1557).

In 1985 she was back in Lisbon at the start of

another European tour, the highlight of which was a massive gathering of tall ships in Amsterdam. In 1986 she was present at the New York OpSail, berthed at the South Street Seaport next to all three of her near-sisterships Gloria, Guayas and Cuauhtémoc, a rare but not unique reunion.

In 1987-88 she sailed round the world and took part in the Australian Bicentennial parade of tall ships in Sydney harbor on 26 January 1988. She also took part in the 1992 Columbus Regatta marking the 500th anniversary of Columbus' discovery of the New World, another transatlantic tall ships race. In 1994 she was at the tall ship gathering in Rouen, France, also in company with her three sisters. She was back in Rouen in 1999 for the "Armada du siècle," and the following year she took part in the OpSail 2000 celebrations in various US Eastern ports.

It is infinitely more pleasant (and reassuring) to see navies engaged in a tall ships race rather than in an arms race – and it certainly seems that some sort of "race" was going on when, in turn, the Mexican Navy decided to follow the Colombian, Ecuadorian and Venezuelan Navies in ordering a Senermar-designed barque from Bilbao's ASTACE yard, and one that would be bigger than the preceding one, the Simon Bolivar, which was bigger than her predecessor, the Guayas which was bigger than the first barque, the Gloria.

The new ship's keel was laid in July 1981 and the hull was launched on 9 January 1982. The completed vessel was handed over to the Mexican Navy on 29 July 1982.

234 top Cuauhtémoc (c. 1495-1525), the last Aztec emperor, executed by Cortes on a trumped-up charge, became a national hero after Mexico's independence from Spain.

234 center The Cuauhtémoc is the fourth and last of the series of school barques built at Bilbao, Spain, between 1967 and 1982.

The ship was named after Cuauhtémoc (c. 1495-1525), the last Aztec emperor, who was executed on orders from Hernan Cortés. The figurehead represents him wearing a green quetzal feather headdress and holding a shield and a club.

The Cuauhtémoc is 8.50 m (27.9 ft.) longer than Venezuela's barque, the Simon Bolivar; she is also 1.40 m (4.6 ft.) beamier and her sail area is 33% greater.

Unlike the previous three barques, which have conventional hoisting upper-topsail, topgallant and royal yards, all of the Cuauhtémoc's yards are standing, staying permanently in their "up" position like the yards on the Polish barquentine Pogoria and full-rigged ship Dar Mlodziezy. The Cuauhtémoc's spanker gaff is also standing, with the sail brailing to the mast. The staysails are intentionally large to give some performance when motorsailing with all square sails furled.

The decks are steel clad with iroko planking. The ballast is lead, as is also the case for the older sisterships. In comparison to those earlier ships, the deck and superstructure arrangement of the Cuauhtémoc is almost back to the traditional layout found for instance on the Sørlandet and Christian Radich, with an inconspicuous charthouse on the poop and an uncluttered waist.

The maiden voyage, starting on 4 August 1982 from Bilbao, was to Vera Cruz on the Mexican Gulf Coast, by way of Vigo, Las Palmas and Santo Domingo. The passage was accomplished entirely

234-235 The standard
length for the lower yards
of square riggers is twice
the maximum width
of the hull.

235 top right The funnel
is decorated with the crest
of the Cuauhtémoc topped
by the national symbol of

Mexico, an eagle eating a
snake. the motto means
"To foster the spirit of
seamanship."

Cuauhtémoc

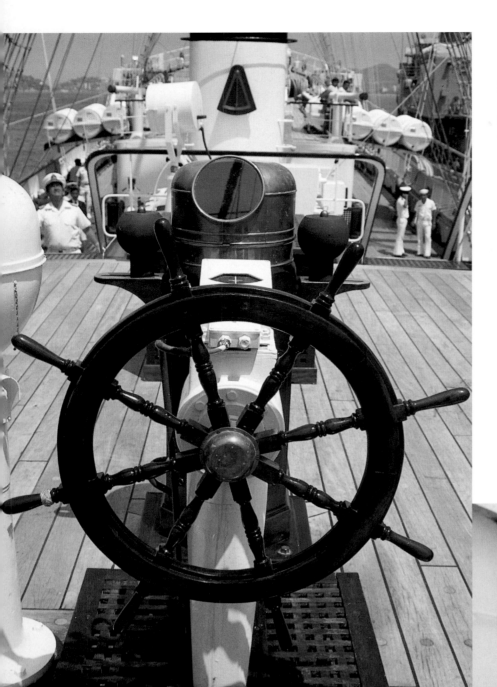

236 bottom A spare stockless bower anchor stowed against the fo'c'sle break. All ships carry one or more spare anchors in the event of loosing one or of having to put out extra anchors in a storm.

237 The Cuauhtémoc is not only the fourth and last of the Bilbao-built barques but is also the largest.

under sail in 18 days and 19 hours, at an average speed of 7.3 knots. The barque is capable of reaching 18 knots given the right wind and sea, a very good speed for a vessel of her type. In December she left Vera Cruz for Acapulco, her homeport on the Pacific coast.

The following year the Cuauhtémoc set sail from Acapulco on 17 July, for a long voyage taking her to Manzanillo, Puerto Vallarta, Mazatlan, Ensenada and San Diego before setting a westerly course to Honolulu and on to Pusan, South Korea, and to the World Sail 93 gathering of tall ships at Osaka in late October. She returned to Acapulco on 18 December by way of San Francisco.

Her first appearance in a European tall ships festival was at Amsterdam in 1985. On that voyage she had previously called at Havana, Annapolis and Oslo, and later called at Hamburg, London, Brest and Lisbon. She took part in all three tall ship festivals at Rouen, France, in 1989, 1994 and 1999.

In 1990 she sailed round the world, covering 26,000 miles in 180 days. In 1992 she took part in the Transatlantic Columbus Regatta from Cadiz to Bermuda, the USA and Liverpool. In 1993 she became a Cape-Horner. In 1996 she was in the Cutty Sark Tall Ships Race in the Baltic, from Rostock to Copenhagen via St. Petersburg and Tallin. The following year she took part in a Tall Ships Race from Hong Kong to Osaka via Okinawa and Kagoshima. In 2000 she took part in the Cutty Sark races from Gdansk to Helsinki, and Stockholm to Flensburg, and she later called at Bremerhaven for the Bremerhaven 2000 tall ship festival.

236 top left The Cuauhtémoc's wheel with hydraulic transmission. The after side of the funnel has a heel indicator.

236 center right The ship's main bell, on the front of the charthouse on the poopdeck, with the builders' plaque behind it.

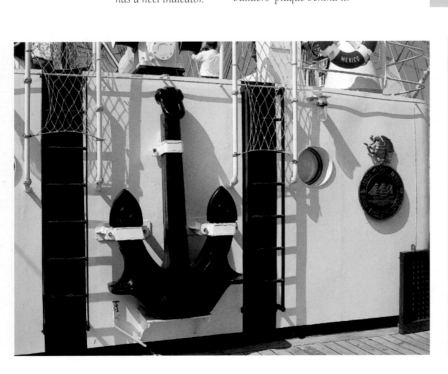

Vessel	CUAUHTÉMOC
Launched	1982
Designer	Senermar (Sener Sistemas Marinos S.A.), Madrid, Spain
Builder	Astilleros y Talleres Celaya (ASTACE), Bilbao, Spain
Owner	Mexican Navy
Flag	Mexico
Rig	Barque
Type	Schoolship
Construction	Steel
Length Extreme	90.50 m (296.9 ft.)
Length Hull	78.50 m (257.5 ft.)
Beam	12.00 m (39.4 ft.)
Draft	5.20 m (17.1 ft.)
Tonnage	
Displacement	1.662 t standard; 1,800 t load
Sail Area	2,200 mq (23,680 sq. ft.)
Engine	1,125 hp Caterpillar
Usage	Naval schoolship
Complement	85 officers and crew; 90 cadets

238 left Unlike in traditional rigging, the upper-topsail, topgallant and royal yards are fixed in height and are not lowered before (or after) clewing up their sails.

238-239 The Dar Mlodziezy and her younger five sisterships were the largest full-riggers in service. They lost that title to the 5-masted Royal Clipper in year 2000.

The first Polish merchant navy schoolship, the Lwow, was put in service in 1921; she was a former British merchant barque built in 1869. The Lwow was replaced in 1930 by the full-rigged ship Dar Pomorza ("Gift of Pomerania"), originally the German schoolship Prinzess Eitel Friedrich built in 1909. The Dar Pomorza survived the Second World War by seeking refuge in neutral Sweden and was recommissioned soon afterwards. In 1972 she was the first Eastern Bloc vessel to take part in the Tall Ships Races, and from then on she was a regular and very popular participant in those races. She was retired in 1981 and is now a stationary museum ship in Gdynia.

The "Dar Mlodziezy" is the Dar Pomorza's replacement. Her name means "Gift of Youth" because her building was helped by financial contributions raised by the youth of Poland. She was designed by the Polish naval architect Zygmunt Choren who had already designed the barquentine "Pogoria" (launched in 1980).

The Dar Mlodziezy is a new generation square rigger and schoolship incorporating many modern features or unconventional ones for a ship of her type. All the yards are fixed, meaning they are not hoisted up their respective mast sections when their sails are set. The masts are built as single tapered tubes, without any doublings. The tops are triangular instead of the traditional D shape, and similar but smaller platforms are placed on the topgallant and royal crosstrees.

The hull is spardecked, meaning that the traditional main weather deck area between the raised poop and fo'c'sle is entirely enclosed, providing an extra accommodation deck, and the poop and fo'c'sle decks are flush with the spardeck linking them. Traditional schoolships have open-plan berth decks where the cadets sleep, eat and study, and where hammocks are slung at night, a direct legacy from the sailing men-o'-war. Even though on many schoolships the hammocks have been replaced by folding bunks, the open plan usually remains. On the Dar Mlodziezy it is compartmented into 25-berth dormitories, which allows to berth together cadets from the same watch who can thus get ready for night time watch changeovers without disturbing those who do not have to get up at such times. There are separate rooms for messing and lectures. The stern has a square transom with windows that provides daylight to the great cabin which serves as mess for the captain and officers and for VIP receptions.

Dar Mlodziezy

239 top right The Dar Mlodziezy cuts a powerful figure under full sail. Although the pole masts and fixed yards are not traditional, the sail plan is.

239 bottom left Opposite. The rope "fouling" the anchor figurehead traces the initials SM, Szkola Morska ("Sea School," the Polish name of the Gdynia Maritime Academy.

239 bottom right The Dar Mlodziezy has a multiple wheel to allow more cadets to take tricks at steering. The dial seen between the spokes is a rudder angle indicator.

The ship was built at the Lenin Shipyard in Gdansk, the very place where, and at the very time when, the Solidarnosc movement appeared that was to result nine years later in the collapse of the Soviet empire. After the change of regime the yard was renamed Gdansk Shipyard and, ironically, became a casualty of the historic changes wrought by its workers: it was closed down in 1997 because it was not profitable.

The Dar Mlodziezy is the first of a series of six sisterships. The five others, also built in Poland, were built between 1987 and 1990 on order from the Soviet Union: Mir (now belonging to Russia), Druzhba (Ukraine), Pallada (Russia), Khersones (Ukraine) and Nadezhda (Russia). The Dar Mlodziezy was commissioned in 1982. She is a very regular participant in the Tall Ships Races and sails very extensively. In 1983 she sailed to Japan; the following year, in a transatlantic Tall Ships Race to Quebec.

In 1987-8 she sailed around the world by way of

240 top Where catheads are found some ships, the Dar Mlodziezy has lookout sponsons that also provide well-placed fixing points for the jib-sheet tackles.

240 center Although not as luxurious as on some of the pre-war schoolships, this great cabin is unexpectedly plush for a ship that was built under a communist regime.

240 bottom The single-tube construction of the masts is plainly visible here. Although sails are established at the conventional places, the rigging is much simplified and streamlined.

241 This photo taken from the main deck of the Dar Mlodziezy allows the full expanse of her sails, filled by the morning breeze, to be appreciated.

Cape Horn, attending the Australian Bicentennial tall ships gathering in Sydney on the way. She took part in the 1992 transatlantic Tall Ships Race; in 1996 she took part in a Tall Ships Race from Hong Kong to Osaka and she took part in the Tall Ships 2000 transatlantic Race. Since 1990 her cadet complement of 150 has been reduced to 120 to make 30 berths available to fee-paying passengers. The latter can take part in the ship's handling and watches if they so wish.

VESSEL	DAR MLODZIEZY		
LAUNCHED	1980	LENGTH Hull	94.80 m (311.0 ft.)
DESIGNER	Zygmunt Choren	BEAM	14.00 m (45.9 ft.)
BUILDER	Stocznia Gdanska im Lenina,	DRAFT	6.37 m (20.9 ft.)
	Gdansk, Poland	TONNAGE	2,385 grt, 355 nrt
OWNER	Gdynia Wyzsza Szkola	DISPLACEMENT	2,946 td
	Morska, Gdynia, Poland	SAIL AREA	3,015 mq (32,453 sq. ft.)
	(Gdynia Maritime Academy)	ENGINES	2 x 750 hp Ciegelski Sulzer
FLAG	Poland	USAGE	Schoolship & "civilian"
RIG	Full-rigged ship		sail training
TYPE	Schoolship	COMPLEMENT	40 crew + 4 instructors + 120
CONSTRUCTION	Steel		cadets + 30 paying trainees and
LENGTH EXTREME	108.80 m (357.0 ft.)		passengers

242 top left A splendid action shot of the Nippon Maru sailing close-hauled on the starboard tack, all her sails nicely set and drawing.

242 bottom left In harbor and when not receiving special guests, the upholstery of this cosy corner is protected with dust covers.

242 center right When steering with such big wheels, one stands to the windward side of them, therefore this original idea of having two steering compasses makes a lot of sense.

242 bottom right A view of the main upper-topsail, lower and upper topgallants and royal, taken from the crosstrees of the foremast.

243 Sailing with all sails set in what appears to be a force 4 or 5 wind. Should the wind exceed force 6 the higher sails would be gradually taken in.

Nippon Maru II

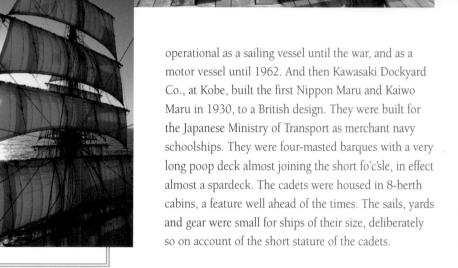

Japan has a merchant navy training ship tradition going back to 1897 when the steam schooner Meiji Maru, a former lighthouse tender, was given a full-rig for use as a stationary training ship. That vessel is now preserved in Tokyo as a museum ship embedded in a dock filled with concrete.

The next sailing schoolship built for the Japanese government was the Tasei Maru, a four-masted barque built in 1904. She operated until the Second World War and was sunk by a mine in 1945, in Kobe harbor.

In 1909 the steam barque Unyo Maru was built at Osaka as a schoolship for the Ministry of Agriculture and Forests (which covered Fisheries). Laid-up well before the Second World War, she became another stationary training ship in Tokyo harbor where she is now preserved as a museum ship.

Next came the Shintoku Maru, a four-masted barquentine built in 1923-24 at Kobe. She remained operational as a sailing vessel until the war, and as a motor vessel until 1962. And then Kawasaki Dockyard Co., at Kobe, built the first Nippon Maru and Kaiwo Maru in 1930, to a British design. They were built for the Japanese Ministry of Transport as merchant navy schoolships. They were four-masted barques with a very long poop deck almost joining the short fo'c'sle, in effect almost a spardeck. The cadets were housed in 8-berth cabins, a feature well ahead of the times. The sails, yards and gear were small for ships of their size, deliberately so on account of the short stature of the cadets.

VESSEL	NIPPON MARU II		
For comparison the figures for Nippon Maru I are given in square brackets.			
LAUNCHED	1984 -[1930]	**BEAM**	13.80 m (45.3 ft.)
DESIGNER	Sumitomo Heavy Industries		[12.95 m / 42.5 ft.]
BUILDER	Sumitomo Heavy Industries Uraga	**DRAFT**	6.29 m (20.6 ft.)
	Shipyard, Yokosuka, Japan		[6.88 m / 22.6 ft.]
OWNER	Ministry of Transport, Institute	**TONNAGE**	2,570 grt [2,257 grt]
	of Sea Training, Tokyo	**DISPLACEMENT**	3,274 td (light); 4,730 td (load)
FLAG	Japan		[4,343 load]
RIG	Four-masted barque	**SAIL AREA**	2,760 mq (29,708 sq. ft.)
TYPE	Schoolship		[2,397 m / 25,800 sq. ft.]
CONSTRUCTION	Steel	**ENGINES**	2 x 1,500 hp Daihatsu; twin
LENGTH EXTR.	110.09 m (361,2 ft.)		propellers (2 x 600 hp, twin prop.)
	[97.03 m / 318.3 ft.]	**USAGE**	Merchant navy schoolship
LENGTH HULL	99.15 m (325.3 ft.)	**COMPLEMENT**	190: 24 officers + 46 seamen +
	[93.52 m / 306.8 ft.]		120 cadets [195: 27 + 48 + 120]

244-245 The Nippon Maru and her sistership the Kaiwo Maru, are the biggest schoolships launched since the Second World War.

244 bottom left When working on an upper-topsail yard in its lowered position, it is more comfortable to walk along the lower topsail yard than to use the footrope.

244 bottom right Instead of the usual horizontal windlass with a gypsy at each end, one for each chain, the anchor chains are here hauled in by separate vertical capstans.

245 top The Nippon Maru's figurehead, named Ranjo, was sculpted by Dr. Nishi and his team of the Tokyo National University of Fine Arts and Music.

245 bottom Detail of
a capstan cap. T.S. stands
for Training Ship.

The word Maru, appended to most Japanese merchant vessels, is untranslatable; it is a term of endearment that also conveys the idea of endeavor. Nippon is the Japanese name for Japan, and Kaiwo means "Sea King."

During the war the two barques continued to train officers, albeit under power only, with their yards taken down. At the conclusion of the war, they were to be seized as war prizes like the German schoolships but, as they were needed for the repatriation of Japanese troops and civilians, they were left under Japanese authority and ownership.

The Nippon Maru was re-rigged and recommissioned in 1952; her sister followed in 1955. Since then, and until their retirement, they performed regular training voyages, usually in the Pacific and occasionally taking part in international tall ship events. In 1960 the Nippon Maru Saile to New York for the hundredth anniversary of Japan's first delegation to the USA.

In 1976, for the American Bicentennial celebrations, she sailed again to New York for OpSail 76 while the Kaiwo Maru sailed to Seattle, Washington State. Both ships took part in the international tall ship gathering at Osaka in 1983. Even though they had plenty of mileage left, the Institute of Sea Training decided in the 1980s to replace them by new four-masted barques. The Nippon Maru was the first to be replaced, in September 1984. In her 54 years of active duty she had trained 11,425 cadets and logged 988,000 miles, the equivalent of 46 times the Earth's circumference. She is now retired as a floating museum at Yokohama, under the management of the Nippon Maru Commemorative Foundation.

The Nippon Maru (II) was designed and built by Sumitomo Heavy Industries. She displays a definite kinship with her predecessor. She was launched on 15 February 1984 and commissioned the same year on 16 September in the presence of the Crown Prince and Princess of Japan. The Nippon Maru (II) represented Japan at the Australian Bicentennial tall ship gathering in January 1988. She took part in the Kagoshima to Osaka Tall Ships Race in 1997 and in Sail Osaka 1997. She was awarded three times the International Sail Training Association's Boston Teapot Trophy for having been the training ship that covered the most miles under sail over a period of 124 hours during the given year.

VESSEL	KAIWO MARU II FOR COMPARISON THE FIGURES FOR KAIWO MARU I ARE GIVEN IN SQUARE BRACKETS.				
LAUNCHED	*1989 [1930]*	**CONSTRUCTION**	*Steel*	**SAIL AREA**	*2,760 mq (29,708 sq. ft.)*
DESIGNER	*Sumitomo Heavy Industries*	**LENGTH**	*Extreme 110.09 m (361,2 ft.)*		*[2,397 m / 25,800 sq. ft.]*
BUILDER	*Sumitomo Heavy Industries Uraga*		*[97.03 m / 318.3 ft.]*	**ENGINES**	*2 x 1,500 hp Daihatsu; twin*
	Shipyard, Yokosuka, Japan	**LENGTH HULL**	*99.15 m (325.3 ft.) [93.52 m /*		*propellers (2 x 600 hp, twin prop.]*
OWNER	*Ministry of Transport, Institute of*		*306.8 ft.]*	**USAGE**	*Merchant navy schoolship*
	Sea Training, Tokyo	**BEAM**	*13.80 m (45.3 ft.) [12.95 m / 42.5 ft.]*	**COMPLEMENT**	*190: 24 officers + 46 seamen*
FLAG	*Japan*	**DRAFT**	*6.60 m (21.7 ft.) [6.88 m / 22.6 ft.]*		*+ 120 cadets incl. up to 20 non-*
RIG	*Four-masted barque*	**TONNAGE**	*2,556 grt; 2,150 nrt [2,257 grt]*		*professional trainees.*
TYPE	*Schoolship*	**DISPLACEMENT**	*4,655 td load [4,343 load]*		*[195: 27 + 48 + 120]*

247 Sailing into the sunset
with all the square sail sets.
Night watches are
generally a peaceful time,
with only the sound of the
wind in the rigging, the
lapping of the bow wave,
the creaking of the spars -
and the hum of generators.

Kaiwo Maru II

246-247 The new Kaiwo
Maru (which translates as
"King of the Sea") was
built by Sumitomo Heavy
Industries in 1989. The
original ship was launched
in 1930.

When the original Nippon Maru was replaced and retired in 1984, the original Kaiwo Maru carried on for an extra five years to the day.

A new pair of slightly larger sisterships replaced those two sisterships. The plans for the new barques were drawn in Japan with computers and the help of tank and wind tunnel testing of models. The old barques having been a success and the purpose and the number of cadets remaining the same, the new design was not that different. While the new barques are 13.06 m (42.8 ft.) longer in their spared lengths, their hulls are only 5.53 m (18.1 ft.) longer. They are wider by 85 cm (33 in.); the draft is actually slightly less and the displacement a little under 9% greater.

The accommodation layout is not fundamentally different. The old barques already had the very modern feature of cadet sleeping quarters divided in 8-berth cabins, with separate mess and teaching rooms, instead of all those activities being conducted in a single big open berth deck with hammocks, a legacy from the days of the men-o'war. The new design makes provisions for the presence of female cadets. On the old ships the exposed part of the main deck was reduced to a residual well deck; this is now entirely covered over by a flush spardeck extending from bow to stern.

The rig height is virtually identical to that of the old barques, but more sail is carried forward, with a longer bowsprit. The yards are longer, partly because of the increased beam and partly because it is no longer necessary to have a light rig for small cadets: prewar Japanese were somewhat stunted by undernourishment and the unprecedented postwar prosperity has seen the average height of the new generations increase by a phenomenal amount. On the old ships the jigger is a single gaff sail; on the new ones it is split by a lower gaff, as on the Kruzenshtern. The masting is conventional, with the lower masts and topmasts being built as one unit and

248-249 The quality
of Japanese steel
shipbuilding can be clearly
seen on this photograph.

249 bottom left Sailing
with all 36 sails set. From
this angle the Kaiwo Maru
looks almost like a tiny
model in a bottle.

249 bottom right
The double wheel
of the Kaiwo Maru
is exactly the same as
on the Nippon Maru.

248 top The three square-
rigged masts each set a
course, lower and upper
topsails, lower and upper
topgallants, and a royal.

248 center The Kaiwo
Maru's figurehead is
named Konjo, a younger
sister of Ranjo sculpted
by Dr. Nishi and his team
of the Tokyo National
University of Fine Arts
and Music.

with a fidded topgallant mast prolonged by the royal pole. The upper topsail, upper topgallant and royal yards are of the traditional hoisting type, but they hoist along tracks. When the Kaiwo Maru II was built, five years after the Nippon Maru II, minor practical modifications were made in the light of experience to improve the sailing qualities. The hull shape and dimensions remained however unaltered.

The prewar barques only had a scrollwork on the bows; the new ones have gilded figureheads. That of the Nippon Maru II is a female figure named Ranjo which, with its elegant, gentle, and dignified pose, symbolises Japanese womanhood. The Kaiwo Maru's figurehead represents a maiden named Konjo and is like a younger sister of Ranjo.

The Kaiwo Maru II was launched on 7 March 1989 and commissioned the following 16 September. The old Kaiwo Maru is kept in Tokyo harbor as a stationary training ship. During her active career she had trained over 11,000 cadets and logged 1,050,000 miles at sea (49 times the Earth's circumference).

On her first full year of operation (1990), the Kaiwo Maru II won the International Sail Training Association's Boston Teapot Trophy for the best 124-hour run under sail of the year, and she won that trophy again in 1995 with the so-far unbroken record of 1,394 miles. To date (end 2000) she has won the Teapot four times, and the Nippon Maru II has won it three times.

The Kaiwo Maru II took part in the Columbus Quincentenary celebrations (New York OpSail 92 and Sail Boston 1992), in the 1997 Kagoshima to Osaka Tall Ships Race, in OpSail 2000, and the Tall Ships 2000 Boston to Halifax race which she won both in her own Class A and overall.

In 1971 Captain Adam Jasser founded the Iron Shackle Fraternity, a sail training organization aimed at youngsters in trouble. It used an old Baltic trader but a larger ship was required. With the help of Krzysztof Baranowski, a round-the-world single-handed Cape-Horn yachtsman who worked for Polish TV, the latter agreed to sponsor the construction of a new training ship. The marine architect Zygmunt Choren, another Cape-Horn racing yachtsman, was asked to draw the plans for this new ship, the barquentine "Pogoria," his first square rig design

that was to be immediately followed by that for the "Dar Mlodziezy."

The Pogoria was built for weatherliness and speed, with an eye on winning in the Tall Ships Races; she has a fine entrance and a long run. She has a high deck for more accommodation volume and, in order not to make her sides appear too high, she has open rails instead of bulwarks. There are two sunk-in deckhouses, one abaft the foremast and one abaft the mizzen. Behind the latter there is a cockpit on deck. The steel masts are built in a single section and, as for the Dar Mlodziezy, all the yards are fixed in height. Originally both the mainsail and mizzen were gaff sails but the Pogoria was found to be carrying too much canvas aft, giving her lee helm, so the mizzen was replaced by a Bermudan sail at the end of her first season.

The Pogoria was the first of a series of near-sisterships. The Polish Navy's schoolship Iskra (1982) and the Bulgarian schoolship Kaliakra (1984) are also barquentine-rigged; the Polish Academy of Sciences research vessel Okeania (1985) has a similar hull but an experimental rig.

From the very start the owners made berths available to Western trainees, as a way of raising much-

250 left The bell is one of the few traditional details about the deck but its bracket is welded steel pipes and plates.

*250 right
The triangular top is a new design for tops. The topgallant crosstrees are covered by a similar platform. The red running rigging was not a deliberate choice but the color of polypropylene rope available at a good price.*

250-251 Among the Pogoria's modern or unusual features are the reverse transom (not retained in her later sisterships), the masts built as a single tapered tube, the yards all at fixed heights and the large number and disposition of the footropes' stirrups. The original gaff mizzen caused too much weather helm and was replaced by a Bermudan one.

Pogoria

needed hard currency. The Pogoria was the first Eastern Bloc ship to do so and set the trend that became widespread in the final years of that geopolitical entity. She took part in the 1980 Tall Ships Race, the first one held after her commissioning.

The Polish Academy of Sciences chartered her for the 1980-81 southern summer, as relief vessel for a Polish scientific station on King George Island in the South Shetlands, off Antarctica. On that voyage she also called at Port Stanley in the Falklands and in South Georgia.

In 1983-84 she sailed for the Polish "Class Afloat" project, on a long clockwise voyage around Africa, with a crossing of the Indian Ocean to Bombay and Colombo before heading for Cape Town via the Seychelles. The trainees on that voyage were school age Poles and a few adult Westerners supernumeraries.

252 From this angle, under full sail, the Pogoria offers a nice profile. Although the sails are filled she is at anchor and the current is pushing her backwards!

253 top The Pogoria has made many long transoceanic voyages and one circumnavigation. She has also sailed to Antarctica.

253 center The modern compass card is reduced to its rim. The wheel has a hydraulic transmission.

253 bottom The Pogoria is one of the world's largest purpose-built adventure sail training vessels.

From 1985 until 1991 she was chartered during the school months by the Canadian Class Afloat for a similar scheme with Canadian youngsters. In 1985-85 she made another circumnavigation of Africa. That voyage ended in Montreal and the Pogoria sailed back to Poland by way of the New York OpSail in July. The 1987-88 Class Afloat charter took her on a round-the-world voyage. Those charters ended when Class Afloat took delivery of its own barquentine, the Concordia, which was being built in Poland during those years.

In 1992-93 the Pogoria, needing a refit but short of funds, was the subject of multilateral negotiations involving the Polish Yachting Association, the Gdynia shipyard and municipality. They resulted in the Gdynia Sailing Foundation becoming part owner and operator, evolving in 1995 into the Sail Training Association Poland (STAP).

The Pogoria took part in the 1993 Tall Ships Race off Norway and in 1994 she sailed to the Great Lakes for a series of maritime festivals. From 1995 the Pogoria took part in Tall Ships Races every year, in the Mediterranean in 1996, winning the Cutty Sark Trophy in 1999.

VESSEL	POGORIA
LAUNCHED	1980
DESIGNER	Zygmunt Choren
BUILDER	Stocznia Gdanska im Lenina, Gdansk, Poland
OWNER	Sail Training Association Poland, Gdynia
FLAG	Poland
RIG	Barquentine
TYPE	Training ship
CONSTRUCTION	Steel
LENGTH EXTREME	46.80 m (153.5 ft.)
LENGTH HULL	42.00 m (137.8 ft.)
BEAM	8.00 m (26.2 ft.)
DRAFT	3.70 m (12.1 ft.)
TONNAGE	289 grt; 41 nrt
DISPLACEMENT	342 td
SAIL AREA	1.050 mq (11,302 sq. ft.)
ENGINE	310 hp Wola Warszawa
USAGE	Sail Training
COMPLEMENT	50: 10 officers (5 permanent, 5 volunteer) + 40 trainees

254 top left
The idiosyncratic bottle-
green sails of the
Alexander von Humboldt
are the corporate color
of the Becks Brewery, one
of the major sponsors
of the "Alex."

254 top right
The Alexander von
Humboldt is the smallest
training ship to have a
double wheel. Its threaded
worm screw gear is of the
same type as found, for
instance, on the Sørlandet.

254 bottom left In the Tall
Ships Races sail numbers,
used for identification, are
not mandatory for square
riggers as those are easy
to tell apart (except
sisterships…).

254 bottom right
The Alexander von
Humboldt has a very
conventional binnacle –
not in front of the wheel
(right) but at the front of
the poop deck.

The Alexander von Humboldt is a distinctively unusual sailing vessel, with her enormously long poop deck extending almost to the foremast, and her bottle-green sails. However any idea that this may have something to do with the fact that she was not originally a sailing ship, but is a converted light vessel, would be misplaced. The first light ships ever used were converted from old sailing vessels and their hull shapes were found to be ideal for riding out storms at anchor at sea, and, so, the same lines were used for later purpose-built light ships.

Thus, in a reversal of history, many former light vessels are excellent candidates for conversion to "tall ship" rigs, and many have been so converted.

The Alexander von Humboldt is one of those. Not only has she the lines of a sailing ship but they have a great pedigree: her designer was none other than Frederick Middendorf, the architect of many of the famous German Cape Horners including the legendary five-masted full-rigged ship Preussen of 1902. She was the first of a series of four sisterships built by Weserwerft Bremen (nowadays AG "Weser"). Her first name was Reserve Sonderburg, meaning that she was the standby light ship for the Sonderburg station (Today's Sonderborg in Denmark), available to replace other light ships of that station when they needed to come in for repairs or yard maintenance.

She was later renamed Reserve Fehmarnbelt and, in 1920, Reserve Holtenau, as she moved around stations mostly in the Baltic. In 1945 she acquired her own station and became the Kiel, replacing the previous light ship of that name which had been sunk by Allied bombs. In early 1957 she was rammed and sunk by a Swedish freighter but she

255 *The hull lines can be seen or, for the underwater body, guessed, and they are those of a sailing ship despite the hull having been built as a light vessel.*

Alexander von Humboldt

VESSEL	ALEXANDER VON HUMBOLDT
LAUNCHED	1906
CONVERTED	1988
DESIGNER	Frederick Middendorf (original); Manfred Hövener and Zygmunt Choren (conversion)
BUILDER	AG "Weser," Bremen, Germany
OWNER	Deutsche Stiftung Sail Training
FLAG	Germany
RIG	Barque
TYPE	Converted light ship
CONSTRUCTION	Steel
LENGTH EXTREME	62.55 m (205.2 ft.)
LENGTH HULL	53.00 m (173.9 ft.)
BEAM	8.02 M (26.3 FT.)
DRAFT	4.88 m (16.0 ft.)
TONNAGE	450 grt
DISPLACEMENT	800 T
SAIL AREA	1,010 mq (10.872 sq.ft.)
ENGINES	510 hp MAN
USAGE:	Sail Training
COMPLEMENT:	25 crew + 35 trainees

256 The long poop can be seen here. The shelter deck under its side does not run through to the same on the other side; the fore and after parts of the poop accommodation are connected.

257 top left The fine entrance of the hull can be seen on this picture.

257 bottom left A shadow theatre is played on the mainsail as trainees climb aloft.

257 top right The Alexander von Humboldt sets a main skysail above the topgallant. The brigantine in the background is the British-registered Eye of the Wind.

258-259 The unmistakable silhouette of the Alexander von Humboldt with her vast sail area captured at sunset.

was back on station in 1959 after 2 years repairs and modernizing. In mid-1967 she was replaced by a lighthouse and once again moved around stations, mainly in the North Sea, but now keeping the name of Kiel. She eventually took up the Amrumbank station in the German Bight. She was decommissioned in 1986 when her station was taken over by an automated light buoy. Laid up in Willhelmshaven, she suffered collision damage but was repaired before towed to Bremerhaven under the name of Confidentia.

The Bremerhaven-based Sail Training Association Germany (STAG) was wanting to convert the Confidentia to a sail training barque. Conversion plans were drawn by captain Manfred Hövener of STAG and these were checked and finalised by Zygmunt Choren, the polish naval architect who had designed the M108 "Dar Mloziezy"

class of full-riggers and the "Pogoria" class of barquentines.

Financial backing came primarily from the Bremen Beck brewery and Egon Harms, a Bremen ship owner and entrepreneur. A special foundation was created for the purpose of converting and operating the ship, the Deutsche Sftiftung Sail Training (DSST).

On 30 May 1988 the Confidentia was commissioned under the name of the German explorer, geographer and naturalist Alexander von Humboldt (1769-1859).

The distinctive green color of the hull and sails is the corporate color of the Beck Brewery. The barque has a traditional German-style double spanker. The yards however are of the modern fixed type favored by Zygmunt Choren, meaning they are not lowered down their relative mast sections when the sails are furled Only the main skysail yard has a halyard to hoist it when setting its sail.

The Alexander von Humboldt operates summer cruises in the North Sea and Baltic and is also a very regular participant in the Cutty Sark Tall Ships Races. She took part in the 1992 Columbus Grand Regatta (the transatlantic tall ships race commemorating the 500th anniversary of Colombus' first voyage) and in the winter of 1998-99 she sailed to the Caribbean and South America to commemorate the 200th anniversary of Alexander von Humboldt's voyage to those parts. In winter the barque normally cruises in the Canaries, predominantly with adult trainees.

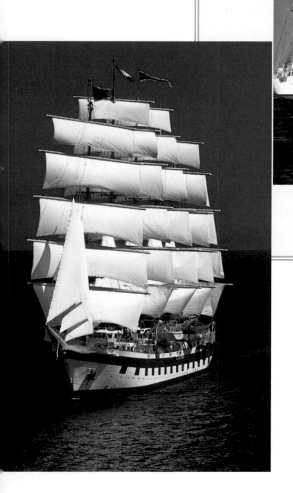

260 top left The Star
Clipper, here seen almost
head on with her sails set,
is operated by a company
from Monte Carlo. She was
built in the Langerbrugge
Shipyards of Ghent in
Belgium.

Cruise Ships

Once upon a time ships, those propelled by
sail, were profitable while still offering a
sense of adventure. This magical combination, capable
of attracting men of all stations far from dry land, no
longer exists. As Alan Villiers says, "beauty has
disappeared from the oceans."

In reality, moves are afoot to revive ancient
customs in this period, at the beginning of one
millennium, as if to deny the demands of progress.

Just as it appeared inevitable that even cruising,
that practice of leaving behind the noise and crowds
of the coasts, was assuming those same frenetic
rhythms, an ancient mode of transport, sail, is coming
to the fore once again as a response to a contemporary
fashion.

Whilst we could hardly talk about a wide-scale
phenomenon (they can in fact still be counted on the
fingers of two hands), there are increasing numbers of

sailing ships being launched or refitted for this
purpose.

They draw inspiration from the glorious ships of
the past, reviving and to a certain extent usurping
definitions such as clipper and windjammer, evoking
irreverent comparisons with legends such as the
Preussen or the Cutty Sark. They are actually a
commercial response to the demand for an alternative
to the perceived monotony of cruises organized
aboard motor ships, with the added alibi of the thrill
of navigation under sail.

Commercial as these enterprises are, there is
nothing romantic about them and no real links with
the past. Villiers is right, beauty has disappeared from
the oceans, and where there is profit there is usually a
distinct lack of adventure. Then again, I cannot see
why a tourist should accept to spend a single day on a
ship heeling at twenty degrees or with her spars

brushing the water as she rolls first left and then right
as she flies through the water at twelve knots. In this
day and age twelve knots is slow for a tourist while
twenty degrees is far, far too steep.

There are around ten vessels that can be classified
as sailing ships which today roam the seas if not the
oceans, in a kind of coastal cruising which takes in the
most popular tourist resorts around the globe.

To this end, shipping companies and lines have
been founded and public and private bodies have
financed the construction or the restoration of
individual ships. The former are dominated by the
major tour companies such as Club Mediterrenée and
Star Clippers; the former has launched the largest of
these vessels, while the latter has a fleet of three sailing
ships of over 300 feet or more. In the second case,
groups have been formed to reconstruct, more or less
faithfully (less rather than more if truth be told) ships

260 top right The Sea Cloud was built in the 1930s to the most exacting standards of luxury and with classic lines. A veteran of the South Seas, this sailing ship is unlikely to be pensioned off until 2010.

260-261 The Star Flyer, seen during a Caribbean cruise, can achieve a cruising speed of 15 knots with peaks of 20.

261 bottom The two large sailing ships Royal Clipper and Star Flyer launched by the same company (the Star Clippers) provide the greatest possible comfort to their passengers.

of the past, or private individuals have restored abandoned vessels such as the Sea Cloud, originally a private yacht, rigged as a bark with the name Hussar.

While this last example has the merit of having saved a relic of the 1930s, in other cases the enterprise has little to do with the history of sailing ships. If they are cited here it is because they are undeniably sailing ships and may be considered as valid promotional vehicles for this type of sailing and, if you like, the first hint of a building wave.

Sailing ships destined for cruising have had to adopt new forms. Most, in fact. apart from the naval vessels, were designed for the transportation of goods; the packets did carry passengers, but they were ships built for speed rather than comfort and while some cabins were truly luxurious, most passengers had to do with bunks in enormous, malodorous dormitories.

In contrast, a cruise ship sacrifices everything in

the name of its guests, guests rather than mere passengers as they are the vessel's very raison d'être. Thus, the hull of the modern day cruise ship resembles those of the great passenger liners rather the classic sailing ships. And when, as in the case of the Star Clippers, there is an undeniable echo of traditional forms, they nonetheless take into account the need to install comfortable cabins and thus have high sides and superstructures designed to house the guests' recreational activities.

As for the rigs of these ships, there again two distinct schools of thought. Given that the use of sails is always considered auxiliary to motorized propulsion if not merely for show and the ships navigate almost exclusively thanks to a "bilge wind" to the "iron topsail," some of them do replicate the square-rigged sail plans typical of the ships of past centuries.

The handling of the sails is, of course, now very different as everything is mechanized and requires no men aloft. While the overall effect may not be to the liking of sailing enthusiasts or historians, it satisfies those simply wishing to see a "sailing ship."

Other ships use rigs openly designed for this use, or rather non-use, and perhaps this is the more acceptable solution: sails that can be rolled on stays and rapidly and effortlessly set or furled according to the conditions or the aesthetic demands of the cruise.

I have seen a ship of this type set sail, so to speak, having entered roadstead and just before dropping anchor, and then calmly furl her full sail plan after having conceded to the onlookers the spectacle of hundreds of square feet of canvas, sadly drooping in the absence of wind that characterizes the evening hours in that sheltered bay.

It is difficult to explain the point of a complex, heavy and therefore expensive sail system on a ship that in any case navigates quite comfortably under the power of its engines alone. It would appear to be a relic of the oil crisis that had raised the hopes of sail enthusiasts were it not for the fact that the ship, a gigantic air-conditioned floating hotel, reveals very different forms of conspicuous consumption other than that demanded by propulsion.

Some of these ships nonetheless boast excellent sailing qualities. Apart from the Sea Cloud mentioned earlier, which was actually born as a sailing yacht, albeit one equipped with an auxiliary engine, and which as such had in the Thirties completed cruises and ocean crossings under sail, the Star Clippers themselves appear to provide respectable performance: a maximum speed under sail of fifteen knots is quoted, with peaks of no less than twenty. This would seem to me to be a little optimistic given that not even the best clippers, under full sail and with commanders willing to see spars fail and masts crack, were capable of similar speeds.

This apart, and it has to be said that these vessels were not built for outright speed, the cruise ships are all very large. They generally have hulls of over 300 feet in length, a dimension that represent the limit for many of the great windjammers. And they all, like almost every other ship built in the last hundred years, have steel hulls. While none of them will really provide the sense of adventure they appear to promise, they may well prove to be profitable.

Stad Amsterdam

The clipper ships of the period 1845-1869 were the most breathtakingly beautiful ships ever built, the apogee of the history of square-riggers. Only three clippers from that era are still in existence today and of those, only the Cutty Sark (1869) has been restored, as a static museum ship.

The town Council of Amsterdam and Randstad, the regional body representing the coastal provinces of the Netherlands, announced in March 1997 that they were joining forces for the building of a clipper ship, the first to be built for nearly 130 years. The ship was to be named Stad Amsterdam ("City of Amsterdam"). The justifications invoked were that the project would provide job experience and training for 150 unemployed and school leavers, that the public could view the progress as the ship was being built, and that the ship would remain a potent symbol for Randstad and Amsterdam.

The company Rederij Clipper Stad Amsterdam was established to manage the project and operate the ship. The clipper was to be used for youth sail training, to be entered in the Tall Ships Races, to run public day cruises and longer passenger cruises, to represent the city of Amsterdam at home and abroad, and to be made available for private quayside and sailing charters.

The initial inspiration for the design was the 1854 clipper Amsterdam, the first iron clipper to have been built in Amsterdam. The project however was not to build a replica but to build a new clipper that could have been designed in the 1860s. combining the best features of many famous clippers including the legendary Cutty Sark, Thermopylae, Flying Cloud and Lightning. The research, analysis and design were contracted to the Dutch naval architect Gerard Dijkstra of Ocean Sailing Development Holland BV.

The keel was laid at the NISTA shipyard, in North Amsterdam, on 16 December 1997. While the hull has very traditional lines, the building method was resolutely modern. Centraal Staal, in Groningen, used a computer-controlled cutting machine to cut the hull plates and frames. Steel elements of the hull and internal partitions were assembled by modules at the yard and the prefabricated modules were in turn assembled to build the ship.

The hull was floated out on 16 December 1998, a year to the day after building had begun. The sleek racy hull was towed two days later next to the Dutch national maritime museum. Rigging and fitting out were carried out there. The design and building of the Stad Amsterdam did not go unnoticed – in 1999 the Brazilian Navy contracted NISTA for a sistership. She had to be finished in time for the Brazilian Quincentenary early summer 2000, meaning she would be commissioned before the Stad Amsterdam. To avoid a "spoiler," the Rederij Stad Amsterdam requested that the Brazilian clipper be not painted black (the color of Stad Amsterdam), and not make a public appearance in Amsterdam before her departure. The color restriction was no problem as the Brazilians had decided to call their ship Cisne Branco ("White Swan"), and they left Amsterdam discreetly for Lisbon in time for the cruise in company to Brazil with Sagres in April 2000. After the commemorations in Brazil the Cisne Branco sailed north to join OpSail 2000.

The Stad Amsterdam made her sailing trials in June 2000. Her first appearance in tall ship events was in July in France, at Brest and nearby Douarnenez. She naturally was the star at Sail 2000 Amsterdam in August. Later she took part in Sail Bremerhaven and Expo Wilhelmshaven. In October she set sail for Recife and Rio and then sailed north for a winter passenger season in the West Indies. She sailed back to Amsterdam by way of Halifax in May 2001 and took part with young trainees in the 2001 Cutty Sark Tall Ships Race Antwerp - Ålesund - Bergen - Esbjerg.

266-267 The deck arrangement, apart from the lack of cargo hatches, is traditional. No "hangars" and "control towers!" Pity about the two big motor-launches-cum-lifeboats necessary for the passenger trade.

VESSEL	STAD AMSTERDAM		
LAUNCHED	1998 (put in service in 2000)	BEAM	10.50 m (34.4 ft.)
DESIGNER	Gerard Dijkstra, Ocean Sailing Development Holland BV	DRAFT	4.80 m (15.7 ft.)
		TONNAGE	698 grt
		DISPLACEMENT	1,036 td
BUILDER	Damen Orangewerft at the NISTA shipyard, Amsterdam	SAIL AREA	2,200 mq (23,680 sq.ft.) - with stunsails
OWNER	Rederij Clipper Stad Amsterdam	ENGINES	1,014 hp Caterpillar + bow thruster
		USAGE	Sail training, passenger cruises, day trips, promotions, charter
FLAG	The Netherlands		
RIG	Full-rigged ship	COMPLEMENT	Crew: 14-25; 36-72 trainees
TYPE	Clipper		or passengers (in 18 cabins)
CONSTRUCTION	Steel		125 passengers on day trips,
LENGTH EXTREME	78.00 m (255.9 ft.)		300 guests at quayside receptions.
LENGTH HULL	60.50 m (198.5 ft.)		

266 bottom left
Impeccably furled sails,
yards braced square,
seamen working with
competence and confidence
aloft, the Stad Amsterdam
is a proud ship.

266 bottom right
The main saloon, below
deck, is airy and spacious.
The rope overhead is
a handhold for use
in heavy seas.

267 top right True to her
inspiration, the Stad
Amsterdam has a lofty and
well proportioned rig, and
sets a big sail area even
without the stun'sails.

267 center right
The passenger cabins are
to excellent modern
standards of comfort
except for size, the price
paid for not covering the
deck in deckhouses.

268 This ultimate yacht is a cross between a clipper and a Cape Horn nitrate carrier. Her rig is lofty and includes a main skysail.

269 top left
Marjorie Merriweather Post (1887-1973), heir to the Post cereal fortune, was a keen appreciator of fine arts and the original owner of the Sea Cloud.

269 center left
Caulking the seams is done by forcing oakum into the seams with chisel and mallet, and then laying a bead of pitch or, nowadays, a synthetic equivalent.

269 bottom left
Each of these two propellers is driven by two 1,500 hp diesel engines providing excellent speed under power as well as under sail.

269 right The long counter stern, unlike the usual elliptical sterns of most steel merchant ships and barques, is part of Sea Cloud's yacht pedigree.

Sea Cloud

The Sea Cloud was built as a sailing yacht – the biggest and most luxurious ever. She was named Hussar II and her hull was painted black, and she was the wedding present of the New York financier Edward F. Hutton to his bride Marjorie Merriweather Post.

The owners two suites (his and hers), and the eleven guest suites, are panelled in woods of exquisite grain, each suite with a different wood and furnished in different style, all with refined furniture and fittings. The en-suite bathrooms have Carrara marble bathtubs and solid-gold taps. The dining saloon, on deck, is like a Medieval banqueting hall; the adjoining library is furnished in the style of English stately home.

From 1932 to 1935 the Huttons enjoyed the yacht on many long cruises to the West Indies, the Galapagos, Tahiti, Hawaii, Alaska, and other such destinations. Their guests included heads of state, royalty, film stars and tycoons.

The couple divorced in 1935. Marjorie kept the yacht but Hutton, who had owned other yachts named Hussar, kept the name. The yacht was renamed Sea Cloud and was painted white. Marjorie Post remarried the same year. Her new husband, Joseph E. Davies, was a politician and a diplomat. They spent their honeymoon on the Sea Cloud. In 1937 Davies was posted ambassador to Moscow and Marjorie followed him with the yacht, berthing it in Leningrad. Joseph Stalin strictly forbade any Soviet national from going aboard.

In 1942 Marjorie Post made the Sea Cloud available to the US Navy. The barque was unrigged; the hull was painted naval grey, and twenty-four guns were mounted on deck. Manned by a crew of 300 sailors, she cruised in the Western Atlantic as an anti-submarine patrol ship and a weather ship.

The Sea Cloud was returned to her owner in 1944

270 top The triangular mizzen course is unusual but was found on some merchantmen. Sheet and tack being a single line, it is easy to brace around.

270 center The taps in the bathrooms of the original owners and guest cabins are solid gold. No detail on the ship was "off the shelf."

270-271 The Sea Cloud has a rakish clipper bow and one feels the whole barque is about to take off and soar behind the eagle figurehead.

271 bottom left No. 1 cabin was Marjorie Post's own suite, the largest and most luxurious. The Carrara marble fireplace is for decoration only: there is no flue.

271 bottom right The original dining saloon and library, in the main deckhouse, are now both used as dining saloons retaining the original decor.

VESSEL	SEA CLOUD		
LAUNCHED	1931	BEAM	14.94 m (49.0 ft.)
DESIGNER	Gibbs & Cox, New York	DRAFT	5.13 m (16.8 ft.)
		TONNAGE	2,532 grt
BUILDER	Germania Werft, Kiel, Germany	DISPLACEMENT	3,075 td
		SAIL AREA	3,160 mq
OWNER	Hansa Treuhand AG, Hamburg, Germany		(34,014 sq. ft.)
		ENGINES	4 x 1,500 hp
FLAG	Malta		Enterprise;
RIG	Four-masted barque		twin propellers
TYPE	Yacht	USAGE	Holiday cruises
CONSTRUCTION	Steel	COMPLEMENT	129: 60 crew +
LENGTH EXTREME	109.50 m (359.3 ft.)		69 passengers
LENGTH HULL	96.29 m (315.9 ft)		

and was back to a white-hulled four-masted barque in 1947. She was sold in 1952 to the Dominican dictator Rafael Trujillo who renamed her Angelita, after his daughter. His playboy son Ramfis took the yacht with him to Santa Monica when he went to follow law studies in California. Following Trujillo's assassination in 1961, his exiled family sold the yacht to Sea Cruises Inc., a Panamanian corporation representing a Mr. John Blue from Florida. Renamed Patria, the ship was overhauled in 1967-68. The following year she was sold to Antarna Inc. and renamed Antarna, still under Panamanian registry. She was refitted for charter work and was chartered a short while to Oceanics, an American school-at-sea venture.

The Antarna was laid-up in Panama from 1974 until 1978 when she was sold to a German consortium. They renamed her Sea Cloud once more and took her to Hamburg for a complete refit and conversion to a luxury cruise vessel. A new deckhouse was built abaft the mizzenmast with 14 passenger cabins, and another 8 cabins were built in a new superstructure above the midship deckhouse, providing a total of 69 passenger berths with the original thirteen suites below the main deck. Those original cabins, along with the deck saloons, had amazingly survived in their original splendor.

Since 1979 the Sea Cloud offers unmatchable style holiday cruises in the Mediterranean in summer and in the West Indies in winter. She was first registered in the Cayman Islands and then in Malta. In 1994 she was sold to the Hansa Treuhand AG shipping company of Hamburg which continues to operate her likewise. That company has had a new ship, the Sea Cloud II, launched in Spain in February 2001.

This ship is 7.3 m (24 ft.) longer than Sea Cloud but rigged as a three-masted barque, and has a 96-passenger capacity. She will be operating in parallel to the Sea Cloud but not for many years as the old Sea Cloud will have to be retired by 2010 when new safety regulations will prohibit the presence of any wood in the accommodation of passenger ships.

Star Clipper and Star Flyer

272-273 *The Star Flyer under full sail. The square sails are hydraulically rolled up like blinds into the yards and there is no need to go aloft.*

272 bottom left *Only the wood paneling, skylights and portholes differentiate this cabin from a luxury hotel suite.*

*272 bottom right
The portholes and the big
skylight that provide light
to the Piano Bar on the
barquentines are the sides
and floor of the sun deck
swimming pool.*

*273 top right When
sailing, the Star Flyer
causes very little
turbulence in the water, a
sign of a hull well designed
for a good turn of speed.*

*273 top left The interiors
of the "Star" barquentines
are lavishly decorated
with mural paintings
in trompe-l'œil.*

*273 bottom A rare
picture of the Flying
Clipper and Star Clipper
sailing together - they
usually operate far apart
from one another.*

Star Clippers Ltd. and its three ships are the brainchildren of Mikael Krafft, a Swedish businessman and yachtsman with a love of clippers and tall ships since childhood. Those ships have sail plans that would look familiar to the sailors of old but they make full use of modern materials and technology: stainless steel for the rigging, steel masts built as a single piece, fixed yards, terylene for the sails, square sails that roll up like blinds inside the yards and all the sail handling being powered and controlled from the deck. The Star Clippers are also fitted with anti-roll and anti-heel tanks for the comfort of passengers.

The Star Flyer is the first of the Star Clippers. Delivered in May 1991, she was followed ten months later her sistership, the Star Clipper. Those barquentines can reach 17 knots under sail and only require 10 deckhands.

They have four full-length decks but their length is such that the hulls remain sleek-looking, and they do not have obtrusive superstructures. The galley, storerooms and crew quarters are on the lower deck. There are 81 passenger cabins on the next two decks and a dining saloon with seating for all passengers on the third deck. The main deck has a Piano Bar, a library, an outdoor Tropical Bar and six staterooms The sun deck, above the piano bar and staterooms

has a swimming pool with a transparent bottom that forms the ceiling of the piano bar below. There are another two staterooms and another swimming pool on the poop deck.

The barquentines operate seven-day cruises with alternating itineraries "A" and "B." The Star Flyer sails in summer from Piraeus, Greece, and in winter from Phuket, Thailand. The Star Clipper sails in summer from Civitavecchia, Italy, and in winter from St Maarten in the West Indies. The ocean passages between the summer and winter stations are naturally also marketed.

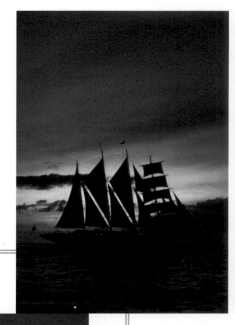

274 top left A square-rigged mast with conspicuously few facilities for climbing and working aloft: the rig is reliably controlled from the deck.

274 bottom left A "modern" variant to dressing a ship over all with flags is stringing up lights as on a Christmas tree. The yards are likewise decorated.

274 right The staysail and trysail sail-plan set between the three after masts is much easier to control than the huge gaff sails that would otherwise fill those spaces.

275 Although far removed from the last cargo-carrying sailing ships, the Star Flyer and Star Clipper are bona fide sailing ships and bona fide merchant navy vessels.

VESSELS	STAR CLIPPER AND STAR FLYER		
LAUNCHED	1991 (commissioned 1991 and 1992)	TYPE	Sailiner
		CONSTRUCTION	Steel
DESIGNERS	Robert MacFarlane, UK (hull), Olivier van der Meer, NL (rig), Studio Acht, NL (interior).	LENGTH EXTREME	108.80 m (357.0 ft.)
		LENGTH HULL	91.40 m (300.0 ft.)
		BEAM	14.60 m (48.0 ft.)
		DRAFT	5.60 m (18.5 ft.)
		TONNAGE	2,298 grt; 869 nrt
BUILDER	Langerbrugge Shipyards, Ghent, Belgium	DISPLACEMENT	2,018 t (light); 2,556 t (load)
		SAIL AREA	3,340 mq (36,000 sq. ft.)
OWNER	Star Clippers Ltd., Monaco		
		ENGINE	1,600 hp Caterpillar
FLAG	Luxembourg (Homeport: Antwerp, Belgium)	USAGE	Holiday cruises
		COMPLEMENT	254: 58 crew + 180-196 passengers
RIG	Four-masted staysail barquentines		

277 top As on more
conventional cruise liners,
there are plenty of launches
to ferry passenger to and
from the shore.

277 bottom
This bar saloon, if ashore,
would have a nautical
flavor. On the Royal

Clipper it feels like it may
be ashore – the ship's
stabilizers ensure there is
very little heel and motion.

VESSEL	ROYAL CLIPPER
COMPLETED	2000
DESIGNER	Robert MacFarlane, UK (hull conversion); Donald Starkey, UK (interior)
BUILDERS	Stocznia Gdanska, Poland (hull); Merwede yard near Rotterdam, The Netherlands (completion)
OWNER	Star Clippers Ltd. (Monaco)
FLAG	Luxembourg (Homeport: Antwerp, Belgium)
RIG	Five-masted full-rigged ship
TYPE	Sailiner
CONSTRUCTION	Steel
LENGTH EXTREME	133.8 m (439.0 ft.)
LENGTH HULL	120.40 m (393.8 ft.)
BEAM	16.46 ft. (54.0 ft.)
DRAFT	5.64 m (18.5 ft.)
TONNAGE	5,000 grt
DISPLACEMENT	-
SAIL AREA	5.050 mq (54,360 sq. ft.)
ENGINES	2 x 2,500 hp Caterpillar; 500 hp bow thruster
USAGE	Holiday cruises
COMPLEMENT	328: 100 crew + 228 passengers

276-277 The Royal
Clipper is only the second
five-masted full-rigger
to have been ever built.
The first was the Preussen
(1902-10) where the deck
awash with water in Cape
Horn snorters provided
another sort of swimming
pool.

276 bottom left
The figurehead of the
Royal Clipper looks
confidently towards the
21st century – square sail
will never loose its appeal.

276 bottom right The
dining saloon on the Royal
Clipper is modern in a way
that suggests tradition.

Royal Clipper

278-279
When the Padua, now the Kruzenstern, was launched in 1926, people thought no more commercially operated merchant square riggers would be built after her. Yet, at the dawn of the 21st century...

The Royal Clipper, the third ship of the fleet is the biggest square-rigger in existence, exceeding the Sedov's hull length by 11 m (36 ft.). She is only the second five-masted full-rigged ship ever built, the first one being the legendary Preussen (1902-1910) of the Laeisz "Flying P" line of Hamburg. The Preussen, the biggest sailing vessel ever built, is very much the inspiration for the present ship, although the latter is not a replica and is shorter by the length of her bowsprit.

The hull was built at the Gdansk Shipyard. It was an abandoned building project for a cruise liner acquired by Star Clippers in 1998 and lengthened on site before being towed to Holland for completion and fitting out. The maiden passenger cruise departed from Cannes on 22 July 2000.

The Royal Clipper carries a staggering suite of 42 sails, of which 26 are square. All the know-how and experience acquired with the barquentines were brought to bear in this new project. The Preussen was sailed by 60 seaman while only 20 are required on the Royal Clipper; the rest of the crew being the officers and hotel staff. The ship can reach 20 knots under sail and 13 knots under power

Inside the hull there is a three-deck-tall atrium the ceiling of which is the transparent bottom of the largest of the ship's three swimming pools. There are 2 owners' suites, 14 deluxe deck suites, each with private verandah, 2 deluxe deck cabins and 96 double cabins. All cabins have an en-suite marble bathroom. TV, radio, satellite telephone, a safe and individually adjustable air conditioning. There are teak benches on the tops where passengers able to climb up to them can have drinks hoisted up to them.

The Royal Clipper operates seven-day cruises, with alternating itineraries "A" and "B," out of Cannes, France, in summer, and out of Barbados, West Indies, in winter.

Replicas

A stela from the 7th-6th century before Christ discovered in the countryside of central Italy carries engraved images of three war ships, presumably Roman or Greek, with the square sail, ram and long rostrum typical of the vessels of the era. That stela remained neglected in a small museum for decades until it fell under the gaze of an enthusiast of naval history. This same enthusiast then laboriously collected sponsorship and donations sufficient to begin the reconstruction of a ship on the basis of those faint ancient traces. Today the rebuilding of a war ship fourth century BC is taking place. It is difficult to say quite what the significance of such operations may be. Certainly, a faithful reconstruction in terms of both materials and methods of construction would have the great merit of verifying and therefore proving or disproving, the hypotheses regarding ancient shipbuilding which in the absence of reliable documentary absence are otherwise destined to remain such. It would also have the merit of making real what has previously only been imagined.

This is the theory. In practice such operations, not only the one mentioned above, are impossible for a series of motives. First and foremost, the lack of precise visual sources indicating true scale and detail inevitably makes these reconstructions the product of the imagination. Moreover, in the absence of design drawings (remember that it was not until the second half of the 19th century that ships began to be built on the basis of drawings!) the realization of individual

is a task without any real logic as it is impossible to build a "true" replica.

It would be appropriate at this point to make certain distinctions. Reconstructing the Roman ships of Nemi, the remains of one of which was salvaged but then destroyed in a fire after a detailed survey had been carried out, represents a perfectly legitimate and praiseworthy project. Creating a reconstruction that is based solely on one's imagination, putting forward the "impossibility" of finding materials identical to those originally employed as an excuse, is fanciful and lacking in historical or scientific justification.

More in general, there is no legitimacy in reconstructing those ships for which there is insufficient information, as in the case of the ship of the stela. Neither is there any motive for building a replica of a type of ship that has survived to the present day. We have the Victory, so why build another ship of the line? It would, instead, be interesting to reconstruct one of ships used by Columbus, but despite a number of so-called replicas, generally built as film props and then promoted as tourist attractions, the task would be difficult because of the unreliability of the available technical information. It would also appear to make more sense to restore that historical patrimony still afloat around the world: the hulks of windjammers or carriers abandoned in the extreme southern latitudes, the few brigs or schooners that, after decades spent on charter work, are rotting away in South American or Central African estuaries.

Lastly, constructing a replica is justifiable where a tradition exists and there is a memory to be honored.

elements and their assembly can at best be interpreted or defined by analogy. Lastly, and this is a crucial aspect, the materials we presume or know the original shipbuilders used are either no longer available or difficult to find.

In the case of the ship depicted on the Italian stela, for example, it is known that the connections between the various planking elements depended on broom fiber cords, something that can no longer be produced.

All this would seem to suggest that the construction of something that no longer exists

280 bottom left The replica of the Kalmar Nyckel, a three-masted pinnace from 1637, 88 feet 6 inches LOA, which once transported Swedish, Finnish and Dutch colonists to the New World. She was reconstructed in 1986 by a foundation constituted by the citizens of Wilmington (USA).

280 bottom right This photograph shows the reconstruction of James Cook's ship. Less than 83 feet long overall, the Endeavour carried the English explorer around the world, by way of Cape Horn and the Cape of Good Hope.

280-281 The Rose is one of the many sailing ships built in the United States as replicas of models with historical significant to the nation. The Rose in fact is based on the design of the early American frigates which still revealed the influence of the original French or English model.

In many countries, in fact, the maritime traditions have been kept alive through the reconstruction of those ships that were particularly significant in the past.

The reconstructed Matthew, the caravel with which John Cabot completed the first exploration of the American coasts of the North Atlantic at the end of the 15th century, has now sailed from England to Canada. The Elizabeth II, the ship aboard which Sir Walter Raleigh sailed along the coast of North Carolina to found new colonies in the following century has recently been rebuilt. The Swedes, for their part, have built a replica of the Kalmar Nyckel, a pinnace from the middle of the seventeenth century that carried many colonists from the Scandinavian peninsula to the New World. Apart from the rich heritage conserved in the various maritime museums in the USA, ships typical of the American coasts have been reconstructed such as the revenue schooner, Sultana.

Today, these replicas, cited purely as examples of the breed, continue to sail, albeit with certain technical and economic difficulties, carrying with them their historical message and testifying, above all, to the irreducible will of those who carried the reconstruction through.

There is no question that we will never have the opportunity of seeing an authentic Roman cargo vessel under sail, nor a Hanseatic cog or a galleon for that matter. And perhaps it is only right and proper that the long gone eras of sail are cloaked in the misty patina of history. Leaving aside the most remote of times, why rebuild a sailing ship of the sixteenth century, just to experience its poor handling qualities? We are already well aware of them and have been left testimony to the infinite and tragic problems they caused in detailed reports. Nothing would be added to what we already know. Nor would such an operation make any contribution to the preservation of the practice of sailing.

Surely it would be better to concentrate our efforts on saving what is still sailing, on allowing ever more sailors to experience the sailing ships that still today participate in regattas races and cruises. on seeking out and publishing the original sources and information relating to the history of the great era of sail.

282 top The launching of the celebrated original Bluenose at Lunenburg, Nova Scotia, on 26 March 1921. She was of the same breed as the fishing schooners at anchor, just a little faster.

282 center In the last Trophy race, in 1938, Bluenose's most serious rival, the Gertrude L. Thebaud, leads her in this picture but not for long. The Bluenose raced to victory once more.

282 bottom The crew of the Bluenose with the trophies they won in the 1935 series of the International Fisherman's Trophy.

282-283 One can feel the rigging vibrating under the the huge press of sail as the racing Bluenose is spurred along by her crew of 29 sea-hardened fishermen.

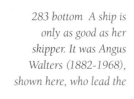

283 bottom A ship is only as good as her skipper. It was Angus Walters (1882-1968), shown here, who lead the

Bluenose to an uninterrupted series of wins from her maiden race in 1921 to the last Schooner Race in 1938.

The Bluenose II is the exact replica of the legendary Grand Banks fishing and racing schooner Bluenose that adorns the Canadian 10-cent coins.

The fisherman of the Canadian Maritime Provinces and of New England had evolved such fast and seaworthy schooners to withstand the sometimes-horrendous seas and winds found on the Grand Banks and to bring their catches to port as quickly as possible.

It was with scornful amusement that those hardy salts watched the vast fortunes being spent on the delicate toys built for the America's Cup. When in 1920 an America's Cup race was postponed because of a mere 23 knots of wind, a Halifax newspaper put up the International Fisherman's Trophy and substantial prize money for a race between real sail carriers, pitting the Canadian fishing schooners against their American counterparts. As with the America's Cup races, there were elimination races to select the finalists, one from each country. The Esperanto of Gloucester, Massachusetts, won the Trophy on 1 November 1920, over the Delawana of Lunenburg, Nova Scotia.

The race became a yearly challenge. With national pride at stake, sponsorship money moved in, but the rules were not relaxed: the crews had to be fishermen and the schooners had to fish commercially before being allowed to contend.

The Bluenose was one such schooner built with the Trophy in mind, her masts somewhat taller and her keel somewhat deeper than on ordinary fishing schooners. Her name derives from Nova Scotians

Bluenose II

being called "Bluenoses" because of the cold damp climate of their province. The Bluenose, designed by William Roué, was skippered until sold abroad by the redoubtable Angus Walters. She was launched in March 1921 and on her maiden fishing trip three weeks later, she landed the biggest catch of the fleet. On 21 October she raced the American Elsie and won the Trophy. Despite determined challenges in the

ensuing years, she never let go of it. Even the splendid Gertrude L. Thebaud was unable to wrest it from her in the 1938 contest. Sadly that was the last challenge, as the war and changing economic and technological conditions put an end to the fishing schooner era.

In 1942 the Bluenose was sold a West Indian company for inter-island trading. She was wrecked on a reef off Haiti on 29 January 1946.

The Bluenose II was built in 1963 for the Halifax brewery Oland & Son Ltd. She is an exact replica of the original, built at the same yard which still employed some of the shipwrights and riggers who had built the original. Among the very few

concessions to modern times, hydraulics for raising the anchor and hoisting the sails, to enable the schooner to be sailed by a crew of 14 instead of the original 29, and auxiliary engines.

After eight years in the charter trade, the Bluenose II was sold in 1971 by the Oland family for $1 to the Government of Nova Scotia which now operates the schooner through the Bluenose II Preservation Trust, a non-profit organization. She sails to other Canadian Provinces, and to ports on the US East Coast, to promote Nova Scotia tourism and business. She also takes part in tall ship gatherings such as the Canadian Windjammer Rally of 1974, the US East Coast OpSails

of '76, '86 and 2000, and Quebec in '84. In '92 she sailed to Toronto for 125th anniversary of the Canadian Confederation and, of course, she was present at the start of the Halifax-Amsterdam race leg of Tall Ships 2000. However she never takes part in any organized or informal racing, out of deference for the mystical reputation of the original Bluenose.

In summer and when in her homeport of Halifax, she operates three two-hour trips a day with up to 80 passengers on deck. She carries a crew of six professionals, master, engineer, three mates and a cook, and twelve young deck hands signed on for the season.

284 top left All the blocks for the Bluenose II were made in Lunenburg, a small harbor town where traditional sea crafts remain practiced to the present day.

284 top right Every detail on the deck of the Bluenose II conforms to the original. The boat with a blue cover is a traditional fishing dory.

284 bottom A slip in the replication: the sails sails are made of Dacron. Longer lasting and not as heavy as cotton or flax, and the Bluenose II sails short-handed.

284-285 The Bluenose II sailing in a breeze without her topsails. Look at the size of the main boom! That mainsail develops many hundreds of horsepower when filled by a good wind.

285 bottom left This photo could be of the original Bluenose in 1921, but it is actually one of the Bluenose II in 1963. Some of the 1921 chippies also worked on the 1963 construction.

285 bottom right The launching of the Bluenose II on 24 July 1963. Same place, but not the same time: the fishing schooners have gone…

VESSEL	BLUENOSE II
LAUNCHED	1963
DESIGNER	William Roué
BUILDER	Smith & Rhuland, Lunenburg, NS, Canada
OWNER	Government of Nova Scotia
FLAG	Canada
RIG	Schooner
TYPE	Grand Banks fishing schooner
CONSTRUCTION	Wood
LENGTH EXTREME	48.92 m (160.5 ft.)
LENGTH HULL	43.58 m (143 ft.)
BEAM	8.23 m (27 ft.)
DRAFT	4.82 m (15.8 ft.)
TONNAGE	191 grt
DISPLACEMENT	285 T
SAIL AREA	1,170 mq
ENGINES	2 x 250 hp Caterpillar
USAGE	Day trips and State of Nova Scotia PR
COMPLEMENT	18 crew + 80 deck passengers

286 Søren Larsen started life in 1949 as one of the last trading schooners. Laid up to die in 1972, she was resurrected in a time warp in 1979.

287 top left This photo, taken in 1948, immortalizes the men working in the Søren Larsen yard, posing on the skeleton of hull.

287 center left The original rig was already somewhat vestigial; had the Søren Larsen been built ten years earlier that she would have been given a proper rig.

287 bottom left Reborn as a late 19th century brigantine, the only anachronisms on this picture are the engine controls (foreground), the liferafts and the exhaust pipe (right).

287 right This brigantine knows the South Pacific inside out and has sailed twice around the world, once by way of Cape Horn.

Søren Larsen

The Søren Larsen began life as a trading schooner, one of the last to be built. She plied the Baltic and North Sea with general cargo, timber and grain. However, as for other European trading schooners, her rig was soon cut down and entirely replaced by the engine. She kept on plying her trade as a motor coaster until laid up in 1972. She was facing oblivion in 1978 when she was found and bought in Denmark by the English brothers Robin and Anthony Davies. They had already restored and operated other Baltic traders including a ketch and a three-masted topsail schooner, the Esther Lohse. As the Esther Lohse before her, the newly-rigged Søren Larsen found employment as a star in the popular 1970s British television series The Onedin Line, about James Onedin, a fictional captain and ship owner in the latter days of sail. Other film work followed, including The French Lieutenant's Woman, The Count of Monte Cristo and Shackleton – the latter movie took the Søren Larsen to Greenland, into the pack ice (but she did not get trapped as Shackleton's Endurance). In 1982-85 she was chartered by the British Jubilee Sailing Trust to run sail training pilot programs for people with physical disabilities, ahead of the construction of the Trust's purpose-built barque Lord Nelson (launched in 1985 and complemented since 2000 by a new barque, the Tenacious). In 1987, under the command of Anthony Davies and with his wife and baby aboard, she was one of a number of square riggers chartered for Australia's bicentennial First Fleet Re-enactment which sailed from Portsmouth that year to arrive in Sydney on Australia Day 200, 26 January 1888, the anniversary of the landing of the First Fleet in Botany Bay.

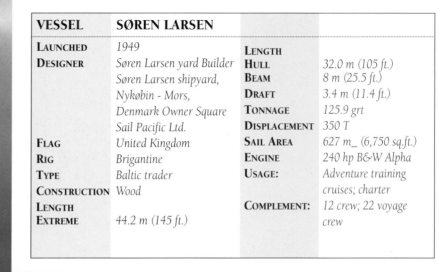

VESSEL	SØREN LARSEN		
LAUNCHED	*1949*	**LENGTH**	
DESIGNER	*Søren Larsen yard Builder*	**HULL**	*32.0 m (105 ft.)*
	Søren Larsen shipyard,	**BEAM**	*8 m (25.5 ft.)*
	Nykøbin - Mors,	**DRAFT**	*3.4 m (11.4 ft.)*
	Denmark Owner Square	**TONNAGE**	*125.9 grt*
	Sail Pacific Ltd.	**DISPLACEMENT**	*350 T*
FLAG	*United Kingdom*	**SAIL AREA**	*627 m_ (6,750 sq.ft.)*
RIG	*Brigantine*	**ENGINE**	*240 hp B&W Alpha*
TYPE	*Baltic trader*	**USAGE:**	*Adventure training*
CONSTRUCTION	*Wood*		*cruises; charter*
LENGTH		**COMPLEMENT:**	*12 crew; 22 voyage*
EXTREME	*44.2 m (145 ft.)*		*crew*

During the voyage difficulties between the Fleet organizers and the master of the fleet's flagship, a replica of the Bounty, lead to the Søren Larsen being designated as the flagship.

The brigantine remained in Australia after the winding up of the First Fleet, and sailed to New Zealand for the first time in 1989. She was based there until 1991, running adventure sailing cruises to remote islands across Polynesia and Melanesia. It was at that time that Anthony Davies became sole owner, giving in exchange to his brother Robin his shares in the jointly-owned barque Kaskelot and his unrestored former three-masted trading schooner Orion (now sailing in Robin Davies' Square Sail fleet as the barque Earl of Pembroke, along with the Kaskelot and the brig Phoenix – Robin Davies is a present-day real James Onedin).

In 1991 the Søren Larsen sailed from New Zealand in company with another British brigantine, the Eye of the Wind. They were the first British square riggers to sail around Cape Horn since 1936. Their destination was Cadiz, in Spain, to take part in the 1992 Columbus Grand Regatta, the tall ships race marking the 500th anniversary of the official discovery of the New World. That race via Bermuda and New York, ended in Liverpool. The Søren Larsen won in her class, a fitting completion of her first circumnavigation. The brigantine then underwent a major refit in England but the South Seas had become her home waters and she sailed back to New Zealand in 1993 via the West Indies, Panama and the Galapagos. From 1994 to 2000 she operated (Austral) summer cruises in New Zealand

waters (which are fabulous) and winter adventure training voyages to the enchanted islands of Polynesia and Melanesia. In 2000 the Søren Larsen sailed to Charleston and Boston via Panama to take part in the Boston-Halifax and Halifax-Amsterdam legs of the Tall Ships 2000 race. She was back in Britain from September to November when she once again headed south, back towards New Zealand via the Canaries, West Indies and Panama. She earns her keep, is beautifully maintained and does real deep-sea sailing – what more could a former trading schooner, already obsolete when built, ask for?

288 top left Running with the wind dead astern under square sails alone: the mainsail would be in danger of gybing; the main staysails useless and the headsails blanketed.

288 top right A plunging view from the crosstrees. The Søren Larsen's rig is sturdy, workmanlike and seaworthy.

288 center The former cargo hold has two-berth cabins along the sides and a congenial saloon in the center. The comfort is basic but luxurious by 19th century standards.

288 bottom left Passengers pay for the privilege of working as crew – going aloft, steering, hoisting sails, scrubbing the decks and galley pots...

289 A tradewind passage anywhere and any time – 1890s or 1990s... The Søren Larsen sails mostly among the Polynesian and Melanesian islands.

In 1577-80, fifty-eight years after Magellan's expedition, Francis Drake (c. 1540 -1596) led the second voyage around the world, a voyage of commercial exploration, trade and state-sponsored piracy. His flagship on that voyage was a galleon named Pelican, which he renamed Golden Hinde to flatter one of his sponsors whose coat of arms included a golden hind, the spelling "hinde" being Drake's. The Golden Hinde was the only ship to complete the voyage out of the five that had set out. Interestingly, after her historic voyage she was preserved as a national monument, just as Magellan's and Elcano's Victoria had been before her, but neither of those early museum ships survived for long the ravages of time.

On his round-the-world voyage Drake was the first European to set foot on a land he named Nova Albion, at a place most historians believe to be the Bay of San Francisco in California.

Thus the Crowley Maritime Corporation of San Francisco had a replica of the Golden Hinde built in 1973 for educational purposes. "Replica" is used loosely here, for unlike the Bluenose replica, there are no plans of the original. They never existed; ships in those days were built by eye, using certain empirical proportions such as beam

Golden Hinde

290 top left This replica of the Elizabethan galleon Golden Hinde has a typical stern gallery that is still found today in the Amerigo Vespucci.

290 center right Sir Francis Drake (c. 1540 - 1596), a national hero in England and a common pirate to the Spaniards, was the epitome of the Elizabethan adventurers.

290 bottom Superseding the lumbering carracks around 1550, the 16th century galleons were the direct ancestors of later ships-of-the-line and frigates.

291 Like her prototype, the modern Golden Hinde has sailed around the world. Note the square spritsail and the absence of staysails.

292 Differences with modern square rigs include fore-topsail braces leading to the main-topmast stay and the futtock shrouds (under the edges of the top) fixed to the lower-mast shrouds.

293 left The master's cabin under the poop deck, is quite cosy. In Drake's day, deckhands had neither hammocks nor bunks; they slept where they could.

293 top right The platforms at the foot of the topmasts, known as tops, were circular until well into the 18th century. On later ships they are D-shaped.

293 bottom right One of two posts in the bows used for making fast the anchor cable or mooring lines. They are known as knightheads even when not sculpted.

294-295 The Golden Hinde and galleons of the period she represents have very poor windward performances but sail well with winds abaft the beam.

VESSEL	GOLDEN HINDE
LAUNCHED	1973
DESIGNER	Loring Christian Norgaard, California
BUILDER	J. Hinks & Sons, Appledore, Devon, England
OWNER	Golden Hinde Ltd.
FLAG	United Kingdom
RIG	Barque
TYPE	Galleon
CONSTRUCTION	Wood
LENGTH EXTREME	36.50 m (120 ft.)
LENGTH ON DECK	31.10 m (102 ft.)
BEAM	7.00 m (23 ft.)
DRAFT	4.00 m (13 ft.)
TONNAGE	156 grt; 96 nrt
DISPLACEMENT	290 td
SAIL AREA	386 mq (4,150 sq. ft.)
ENGINE	295 hp Cummins
USAGE	Itinerant educational exhibit, receptions, re-enactments
COMPLEMENT	18 (when sailing)

to length, etc. The Californian naval architect L.C. Norgaard was commissioned to draw plans for the reconstruction, based on period documents and iconography.

The building, contracted to the yard of J. Hinks & Son in Appledore, Devon, England, was done using hand tools identical to those used in Elizabethan times, and using period techniques and materials, although the hull timber is iroko, more durable than oak. The original suite of sails was flax (now replaced by Duradon, a synthetic cloth that looks like natural canvas). The ship also carries 18 working replica guns and has replica period furniture and fittings. As for concessions to the 20th century, there is a small and well hidden engine room, and the tiller is actuated by a wheel instead of a whipstaff, the hinged vertical lever used on galleons and other large ships until well into the 18th century.

The Golden Hinde was opened to public visits in a number of English ports before sailing for San Francisco in 1974. She was a commercially successful exhibit in her first years in San Francisco but public interest soon waned. In 1979 she sailed to Japan, via Hawaii, to star as the Erasmus in the television serial Shogun. After the filming she sailed back to England by way of Hong Kong where, on advice from the police, she was issued with boarding nets and tear gas canisters to deter possible pirate attacks in the South China sea and Indonesian archipelago. Drake's galleon was certainly likewise fitted, with nets over and around the decks to deter boarders, and stinkpots, filled with sulfur, that would be set alight before being lobbed at the deck of an attacker.

The Golden Hinde reached Plymouth, England, in the spring of 1980, having thus circumnavigated the world like her namesake, but by way of Panama and Suez. From 1980 to 1985 she visited many British ports and took part in a number of harbor festivals. In 1984 she was sold to two Britons, one of whom later became sole owner. They carried on exploiting her as an itinerant educational exhibition. The galleon left England in October 1985 for exhibition work at Charlotte Amalie and St. Thomas in the Virgin Islands, from whence she sailed, under tow to save time, to Vancouver for Expo 86. She remained at Vancouver from May to October 1986, after which, until September 1991, she visited numerous US West and East Coast ports. She returned to England in October that year and has since then been doing much the same work, with individual visitors and school parties, also offering re-enactments and "pirate parties," and being hired out for corporate functions, wedding receptions and film charters.

ALOFT
Of men or sails working or set on the masts and spars.

BEAM
Structural element supporting the deck.

BEAR AWAY, TO
Steer the ship away from the wind, also sail fuller.

BERMUDIAN
Rig characterized by triangular spankers.

BILGE
Internal part of the ship below the lowest deck.

BONAVENTURE
The sternmost mast of a sailing ship rigged exclusively with fore-and-aft sails.

BONNET
From the French "bonnette," additional section of a square sail.

BOOM
The spar to which a spanker is bent.

BOWSPRIT
Part of the mast system located at the prow of the ship.

BRACE
Part of the running rigging allowing yards to be trimmed.

BRACE UP, TO
Haul on rope attached to a yard to trim the yards to the wind.

BULWARK
Rail in the form of a solid parapet along the sides of the deck.

CALM
An absence of wind.

CAULKING
Sealing of the joints between the planking elements.

CLOSE-HAULED
Point of sailing against the wind.

CUTWATER
Part of the prow of a ship, below the bowsprit.

EASE, TO
Release a halyard to adjust a sail.

FOOTROPE
Rope set below a spar and used as a foothold by the seamen working aloft.

FORE OR AFT
Respectively to the front or to the rear of a ship.

FORE-AND-AFT
Rig characterized a longitudinal sail plan.

FORECASTLE
Raised part of the main deck at the prow.

FOREMAST
The foremost mast of a ship.

GAFF
The spar to which the top of a fore-and-aft sail is attached.

GAFF TOPSAIL
The sail placed above a spanker in a fore-and-aft-rig.

HALYARD
Line used to hoist a sail.

HEAVE TO, TO
Adjust the rig to bring the ship to a halt or to cause it to move slowly.

HOIST, TO
Raise sails for example using ropes.

JIB
Triangular sail rigged at the prow.

JIBBOOM
Extension of the bowsprit to which the jib or flying jibs are attached.

LATEEN SAIL
Triangular sail the upper edge of which is rigged on a lateen spar.

LATEEN YARD
The yard to which a lateen sail is attached.

LEEWARD AND WINDWARD
Said of something or a ship respectively set where the wind is blowing to or where it is blowing from.

LEEWAY
Lateral movement of a ship induced by the wind when beating.

LOWER MAST
The lowest part of a sectioned mast.

LUFF
The edge of a sail next to the mast or stay supporting it.

LUFF, TO
Steer a ship closer to the wind.

MAIN COURSE
Or main sail, the largest and lowest sail on a foremast or main mast.

MAIN MAST
The tallest mast on a ship.

MAST
When divided into sections composed of lower mast, topmast, topgallant and royal mast.

MIZZEN MAST
The mast stepped at the stern of the ship.

PANEL
One of the strips of canvas making up a sail.

PLANKING
The surface skin of the hull, generally in the form of wooden planks.

QUARTER
One of the points of the compass.

QUARTERDECK
Raised part of the main deck, generally at the stern.

RATLINES
Ladder composed of ropes or metal wires set across the shrouds.

REACHING
Point of sailing with the wind approximately at right-angles to the ship.

REEF, TO
Reduce the area of a sail exposed to the wind.

RIB
The transverse structural element of a ship.

RIDE, TO
...at anchor, when a ship is anchored.

RIG
Defines a ship's sail plan and mast system.

RIGGING
Ropes or cables, known as running r. when used to trim the sails and standing r. when supporting the masts.

ROLL
The transverse movement of a ship about an axis parallel to the direction of motion, induced by the waves.

ROYAL MAST
The highest part of a sectioned mast.

SAIL FULLER
Steering maneuver that turns the prow of the ship away from the direction of the wind.

SEAM
The join between planking elements.

SET UP, TO
Put under tension part of the running rigging.

SHEET
Part of the running rigging attached to the lower corner of a sail and extending it sternwards.

SHORTEN SAIL
Gather and tie a sail to the spar or mast supporting it.

SHROUDS
Part of the standing rigging providing lateral support for the masts.

SPANKER
Trapezoidal or triangular sail rigged longitudinally astern of a mast.

SPRITSAIL
A sail extended by a yard set beneath the bowsprit.

STANCHION
Upright support for the rail placed around the main deck.

STAY
Part of the standing rigging providing longitudinal support for the masts.

TACK
Part of the running rigging attached to the fore corner of a fore-and-aft sail.

TACK, TO
Change the direction of the ship into and through the wind.

TILLER
Bar governing the rudder.

TONNAGE
The conventional measurement of the size of ship.

TOPSAIL
Square sail set above the main sail.

TOPSIDES
The part of the hull above the waterline.

TRANSOM
The flat surface forming the stern of a ship.

UNDER BARE POLES
Proceed with no sails aloft due to fierce winds.

WETTED AREA
The submerged part of the hull.

WINCH
Mechanical aid for sail handling.

YARD
Spar supporting the upper edge of a square sail.

YARDARM
The extremity of any horizontal spar.

BIBLIOGRAPHY

Anderson R. & C., *The sailing ship*, New York, 1947

Bass F. G., *A history of seafaring, based on underwater archaeology*, Londra, 1972

Caddeo Rinaldo, *Le navigazioni atlantiche di A. da Ca' da Mosto*, Milano, 1928

Carrozzino R., *Tall ship 2000*, Genova, 2000

Casson, Edward Och Franzen, Anders, *Wasa - Fynd och bargning*, Stoccolma, 1959

Casson L., *Speed under sailn of ancient ship*, New York, 1959

Casson L., *The earliest two masted ship*, New York, 1964

Casson L., *New light on alient rigging and boat building*, New York, 1964

Casson L., *The size of ancient merchant ship*, New York, 1964

Chapelle H. I., *The history of american sailing ship*, New York, 1936

Chapelle H. I., *The american fishing schooners*, New York, 1936

Chapman F. E. Af, *Architectura Navalis Mercatoria*, Stoccolma, 1768

Cipolla C.M., *Guns and sails in the early phase of european expansion*, Torino, 1969

Clowes. G. S. L., *Sailing ship, their history and development*, Londra, 1932

G. Dela Roerie & J. Vivielle, *Histoire des navires de la rame a l'a helice*, Parigi, 1946

Derby W.L.A., *The tall ship pass*, Londra, 1937

Gropallo T., *Ultima vela*, Genova, 1969

Howarth D., *The men of war*, New York, 1978

Jeannin, P., *Le navire et l'économie maritime*, Parigi, 1965

Keble Chatterton, E., *Ship models*, Londra, 1923

Landstrom Bjorn, *Skeppet*, Stoccolma, 1961

Lane Frederic C., *Le navi di Venezia*, 1983

Lubbock Basil, *The china clippers*, Glasgow, 1919

Lubbock Basil, *The last of the windjammers*, vol 1 e 2, Glasgow, 1927

Lubbock Basil, *The western ocean packets*, Glasgow, 1956

Moretti Maric, *La tomba della nave*, Milano, 1961

Randaccio Carlo, *Storia navale universale antica e moderna*, Roma, 1891

Solmi A., *I conquistatori degli oceani*, Novara, 1984

Solmi A., *Gli esploratori del Pacifico*, Novara, 1985

Schiavoni G., *La nave a vela*, Venezia, 2000

Torr Cecil, *Ancient ship*, Chicago, 1964

Tre Trycare, *L'arte navale*, Stoccolma, 1963

Uccelli Guido, *Le navi di nemi*, Roma, 1950

Van Konijneirburg E., *L'architecture navale depuis ses origines*, Bruxelles, 1905

Vecchi Augusto Vittorio, *Storia generale della marina militare*, Firenze, 1892

Vicino Michele, *La nave nel tempo*, Roma, 1927

Vingiano Giuseppe, *Storia della nave*, Roma, 1955

Wipple A. *Fighting sails*, New York, 1973

Wipple A.. *The clipper ships*, New York, 1980

Abranson Erik C, *Sailing Ships of the World*, London, 1992

Brouwer Normar, *The International Register of Historic Ships*, Peekskill, NY, 1999

Dickinson Jonathan C., *Sail Tall Ships! (A Directory of Sail Training and Adventure at Sea)*, Newport, RI, 2000

Ollivier Puget et Jean-Noël Darde, *Partir sur les grands voiliers*, Paris, 2000

Schnuffelen Otmar, *Die letzten grossen Segelschiffe*, Bielefeld, 1990

Tre Trickare, *The Lore of Ships*, New York, 1973

Tsanov Miroslav, *Uchebni vetrohodni korabi*, Sofia, 1990

Underhill Harold A., *Sailing Ships and Rigging*, 1938 (reprinted 1963)

MAGAZINES

American Neptune
Archeology
Classic boat
Mariner's mirror
Maritime
Mondo Sommerso
Nautical quaterly
Yacht Digest

INDEX

1: B.Astorg/D.P.P.I.;
2-3: F.Pace/D.P.P.I.;
4-5: Livio Bourbon / Archivio White Star;
6 top: Christie's Images ;
6 bottom: Sotheby's Picture Library;
7: Eudenbach/Stock Newport;
8 left: Alexis Komenda;
8-9: Mcallen/Stock Newport;
9 right: Van der Wall/Stock Newport;
10-11: Tsuneo Nakamura/Volvox Inc;
12-13: Sotheby's Picture Library;
14-15: Archivio Scala;
15: Erich Lessing/Contrasto;
16 and 17: Archivio White Star; 1
18 and 19: Archivio White Star;
20 top: AKG;
20 bottom and 20-21: Erich Lessing/Contrasto;
22-23: John Batchelor Illustration;
24 top, 24 center, 24-25 center, 24-25 bottom: John Batchelor Illustration;
25 bottom: Archivio White Star;
26 and 27: The Bridgeman Art Library;
28 top: Double's;
28-29: NY Carlsberg Glyptotek, Copenaghen;
29 top: Alfio Garozzo/Archivio White Star;
30-31: Double's;
31 top: Archivio Fotografico Foglia;
31 bottom left:Archivio Scala;
31 bottom right: Erich Lessing/Contrasto;
32 top: Cameraphoto;
32-33: John Batchelor Illustration;
33 top: Archivio Scala;
34 top: John Batchelor Illustration;
34-35 top: Archivio Dagli Orti;
34-35 bottom: John Batchelor Illustration;
36 top: Archivio Scala;
36 center, 36 bottom: John Batchelor Illustration;
37: Archivio Scala;
38 and 39: John Batchelor Illustration;
40 top: Cameraphoto;
40 center: Peabody Museum;
40 bottom: John Batchelor Illustration;
40-41: National Maritime Museum;
42 and 43: John Batchelor Illustration;
43 top: Archivio Dagli Orti
44-45: Archivio Dagli Orti;
45 top: AKG;
45 bottom: Archivio Dagli Orti;
46-47: Erich Lessing/Contrasto;
46 bottom: Art Archive;
47 top: Giancarlo Costa/Archivio White Star;
47 bottom: Museo Correr;
48 top: Erich Lessing/Contrasto;
48 bottom, 48-49: Cameraphoto;
50 left: The Pepys Library – Magdalene College, Cambridge;
50 right and 51: National Maritime Museum;
52 top: National Maritime Museum;
52 center, 52 bottom: The Pepys Library – Magdalene College, Cambridge;
53: Museo Naval, Madrid;
54 top, 54 center: The Pepys Library – Magdalene College, Cambridge;
54 bottom:AKG;
55 top, 55 bottom: The Pepys Library – Magdalene College, Cambridge;
56 bottom: The Bridgeman Art Library;
56-57, 57 top: National Maritime Museum;
58 top: Christie's Images;
58 center: Sotheby's Picture Library;
58-59, 59 bottom: Christie's Images;

60 bottom: National Maritime Museum;
60-61: Peabody Museum;
62-63, 63 top left, 63 center: J.Jonson/Sjöistoriska Museet, Stokholm;
63 top right, 63 bottom: Giancarlo Costa/Archivio White Star;
64-65, 65 bottom: Giancarlo Costa/Archivio White Star;
66 top, 66 center, 66-67 top: Christie's Images;
66-67 bottom: J.Jonson/Sjöistoriska Museet, Stoccolma;
68 top, 68 center: Hans Hammarskiöld;
68-69: Focus Team;
69 top left, 69 top right: Vasa Museet, Stokholm;
70 top left, 70 center: Hans Hammarskiöld;
70 bottom, 70-71: Vasa Museet, Stokholm;
72-73, 73 top left: Hans Hammarskiöld;
73 top right, 73 center: Vasa Museet, Stokholm;
74 left, 74 bottom right: Hans Hammarskiöld;
74 top right, 75: Vasa Museet, Stoccolma;
76-77, 76 bottom left: National Maritime Museum;
78-79, 79: National Maritime Museum;
80-81: John Batchelor Illustration;
82 top: AKG;
82 right: Mary Evans Picture Library;
82 center left, 82 bottom left: Flagship Portsmouth Trust;
83: Topham Picture Library/ICP;
84-85, 85 bottom right: Christie's Images;
85 bottom left: Mary Evans Picture Library;
86 top, 86-87: Fine Art Photographic Library;
86 center, 87 bottom: Sotheby's Picture Library;
88 center, 89 right: Fregatten Jylland;
88 bottom: Fine Art Photographic Library;
88-89: National Maritime Museum;
90-91 top: Peabody Museum;
90-91 bottom: : John Batchelor Illustration;
91 top: Mary Evans Picture Library;
91 center: Giancarlo Costa/Archivio White Star;
92 bottom: J.Jonson/Sjöistoriska Museet, Stokholm;
92-93: Giancarlo Costa/Archivio White Star;
93 top right: AKG;
94 top: Peabody Museum;
94 center, 94 bottom: The Bridgeman Art Library;
94-95: The Royal Exchange Art Gallery;
96 left: Fine Art Photographic Library;
96-97: Sotheby's Picture Library;
97 top: Peabody Museum;
97 bottom: Derek Bays Collection;
98 top left, 98 top right, 98 bottom: Peabody Museum;
98 center, 98-99: Fine Art Photographic Library;
100 top, 100 bottom: Peabody Museum;
100 center: National Maritime Museum;
101: Bygones Designs;
102 top: The Cutty Sark Trust;
102-103: Brown, Son & Ferguson Ltd;
103 top, 103 bottom: National Maritime Museum;
104-105 top, 104-105 bottom: John Batchelor Illustration;

105 top: Peabody Museum;
106 top: The Cutty Sark Trust;
106 bottom left: Peabody Museum;
106 bottom right, 106-107, 107 bottom right: National Maritime Museum;
108 top left, 108 top right, 108 center right, 108 bottom left, 108 bottom right: Alexis Komenda;
109: Tsuneo Nakamura/Volvox Inc.
110 and 111: US Naval Academy;
112 top: US Naval Academy;
112 center, 112 bottom, 112-113: US Naval Historical Foundation;
114-115: National Maritime Museum;
115 top: W. Hester Collection, University of Washington Library;
115 bottom: A.Siliotti/Geodia;
116 top: Fullriggeren Sorlandets Venner
116 center: San Francisco Maritime Museum;
116 bottom: W. Hester Collection, University of Washington Library;
117: The Bridgeman Art Library;
118 top: The Gibson Family Collection, Isles of Scilly;
118 bottom left: San Francisco Maritime Museum;
118 bottom right: National Maritime Museum;
118-119: W. Hester Collection, University of Washington Library;
120-121: San Francisco Maritime Museum;
121 top: A.Villiers/Popperphoto/Vision;
121 bottom: The Gibson Family Collection, Isles of Scilly;
122 and 123: Deutsches Schiffahrtsmuseum, Bremerhaven;
124 top right: San Francisco Maritime Museum;
124 left: Museum of History and Industry, Seattle;
124-125 bottom: G.Costa/Archivio White Star;
126 bottom left, 126 bottom right, 126-127: Deutsches Schiffahrtsmuseum, Bremerhaven;
127 right: John Batchelor Illustration;
127 bottom left: Deutsches Schiffahrtsmuseum, Bremerhaven;
128: Benjamin Mendlowitz Marine Photography
129: G.M.Raget/Sea & See;
130 right, 130 left: Deutsches Schiffahrtsmuseum, Bremerhaven;
131: Peabody Museum;
132 top left, 133 bottom right: Alexis Komenda;
132-133: B.Pigott/D.P.P.I.;
134-135: Tsuneo Nakamura/Volvox Inc.;
135 right: Borlenghi/Stock Newport;
135 left: Tsuneo Nakamura/Volvox Inc.;
136 left, 136-137, 137 bottom left: Tsuneo Nakamura/Volvox Inc.;
137 bottom right: Vapillon/Stock Newport;
138-139: PPL Photo Agency;
138 bottom left: J.Vapillon/Sea&See;
138 bottom right: C.Borlenghi/Sea&See;
139 left: Alexis Komenda
139 center: B.Stichelbaut/D.P.P.I.;
140 and 141: B.Stichelbaut/D.P.P.I.
142 bottom left, 142 bottom right: Alexis Komenda;

142-143: De Tienda/D.P.P.I.;
143 top right, 143 bottom: Thad Koza;
144 top: Thad Koza;
144 center: Tsuneo Nakamura/Volvox Inc.;
144 bottom: Raycroft/Stock Newport;
145: Monika Kludas/Geomarin;
146 top: Tsuneo Nakamura/Volvox Inc.;
146 center: De Tienda/D.P.P.I.;
146 bottom: Ollivier Puget;
147: Grant/Stock Newport;
148 top, 149 bottom right: Tsuneo Nakamura/ Volvox Inc.;
148-149: B.Stichelbaut/D.P.P.I.;
149 top right: Grant/Stock Newport;
149 bottom left: Livio Bourbon/Archivio White Star;
150 and 151: Ollivier Puget;
152 top: B.Stichelbaut/D.P.P.I.
153: B.Astorg/D.P.P.I.;
152 center right, 152 bottom: Tsuneo Nakamura/Volvox Inc.;
152 center left: Nigel Pert;
154 top left, 154 center left: Tsuneo Nakamura/Volvox Inc.;
154-155: Alexis Komenda;
155 top right: Beken of Cowes;
155 bottom: Tsuneo Nakamura/Volvox Inc.;
156 bottom left: B.Stichelbaut/D.P.P.I.;
156-157: E.Cattin/D.P.P.I.;
156 bottom right, 157 center right: Tsuneo Nakamura/ Volvox Inc.;
157 top right: Stiftelsen Skoleskipet Christian Radich;
158 top left, 158 bottom, 159: Tsuneo Nakamura/ Volvox Inc.;
158 center right: F.Pace/D.P.P.I.;
158 center left: Thad Koza;
160: Tsuneo Nakamura/Volvox Inc.;
161 top, 161 center left, 161 center right, 161 bottom: Skoleskibet Georg Stage;
162 top: Max Mudie;
162 left, 163: Uwe Delfs Jespersen;
164 top: Benjamin Mendlowitz Marine Photography;
164 center: Topham Picture Library/ICP;
164 bottom: Thad Koza;
164-165: Beken of Cowes;
166 top: Beken of Cowes;
166 bottom left: Ollivier Puget;
166 bottom right, 167: Tsuneo Nakamura/Volvox Inc.;
166-167 bottom: The Danish Maritime Authority;
168 top, 168 center, 168 bottom: Tsuneo Nakamura/Volvox Inc.;
168-169: Roberto Merlo;
170 top: Max Mudie;
170 bottom: Tsuneo Nakamura/Volvox Inc.;
171: Alexis Komenda;
172 top: E.Layani/Sea & See;
172 bottom, 173 bottom right: Chris Queeney;
172-173: Grieser/Stock Newport;
173 bottom left: Polo/Overseas/Farabolafoto;
174 bottom: Tsuneo Nakamura/Volvox Inc.;
174-175: R.Pigott/D.P.P.I.;
175 top right, 175 bottom left, 175 bottom right: Monika Kludas/Geomarin;
176 top, 177 bottom left: Ollivier Puget;
176 bottom: Tsuneo Nakamura/Volvox Inc.;
176-177: G.M.Raget/Sea & See;
177 bottom right: Nigel Pert;
178 top, 178 bottom left, 178 center right:

Tsuneo Nakamura/Volvox Inc.;
179: Sea & See;
180-181, 180 bottom left , 181 center right:
  G.M.Raget/Sea&See;
181 bottom left: C.Borlenghi/Sea&See;
180 bottom right, 181 top left: Ollivier
  Puget;
182-183, 183: Tsuneo Nakamura/Volvox
  Inc.;
184 and 185: Tsuneo Nakamura/Volvox
  Inc.;
186 and 187: Livio Bourbon/Archivio White
  Star;
188 top, 188 center, 189: Tsuneo
  Nakamura/ Volvox Inc.;
188 bottom: Livio Bourbon/Archivio White
  Star;
190 top left: Livio Bourbon/Archivio White
  Star;
190 top right:Villarosa/Overseas/Farabolafoto;
190 bottom: Roberto Merlo;
190-191: Tsuneo Nakamura/Volvox Inc.;
192 top left: Ferraris-Marré;
192 top right, 193: Livio Bourbon/Archivio
  White Star;
192 center: J.Smith/Sea & See;
192 bottom: Wilson/Stock Newport;
194 and 195: Livio Bourbon/Archivio White
  Star;
196 top: Ferraris-Marré;
196 center left, 196 center right, 196
  bottom, 197: Livio Bourbon/Archivio
  White Star;
198 top, 198 center, 198 bottom: 198-199,
  199 bottom right: Livio Bourbon/Archivio
  White Star;
199 bottom left: Antonio Attini/Archivio
  White Star;
200-201: Antonio Attini/Archivio White
  Star;
200 bottom left, 200 bottom right, 201 top
  left, 201 bottom: Livio Bourbon/Archivio
  White Star;
201 right: Ollivier Puget;
202 top: C.Borlenghi/Sea & See;
202 center, 202-203: Tsuneo
  Nakamura/Volvox Inc.;
203 top: Livio Bourbon/Archivio White Star;
204 top: Tsuneo Nakamura/Volvox Inc.;
204 bottom: Beken of Cowes;

204-205: Monika Kludas/Geomarin;
205 bottom left: N.Martinez/Sea & See;
205 bottom right: Livio Bourbon/Archivio
  White Star;
206-207, 207 top, 207 center: Tsuneo
  Nakamura/Volvox Inc.;
207 bottom: Livio Bourbon/Archivio White
  Star;
208 top, 208-209, 209 bottom right:
  Tsuneo Nakamura/Volvox Inc.;
208 bottom left: The Bridgeman Art Library;
210 top left, 211: Tsuneo Nakamura/Volvox
  Inc.;
210 center right: C.Borlenghi/Sea & See;
210 bottom left: Van der Wal/Stock
  Newport;
212 top, 212 center, 212-213, 213 bottom
  right: Tsuneo Nakamura/Volvox Inc.;
213 bottom left: Livio Bourbon/Archivio
  White Star;
214: F.Pace/D.P.P.I.;
215 top: Topham Picture Library/ICP;
215 left: Nigel Pert;
215 center right: Tsuneo Nakamura/Volvox
  Inc.;
215 bottom right: R.Nobbio/Sea & See;
216-217, 216 bottom, 217 top left, 217
  center right: Tsuneo Nakamura/Volvox Inc.;
217 bottom: Farabolafoto;
218 top, 218 bottom left, 218 bottom
  center, 219: Tsuneo Nakamura/ Volvox
  Inc.;
218 bottom right: Livio Bourbon/Archivio
  White Star;
220 bottom left: Ollivier Puget;
220-221: B.Astorg/D.P.P.I.;
221 top: Tsuneo Nakamura/Volvox Inc.;
221 bottom: C.Borlenghi/Sea & See;
222 top, 222-223: Tsuneo
  Nakamura/Volvox Inc.;
222 bottom: Polo/Overseas/Farabolafoto;
223 bottom: R.Nobbio/Sea&See;
224 and 225: Tsuneo Nakamura/Volvox Inc.;
226 top: Tsuneo Nakamura/Volvox Inc.;
226 center, 226-227: Livio
  Bourbon/Archivio White Star;
228 left: Thad Koza;
228 bottom right: Tsuneo Nakamura/Volvox
  Inc.;
228-229: F.Pace/D.P.P.I.;

229 bottom: Ollivier Puget;
230 top: Beken of Cowes;
230 center, 230 bottom: Ollivier Puget;
231: G.Gurney/Sea & See;
232 and 233: Tsuneo Nakamura/Volvox
  Inc.;
234 and 235: Tsuneo Nakamura/Volvox
  Inc.;
236 and 237: Tsuneo Nakamura/Volvox
  Inc.;
238 left: Livio Bourbon/Archivio White Star;
238-239, 239 top right, 239 bottom right:
  Tsuneo Nakamura/Volvox Inc.;
239 bottom left: Ollivier Puget;
240 top: Ollivier Puget;
240 center: Tomlinson/Stock Newport;
240 bottom: Raycroft/Stock Newport;
241: Tomlinson/Stock Newport;
242 top left, 242 center right, 243: Tsuneo
  Nakamura/Volvox Inc.;
242 bottom right, 242 bottom left:
  Yokohama Maritime Museum;
244 bottom left, 244-245, 245 top: Tsuneo
  Nakamura/Volvox Inc.;
244 bottom right, 245 bottom: Thad Koza;
246 and 247: Tsuneo Nakamura/Volvox Inc.;
248 top, 248-249, 249 bottom left: Tsuneo
  Nakamura/Volvox Inc.;
248 center: Ollivier Puget;
249 bottom right: Thad Koza;
250 right: Tsuneo Nakamura/Volvox Inc.;
250 left: Tsuneo Nakamura/Volvox Inc.;
250-251: E.Cattin/D.P.P.I.;
252: Ferraris-Marré;
253 top, 253 bottom: Monika
  Kludas/Geomarin;
253 center: Tsuneo Nakamura/Volvox Inc.;
254 top right, 254 bottom left, 254 bottom
  right: Tsuneo Nakamura/Volvox Inc.;
254 top left: Monika Kludas/Geomarin;
254-255: Beken of Cowes;
256: F.Pace/D.P.P.I.;
257 top left, 257 bottom left: Monika
  Kludas/ Geomarin;
257 top right: Alexis Komenda;
258-259: Tsuneo Nakamura/Volvox Inc.;
260 top right: Sea Cloud Cruises;
260 top left, 260-261, 261 bottom: Harvey
  Lloyd/Helios Productions;
262 and 263: Harvey Lloyd/Helios

Productions;
264 and 265: P.Nijdeken/Rederij Clipper
  Stad Amsterdam;
266 bottom left, 266 bottom right, 267
  center right: P.Nijdeken/Rederij Clipper
  Stad Amsterdam;
266-267, 267 top right: Nigel Pert;
268 and 269: Sea Cloud Cruises;
270 and 271: Sea Cloud Cruises;
272-273: Harvey Lloyd/Helios Productions;
272 bottom left, 272 bottom right, 273 top
  left: M.Martini/Star Clippers Company;
273 top right; 273 bottom: Harvey
  Lloyd/Helios Productions;
274 top left, 274 top right, 274 center, 274
  bottom: Harvey Lloyd/Helios Productions;
275: Star Clippers Company;
276 bottom left, 276 bottom right, 276-277
  277 bottom: Harvey Lloyd/Helios
  Productions;
277 top: F.Pace/D.P.P.I.;
278-279: Harvey Lloyd/Helios Productions;
280 bottom left: Thad Koza;
280 bottom right, 280-281: Tsuneo
  Nakamura/Volvox Inc.;
282 and 283: J.Kingwell/Knickle's Studio &
  Gallery;
284 top left: Ollivier Puget;
284 top right, 284 bottom: Benjamin
  Mendlowitz/Noah Pubblications;
284-285: Thad Koza;
285 bottom left, 285 bottom right:
  J.Kingwell/Knickle's Studio & Gallery;
286, 287 top left, 287 center, 287 bottom
  left: I.Hutchinson/Tall Ship Soren Larsen;
287 right: Max Mudie;
288 top left: Beken of Cowes;
288 top right, 288 center, 288 bottom left,
  289: I.Hutchinson/Tall Ship Soren Larsen;
290 top left: Tsuneo Nakamura/Volvox Inc.;
290 center right, 290 bottom: Golden
  Hinde Ltd.;
291: Beken of Cowes;
292: Nigel Pert;
293 top right: Topham Picture Library/ICP;
293 left, 293 bottom right: Golden Hinde
  Ltd.;
294-295: Beken of Cowes;
304: Tsuneo Nakamura / Volvox Inc.

AKNOWLEDGEMENTS

A special thank goes to:
*Commander-in-chief Ugo Bertelli, chief of Staff of the
Italian Navy above the sail training ship 'Amerigo
Vespucci';
The Italian Navy Staff Records Office - Rome;
The Naval Academy of Rome Records Office.*

The Publisher would also like to thank:
American Sail Training Association (ASTA);
Biblioteca Centrale Sormani, Milan.
Bluenose II Preservation Trust;
Den Selvejende Institution Fregatten Jylland:
Flagship Portsmouth Trust (Alison Henderson);
Golden Hinde Sailing Galleon Museum;
Institute for Sea Training of the Ministry of Transport
  - Yokohama (Tsutomu Kawaji);
International Sail Training Association (ISTA);
Museo della Scienza e della Tecnica, Milan;
Rederij Clipper Stad Amsterdam (Cees Rosman);

Sail Training Association Danmark;
Sail Training Association Germany (Willi Schaefer);
Sea Cloud Cruises (Anja Ringel);
Star Clippers Company - Munich
  (Ingrid Prendergast);
Stiftelsen Fullriggeren Sorlandet;
Stiftelsen Skoleskipet Christian Radich;
Tall Ship Soren Larsen (Ian Hutchinson);
The Danish Maritime Authority (Anne Meyer);
Vasa Museet (Maria Andersson);
"Volies de légende" magazine (Thierry Montluçon);
Yokohama Maritime Museum.

*304 The sails are bent on
the spars just as they were
four thousand years ago;
the first canvas to catch the
wind on an Egyptian ship
was the square sail
supported by a horizontal
spar like these on the
Nippon Maru II sailing in
the last century of the
second millennium.*